Present Tense

Present Tense

A Poetics

*Armen Avanessian and
Anke Hennig*

*Translated by Nils F. Schott with
Daniel Hendrickson*

Bloomsbury Academic
An imprint of Bloomsbury Publishing Inc

B L O O M S B U R Y
LONDON • NEW DELHI • NEW YORK • SYDNEY

Bloomsbury Academic
An imprint of Bloomsbury Publishing Inc

1385 Broadway	50 Bedford Square
New York	London
NY 10018	WC1B 3DP
USA	UK

www.bloomsbury.com

BLOOMSBURY and the Diana logo are trademarks of Bloomsbury Publishing Plc

Originally published as "Präsens: Poetik eines Tempus"
© 2012 diaphanes, Zurich
All rights reserved by diaphanes AG
This English language translation © Bloomsbury Academic 2015

Translation © Armen Avanessian and Anke Hennig, 2015

All rights reserved. No part of this publication may be reproduced or transmitted in any form or by any means, electronic or mechanical, including photocopying, recording, or any information storage or retrieval system, without prior permission in writing from the publishers.

No responsibility for loss caused to any individual or organization acting on or refraining from action as a result of the material in this publication can be accepted by Bloomsbury or the author.

Library of Congress Cataloging-in-Publication Data
Avanessian, Armen.
Present tense : a poetics / Armen Avanessian, Anke Hennig ; translated by Nils F. Schott with Daniel Hendrickson.
pages cm
"Originally published as Präsens : Poetik eines Tempus, 2012 Diaphanes, Zurich" – Verso title page.
Includes bibliographical references and index.
ISBN 978-1-62892-765-8 (hardback)– ISBN 978-1-62892-764-1 (paperback)– ISBN 978-1-62892-766-5 (E-pub)– ISBN 978-1-62892-767-2 (ePDF) 1. Time in literature. 2. Fiction–Technique. 3. Narration (Rhetoric) I. Henning, Anke. II. Schott, Nils F., translator. III. Hendrickson, Daniel, 1963- translator. IV. Title.
PN56.T5A9313 2015
809'.93384–dc23
2015009344

ISBN: HB: 978-1-6289-2765-8
 PB: 978-1-6289-2764-1
 ePub: 978-1-6289-2766-5
 ePDF: 978-1-6289-2767-2

Typeset by Fakenham Prepress Solutions, Fakenham, Norfolk NR21 8NN

CONTENTS

Acknowledgments vii

Introduction 1

1 The present-tense novel 15
   Precondition: Classical narrated fiction and discourse 17
   Modernity: The emergence of the present-tense novel 28
   Altermodernism: The shift to the present tense of the past 58

2 Readings in methodology 89
   Findings from the phenomenology of literature 92
   Revising the approach to time in narratology and
      fiction theory 100
   Narratological revisions: Gérard Genette 101
   Deixis 114
   Deictic shifts 120

3 The imaginary present tense 141
   The present tense of interior monologues 146
   Pathographies of fiction 148
   Tense confusion—Strindberg's indistinguishable present tense
      of delusion 178

4 Tense philosophy 187
   Philosophy of time 189

Conclusion 219

Glossary 223
Notes 233
Index 281

ACKNOWLEDGMENTS

This book was first published in German in 2012. For their work in making this translation possible, we would like to thank Bernd Klöckener, who edited the book both in German and in English, Haaris Naqvi, our publisher, and Nils F. Schott, our translator.

Introduction

A screaming comes across the sky. It has happened before, but there is nothing to compare it to now. It is too late. These sentences immediately provoke an experience of literary fiction, even if you don't know that they come from a novel published in 1973. This effect will seem mysterious to anyone still convinced that the present tense is not capable of producing fiction.[1] Even the various avant-gardes whose anti-narrative and anti-fictional writing in the present tense was intended to confirm the end of the novel made this conviction manifest. To this day most conceptions of "fiction" are based, explicitly or implicitly, on the model of narration in the past tense. Fiction is said to be inconceivable without narrative retro-spection and a present-ification of what is past.

Yet the history of narration in the present tense now spans more than a hundred years. Along this history's eventful course, present-tense narration has developed its own literary universe. Literary prose written entirely in the present tense can be found even before the avant-garde's factographies, in the interior monologues of Édouard Dujardin or Arthur Schnitzler. Present-tense novels in the tradition of German New Objectivity and around the *nouveau roman* movement continue the nihilistic gestures of the avant-gardes (examples include texts by Samuel Beckett and Peter Weiss narrated in the first person). Finally, toward the end of the twentieth century, fictions narrated in the third person appear among the texts written in the present tense. These have a distinct tendency to create a non-contemporaneity in the experience of the present. The present tense used in Claude Simon's and Thomas Pynchon's history novels is a present tense of the past. Looking back at the history of the present tense as narrative tense, we see that in the twentieth century literature has developed procedures that make it possible for the present tense to create fiction and narratively to unfold a past without having to bring it into presence.

The fact that so far it has not been possible to write this history is due not only to the dominance just mentioned of an understanding of "narration" and "fiction" developed by means of the past tense. What have been equally inhibitive are theories that emphasize—sometimes quite contrary to their authors' intentions—terms such as *presence* and *absolute present tense* to highlight certain genuinely modern aesthetic phenomena (e.g. instantaneousness, suddenness, momentariness). These theories continually uphold the liminal situation of modernity; in their confrontation with traditional narration, they inscribe an unremitting aesthetic interruption into the present tense and thus institutionalize a constant break with tradition. While the present tense has received contradictory attributes and has been claimed to support quite diverse positions, conceptions of the present tense are always derived from the moment of this break. Whether, under the dictate of an aesthetic of liveliness,[2] this is declared to be an expression of the extreme timelessness of "moments of being" (Virginia Woolf); whether the present tense appears as the literary comrade-in-arms of a general avant-garde objection to a "lively experience" inspired by the metaphysics of presence; whether it is welcomed as an ally in the battle against an entanglement in the past (against presentification or the bringing-into-the-presence of the past in bourgeois narrated fiction)—as long as the meaning of the present tense is determined by the phenomena it breaks with, it is impossible to recognize either its own systematics or the historicity that it develops in the course of the twentieth century.

Beside these considerations from literary history, the historicity of terms such as *narration, (hi)story, fiction, reference,* or *present* is significant for a poetics of the present tense as a narrative tense as well. In the tension between these concepts, the present tense is outlined, misjudged, or precisely called upon, and, finally and fundamentally, transforms the conceptual field. To explain such a transformation, we not only have to take into account the linguistic and philosophical theoretical foundations of tense and time, but above all we must think narratology and fiction theory together.

The tenses of language do not depict the future, the present, or the past. Nor do they refer to time. Tenses create an understanding of time in the first place. Language has a tense system with which it produces chronology and thanks to which it has its own elementary, grammatical narrativity. The chronological understanding of time, which is acquired through language, can in turn be shifted by a poetic use of tense. And this, precisely, is what we call fiction. Literary fictions always—and in various ways, depending on which tense dominates in them—refer to the grammatical event of the emergence of time or of a chronological understanding of time.

Walter Benjamin speaks of the movement

> by which my hand slid the letters into the groove, where they would be arranged to form words. My hand can still dream of this movement, but it can no longer awaken so as actually to perform it. By the same token, I can dream of the way I once learned to walk. But that doesn't help. I now know how to walk. There is no more learning to walk.[3]

Considering the enduring attraction of traditional narration, a poetics of literary tenses will have to contradict Benjamin's claim about the impossibility of repeating experiences. In the fictional constitution of time, this attraction allows us time and again to experience what the acquisition of language means for us. We will see that learning a new kind of reading in the present tense corresponds to such a learning-over-and-over-again of reading in the past tense.

In the first chapter, "The present-tense novel," we trace the innovative transformations of literary forms that have led to novels in the present tense. This will involve elaborating the historical background of narration in the past tense, in which the fictional present emerges by presentifying a story conceived of as past. Against this backdrop, it will then be possible to perceive the problems that emerge for the present tense as a persistent narrative tense as it begins to establish itself in modernism (for instance in the work of Robert Walser, Andrei Bely, Virginia Woolf, and William Faulkner). Difficulties arise above all in attempts to integrate the two narrative levels into one present, a single present supposed to provide space both for experience and for telling its story. The impossibility to experience and to tell the story at the same time leads to a new coordination of the fictional and factual layers of narration. The ostensibly anti-narrative present tense abandons the aporia of contemporaneously experiencing and telling the story (what we call the aporia of synchrony), which up until that moment has served to legitimize the retrospectivity of narration. Experience and narration become paradoxically synchronous with one another.

First, modern narration becomes aware of the fact that, due to the fictionality of narration, events do not in fact precede the telling of the story. Rather, the narrated events, the *fabula*, split off as an asynchronous moment of an always-present reading. The present-tense novel, as it is established in the last decades of the last century—in English, for instance, by J. M. Coetzee or Thomas Pynchon, the author of our opening quotation—is acutely aware of this. It finally discovers possibilities of narrating the past as such by analyzing the procedures readers use to construe the course of the *fabula* from out of the *sujet* at hand. This triggers a mechanism of asynchrony that is directly opposed to the mechanism of presentification in the epic past tense of classical narrated fiction.

We will show that the presentifying meaning of the epic past tense does not already arise from the contemporaneous form of time that is fiction. It arises only from the interaction of fiction with retrospective narration. And, depending on whether it is the narrative or the fictional aspect that dominates, the result is either a matrix of narrated fiction that generates presentification in the past tense (narration—fiction—past tense) or an order of fictional narration that produces an asynchrony in the present tense (fiction—narration—present tense).

In the figuration of time that is asynchrony, the fictional dimension comes to the fore, while in retrospection, it is narration that dominates. We thus speak of a historical shift of dominants within the relations between narration and fiction, of a progression from narrated fiction to fictional narration. Not the least of its requirements is a regrouping of the persons within the cosmos of narration: the *she–he* of the characters, the *I* of the narrator, and the *you* of the reader. Once the responsibility for constituting the fiction has been transferred to the reader, narrators, too, can mingle with the characters. The experience of a third person's subjectivity in the novel is thus liberated from any hierarchical mediation by means of empathy with the characters, guided by the narrator. Subjectivity in the novel instead arises in a dialogue with the other.

The second chapter, "Readings in methodology," examines various methods employed in describing narration and fiction as to which concepts conceal the productivity of present-tense narration, which methods can be further developed to describe its functions, and which other, forgotten tools have to be updated. We start with two sidelined literary phenomena we encounter in the first chapter and that cannot be understood by means of a (conventional) narratological approach: on the one hand an asynchronous present (in Thomas Pynchon) and on the other a synchronous succession (in Claude Simon). This highlights a blind spot in narratology, which fails to notice that determining the role of temporality in narration is tied to realizing that fiction is a form of time and to sorting out its interaction with narration.

From different perspectives, narratology and fiction theory follow one and the same development. In every concrete literary historical analysis, however, significant interferences arise because neither of the two theories, taken on its own, is in a position to define the line that divides narrativity and fictionality or to settle the matter of whether there can be any fiction that is not produced by narrative procedures at all.

Narratology has related the use of tenses in the novel to a fundamental retrospectivity of narration (and therefore has judged the present tense to be problematic), whereas fiction theory has focused on the presentification of an (implicitly) past event (and thus attributed the capacity to cause such a presentification to the past tense alone).

Our revision of the methods of fiction theory and narratology serves primarily to locate their respective points of contact in order to bring them together in an integrated *fiction-narratology*. For this purpose we go back to and reinterpret concepts from deictic shift theory. We propose a new approach that extends fiction-narratology by the deictic categories of tense, space, and person.

Theories of deixis describe the practice of everyday linguistic indication, in which any reference is dependent on the coordinates of space, time, and person, which come together in an *origo* (*I–here–now*). Using Jakobson's term *shifter*, which stands at the historical beginning of deictic shift theory and echoes the avant-garde device of shifting (Russian *sdvig*), we reactualize the aesthetic dimension of deixis. In so doing, we provide narration with a new linguistic foundation and open it up to reception. The shift from the parameter *tense* to the parameters *space*, *time*, and *person* allows for clarifying the relationship between production, figuration (of time), and reception. We will show that fictional narration characteristically shifts the three dimensions of the deictic system of reality, and along with them also shifts the pivot points of linguistic reference. Literary fiction does not create any worlds; it shifts our linguistic reference to (a) reality.

From this perspective, literary fiction can be conceived of as a grammatically structured understanding of time. The novel, always defined by the contradiction and collaboration of narration and fiction, is also governed by the conflict between their respective forms of time. Narration, with its tendency toward retrospectivity, and fiction, with its manifestations in the contemporaneous, form a single figure. Yet in this figure as it is manifest in classical presentification (in the past tense) or recent asynchrony (in the present tense), narration and fiction paradoxically exclude, integrate, and encompass each other.

The third chapter, "The imaginary present tense," presents the benefits of the analytical instruments developed thus far for a phenomenology of literature. Contrary to the assertion of traditional narratology that the present tense is restricted to a small number of cases of a vivifying, so-called historical present tense, we propose a change in perspective. This new look at the history of literature reveals a number of previously unheeded present tense phenomena well before modernism. Sequences of delusion, hallucination, and dreams (in, among others, E. T. A. Hoffmann, Nikolai Gogol, August Strindberg) announce an initially uncontrollable drift in imagined spatial and temporal worlds that would achieve a fixed literary form only in internal monologue. Alongside its documentary character, i.e., the recording of facts, stories, or mental processes, the present tense here evinces two further functions. On the one hand, it accompanies the realistic novel's history of internalization. There, mimesis increasingly moves from the actions of persons to their inner lives, and it takes on the function of a representation of consciousness. On the other hand, the parallelism of the fictional world with the world of delusion indicates that the present tense used in contemporary simultaneous narration—as we encounter it, for instance, in J. M. Coetzee's present-tense novels—has its origin in techniques of creating simultaneous perspectives (focalization/focus) first perfected in the psychological novel. We will describe this with reference to Fyodor Dostoevsky's *The Double*.

Examining the imaginary present tense of the nineteenth century thus makes it possible to trace how the narration and fiction of the text are affected by attempts of the imaginary to break out, how delusion or hallucination enter into both the narrative and fictional strata of the text and affect the long-established system of narrated fiction itself. What appears is an imaginary (with its temporal mode of non-contemporaneity) whose narrative integration and fictional formation will only be achieved in the prose writing of the century that follows.

In the fourth chapter, "Tense philosophy," we will discuss philosophical conceptions of time (Russell, Deleuze, Rödl) that make it possible for the language of contemporary present-tense novels to blend with their knowledge. We will connect these conceptions with the reflections of the linguist, Gustave Guillaume, on the "chronogenesis" induced by language, that is, the capacity of language to form our understanding of time in the first place. This resolves the question of whether the analytical approaches previously discussed were working with an understanding of time or an understanding of the linguistic nature of temporal statements. According to Guillaume, our chronological understanding of time does not originate in everyday life. It is acquired through language and reactualized in every usage of tense. Our poetics of narrated fiction refers to this grammatical event.

The appeal of literary fiction derives from the identification of this event with the promise of language to provide access to an order of time, with the promise of an imaginary completeness. This is a mirror stage of appropriating language in its power over time—a power reactualized in every fiction generated by the past tense. This mirror stage cannot be abolished once and for all by a switch to the present tense. But neither can it be spelled out by taking recourse to ideas from the philosophy of time, the way the authors of classical modernity (Marcel Proust, James Joyce, Robert Musil) tried to do, the very authors usually cited whenever "time and narration" are at issue.

Ahead of every present, a "present tense of asynchrony" finds a past, and, in order to express the non-present moment of this past, it splits the present. The concept of asynchrony provides an answer to the question of how it is possible to narrate the past. The thesis of the classical novel is: *The past can be narrated*. The anti-thesis of modernity, obsessed as it is with the present, says: *The past cannot be narrated*. The infinite judgment of contemporary present-tense novels is: *Narration is—past*. This "past present tense," which we call *alter*modern present tense, continues the innovations of modernism, which were initially interpreted as purely antifictional, and, in a critique of classical narration, renews the genre of the novel.

We cannot acquire language to usurp time, as the classic tradition assures us in its fear of losing language altogether and of falling into the eternal silence of time. Yet altermodern poetics does not follow the agenda of those avant-garde manifestos that advocate a reversal of time in a revolution of language either. The asynchrony of the altermodern present tense does not let language arrive again and again nor does it let narration return. Instead, it simply draws attention to the fact that every decision alters the present (of writing).

This transformatory aspect also explains why we call this book a *poetics*. Given our analyses of the present tense as a narrative tense, we could conceivably also call it a study in (historical) narratology. In addition, the second chapter and its orientation toward fiction theory, the third chapter and its search for traces of the imaginary, and, finally, the overarching question of time all touch on core themes of philosophical inquiry. And given the excessive metaphorization and emphatic evocation of the present tense, particularly in German debates on aesthetics over the last decades, it might seem a matter of course to speak of an *aesthetics* of the present tense. Yet in the aesthetic debates over "absolute present" and "presence," the present tense itself is hardly ever thematized.[4] In our view, this is not a coincidence. It testifies to a systematic blindness on the part of aesthetic theory to a genuinely temporal-poetic dimension, a blindness in turn imputable to a rebalancing of the relation between aesthetics and poetics. Why then do we not understand our study as a philosophical one or, more narrowly, as an aesthetic one?

Giorgio Agamben describes how the Western aesthetic tradition builds on a peculiar understanding of poetics that must reject or exclude certain aspects or dimensions of the poetic. The central experience of poiesis, production into presence, is replaced by the question of the "how," that is, of the process through which the object has been produced. In terms of the work of art, this means that the emphasis shifts away from what the Greeks considered the essence of the work—the fact that in it something passed from non-being into being, thus opening the space of truth (*a-lētheia*).[5]

Under the aegis of aesthetic thought, the concept of poetics is restricted to the question of *how* something is made. Poetics then appears as something essentially practical. It is placed not only in opposition to aesthetics but also in contradiction to the original meaning of *poiesis*—the crossing of the boundary of non-being and being.

Of course we do not seek to regain, in a quasi-Heideggerian gesture, a forgotten dimension of *poiesis*. We are concerned with the poietic dimension of time (of temporality). Our study is a poetics of tense because it describes a process of *poiesis* that concerns the emergence of time. This emergence of (chronological) time thanks to the tenses is not some sort of bringing-into-appearance in the sense of mimesis, nor is it accessible to (aesthetic) experience. As we will show, the difference between the past tense and the present tense in terms of the *poiesis* of language is this: in the past tense, time passes and can be (spatially) presentified, while the present tense has the privilege of opening up time and of making the constant emergence of the past legible. The present tense institutes not only a present (as the past tense does) but time in general. It asks how something moves from non-being into being, and it does so by asking the question of the being or non-being of time.

Literary language is not content merely to formulate a thesis *about* time or to communicate an experience *of* time. It is essentially a *poiesis* of time. When we read, we do not simply withdraw from the temporal contexts of practical (social, political, historical) involvement with the world in order to have an aesthetic experience. Instead, we practice a poietic craft. Training this craft and making its procedures largely automatic creates a stable experience of time.[6]

Starting from these definitions, we can now address the well-known objections to poetics, understood as the "study of literature as the art of language." These objections always aim at poetics' alleged fixation on the practice or making of literary works.

The most common complaint about poetics as a methodology is an alleged restriction or even reductionism. This is said to be manifest in (1) its *renunciation of the dimension of experience* (poetics is said to argue only on the level of the aesthetics of production); (2) its *lack of a historical dimension* (poetics is said to take historical contexts into account only by way of a theory of genre); (3) the *normativity of poetics* (its origin in the study of verse or in rhetoric is said still to be at work in the "poetics of prose" that is narratology); (4) the *immanence of poetic analyses* (poetics is said to obsessively mark itself off from social meaning, political tendencies, and intermedial constellations). We do not seek to refute these objections historically here but to provide a systematic outline of what the necessity of poetics consists in.

1 The reproach that poetics *lacks a dimension of experience* corresponds to the already mentioned assumption that poetics can be subsumed under aesthetics. This, however, misrecognizes the creative act of the linguistic *poiesis* of time and declares what is linguistically created to be a subdomain of what can be experienced by the senses.[7] What is lost here is the knowledge that every *poiesis* opens up a truth that does not precede it. In fixating on that which appears in what is made, aesthetics becomes blind to the fact that anything *appears* at all.

   From this point of view, the carefully cultivated competition between an aesthetics of the work of art, focused on production, and aesthetic contemplation, tied to reception, obscures the fact that these two poles condition one another. Authorial poetics of literary and cultural studies on the one side, philosophical reflection on literature on the other usurp, apparently "without alternative," a shared terrain of literary theory. The poietic dimension of the production of time that is accessible only to linguistics cannot appear under the pragmatic imperatives of an aesthetics of the work or of an aesthetics of experience. The aesthetics of experience thus runs counter to its most basic intentions, namely to restore the experiential dimension to its rightful place.[8] Neither authors nor readers can have the productive "experience" of time that occurs on the linguistic level, nor can they have experience of the production of time, prior to language—that is possible only with language and in language. Accordingly, readers and authors do not communicate shared experiences but are co-producers of a course of time.[9]

2 We can address the second objection to poetics, that it *lacks a historical dimension*, with reference to Dmitry

Likhachev's reflections on the poetics of time and the core of literariness from the 1960s. In his *Poetics of Artistic Time*, he writes: "Literature, to a higher degree than any other art, becomes the art of time. Time is its object, its subject, and its tool of representation."[10]

Already three decades earlier, Jeremiyah Joffe attributes a temporal dimensionality to the literary work. The artwork is not simply located in history by the point in time of its creation; instead, thanks to its temporal dimensionality, it takes part in the creation of history. According to Joffe, the work is not localized in a chronology to be presupposed. The point in time at which it is created does not simply place it in relation to a state of history. Rather, the work takes part in a law of development. A literary work thus features two axes in the historical process accessible to poetic analysis. On this basis, the differences between (a) literary history, (b) historical poetics, and (c) time-poetics can be articulated as follows:

(a) The simple positioning of works in a presupposed chronology defines the perspective of literary history, for instance when it sequentially lists the evidence it finds of the use of the historical present tense in the history of styles from Virgil to Dickens.[11] In the present study, such a development in the course of literary history is significant wherever we locate the texts that we examine in a history of the present-tense novel according to when they were created.

(b) The dual anchoring in history, which no longer presupposes a chronology, is characteristic of a historical poetics. We will show how in the twentieth century the literary present tense successively develops a system that transforms from a literary history of the novelistic present tense into a historical poetics of the present-tense novel at precisely the moment in which the latter can be constructed as a poetic phenomenon. Poetics aims at innovations that are tangible in individual works in order to then place them within the new, previously non-existent, perspective of a poetics of time. To this extent, every text that succeeds as a present-tense text is a challenge to poetological knowledge. It is only in the last few decades that the object of a poietic study of the present tense (the time figuration of *asynchrony*) emerges conclusively from the (present-tense) material we examine.

(c) In the time-poetic reading of this material, finally, points of transformation take center-stage. For a transformative poetics of time, the present tense no longer appears simply as a motif or successively works its way down to its own foundation. Instead, it stands in a bipolar relationship to the past tense at all stages of its development.

3 The historical and temporal dimension of a poetics of time is also the starting point for challenging the third objection, the alleged *normativity of genre poetics*. There is precisely no binding norm for writing to be derived from our observation that the present-tense novel achieves the stability of a genre. The fact that contemporary writing is by no means exclusively (probably not even largely) writing in the present tense therefore does not need to be "explained away" by claiming that the past tense is untimely and antiquated. Writing in the past tense is not a matter of sedimented high culture falling prey to exploitation by the culture industry, nor is it encountered only in "popular" novels.

The fact that the shift of dominants from narration to fiction would not have been possible without the catalyzing function performed by the present tense does not imply a historical or normative devaluation of the past tense. As the novel written exclusively in the past tense has run its course, we are witnessing a resurrection and reinterpretation of the novel as such. The fact that this happens under the aegis of the present tense does not mean that it is now illicit to write novels in the past tense. Quite to the contrary, it is precisely the new horizons opened up by the altermodern present that retrospectively give new luster to the knowledge of the novel written in the past tense. Only now does the *presentification* of the epic past tense clearly appear as *one* genuine knowledge or *one* legitimate literary operation among others. It is precisely in its (alleged) naïveté that traditional narration in the past tense is immensely efficient at handling the linguistic-ontologically unavoidable, fictional *chronology of time*.

4 The truth-opening aspect of poetics also throws a different light on the fourth objection concerning the *immanence of poetic analyses*. Poetics is reproached for being incapable of considering either general cultural or media constellations in which art emerges. What is the relation of poetics and con-temporality?

With Agamben, we pointed earlier to a pre-aesthetic dimension of poetics recognizable in Greek antiquity. In the context of contemporary art, Peter Osborne has recently pointed out the function of a post-aesthetic poetics: "the generic post-medium concept of art reincorporates 'literature,' returning it to its philosophical origins in early German Romanticism. Post-conceptual art articulates a post-aesthetic poetics."[12] A generic model of art not only includes literature in a new way; post-conceptual art *creates* (in the sense of *poiesis*) the fiction of a global, social, political, and historical present:

> In this respect, in rendering present the absent time of a unity of times, *all constructions of the contemporary are fictional*. More specifically, the contemporary is an *operative* fiction: it *regulates the division* between the past and the present (via its sense of the future) within the present.[13]

Such a contemporaneity, that which expands the space of political and social negotiations to a global space and thereby makes the world a whole world, is an effect of fiction as we understand it here. Fiction does not begin with any fabrication of apparent worlds or the creation of second worlds opposed to reality. Nor does it reveal a fundamental "semblance" of reality. Instead of dismissing reference in a post-modern gesture, fiction shifts reference. Our concept of fiction does in fact aim at immanence. Yet this immanence is not the immanence of the *artwork*, dissipating in the aesthetic contemplation of artistic or literary structures. It is a radical immanence to the *world*. In our poetics of the present tense, the literary language of fiction aims at the form of time that is "contemporaneity" and that outlines the space of political and social engagement. Poetics deals with the knowledge of language in general and, in this book, with the knowledge of tenses.

In relation to Jacques Rancière's concept of a *poetique du savoir*, Rüdiger Campe has recently emphasized that poetics "for its part has a place in knowledge or over against knowledge." In its utopian or seditious deviation from the *adaequatio* of the true word, the "poetological" co-determines "the historicity of knowledge in knowledge and over against knowledge."[14] This is also the sense in which the present-tense novel gives us a poetics of tense to read. Taking seriously the two-dimensional image of time of this poetics also leads to a new poetics of history: it leads to the discovery of an unpredictable past. A new history, which the asynchronous present tense calls for, is as unpredictable as the future.

1
The present-tense novel

At the beginning of the twentieth century, the present tense is still considered to be the tense of the factual. In this first chapter, we would like to trace how the present tense becomes fictionalized in a process that integrates it into the novel and how, in this process, it takes over a function previously reserved for the past tense. We will elaborate this move with the help of excerpts from a number of literary works by, for instance, William Thackeray and Émile Zola for narrated fiction; Sergei Tretyakov for factographies; Virginia Woolf for classical modernity; Robert Walser and Wolfgang Hildesheimer for the modern present tense; and Claude Simon and Thomas Pynchon for altermodernism. In the first steps of the change of tense from past tense to present tense the modern novel operates, it does not break with the way the tenses function in classical fiction. The present tense maintains the function of factuality, which is why, in prose texts, it designates nothing but the "prosaic" present. In fact, the increased appearance of present tenses in the novel is bound up with an emphasis on the present as well as with ideal notions of the documentary and the factual.

In the wake of modernity's reference to the present, we observe an imagination of time past. In altermodernism, the present tense in the novel acquires another, a new and previously inconceivable, significance. The relevant factor here is, above all, a breaking point in classical narrated fiction that results from using past tenses to constitute fiction, for the epic past tense precisely does not signify the past but transforms it into a fictional present. Due to the presentifying effect of the epic past tense, the past could never appear as such in the novel. Altermodernism, then, experiments with the present tense as with a tense thanks to which the past can be imagined *as having passed*.

We can only understand what happens in the process if we recognize that the literary techniques of fiction and of narration condition one another. The experience of a fictional present in nineteenth-century narrated fiction presupposes the organized interplay of prospectivity on the level of the *fabula* and retrospectivity on the level of the *sujet*. Reconstruction in narration goes back to before the moments of a prospective course of events. In so doing it presentifies these unforeseeably futural moments—the technique of fictional presentification and the processes of retrospective narration act together. Looking at "narration in the present tense," we thus retrace the structural shifts (between *fabula* and *sujet*) in the modern and altermodern novel that lead not only to a fictionalization but also to a "narrativizing" of the present tense, to the constitution of a narrative present tense. Narratologically, this development takes place in two stages.

First, the modern present tense abandons the narratological dogma of retrospectivity. (At this stage, however, the question of whether the present tense has its own form of time does not come up.) The assumption that there is an orderly interplay in which the prospective course of the *fabula* is retrospectively recovered by the *sujet* is abandoned. *Fabula* and *sujet* are paradoxically synchronous. This can be seen in the interior monologue as well as in factualist procedural protocols that claim to record the chronological progress of an implicitly factual action in parallel with this progress. When and wherever it succeeds in doing so, modern narration becomes aware of the fact that such an endeavor involuntarily produces fictionality. At the same time, it makes it possible to realize that the retrospection presupposed by the texts of narrated fiction (*qua* epic past tense) is not an imperative of "pure narration." Rather, retrospection *as such* is already fictional. Initially, this means no more than that there is no fictional text in which the narrated factually precedes the narration—a fact that seems so obvious that it has hardly ever been contested. Once it is taken seriously, however, it leads to the recognition that narration and fiction are forms of time that can enter into completely different configurations.

In a second step, the altermodern present tense relates to the breaking point that had emerged under the aegis of classical fiction and had served a presentifying past tense to block the experience of the past as such. The altermodern present-tense novel attempts to narrate the past by analyzing the processes by means of which the reader constructs the course of a *fabula* from a *sujet* at hand. In the practice of reading, *fabula* and *sujet* show themselves to be always synchronously present. This is the case even when the relation between the two is one of retrospection because the *sujet* "looks back" at the *fabula*. It is against this background that we describe the history of the present tense and of the re-foundation of the novel made possible by its employment.

Precondition: Classical narrated fiction and discourse

In order to present changes in time relations and especially changes of tense in the modern and altermodern novel, we first have to look into the preconditions of the developments of tense that interest us. Classic nineteenth-century narrated fiction can serve as a foil here. This kind of fiction is characterized by narration in the fictional past tense, in which narrative retreats in favor of what is narrated, the *sujet* in favor of the fictional *fabula*. Here, the field of inquiry has been staked out by Käte Hamburger and Harald Weinrich.

Käte Hamburger opens her discussion on the use of tenses in the novel with the fundamental thesis that in the novel, the past tense changes its meaning. It loses "its grammatical function of designating what is past,"[1] and instead marks the entry into a timeless present of fiction. According to Hamburger, literary tenses are to be regarded both as producing fiction and as themselves fictional. The irregular use of tense in literature is responsible for opening up the experience of fiction for the reader: "Tomorrow was Christmas."[2] This also means that the temporal meaning of literary tenses is not to be confused with an extra-fictional temporal meaning: The detemporalized tense *past tense* no longer signifies the past but the fictional here and now. Whether the unfolding of events is narrated analeptically or proleptically, all of its moments are equally *fictionally present* although they are in the past tense.

In Hamburger's approach, which aspires to ground fiction in linguistic theory, two other theorems are relevant, even if the theorem of tense-structured fictionality retains the greatest significance for the development of literary history (from the past tense to the present tense) as well as for narratological discussions (of fictionality, of third-person/first-person narration, of deixis). The first of these theorems holds that the entry into the "timeless present" of fiction involves a disappearance of narration,[3] which makes it impossible to interpret the fictional sentences as propositions (of whatever kind) by a narrator. They become fictional because they lose their propositional character.[4] This is why, for Hamburger, only third-person narratives can be fictional, and first-person narratives cannot. The latter can only be considered to be fictitious.

Contrary to John Searle's assumption that there is no linguistically tangible characteristic of fiction, Ann Banfield has radicalized Hamburger's theorem. For her, fictional sentences are "unspeakable sentences."[5] No one speaks the sentences of fiction, and it is not even possible to imagine a communicative situation in which they could be spoken.[6] Between this much-discussed thesis[7] and the question of the (time-figuring) function performed by tenses in fictional texts, it is possible to establish only an *ex negativo* correlation. From this perspective, the only thing that can be said about "unspeakable" sentences is that they lack a concrete temporal connection (what Hamburger conceptualizes as the "timelessness of fiction"), while "speakable" sentences come with a tangible temporality and a connection with a tangible present or past.

The relation to time is similarly mediated in the case of the retreat of narration behind the narrative (or of the *sujet* behind the *fabula*) discerned by Hamburger, in which the medium of narration renders itself invisible in the service of the narrative. Since what is conveyed by the medium is never found in the place and at the time in and at which it is presented to us by the medium, the narrative can be seen not only as timeless, but also as placeless. In the narratological version of this principle, the *sujet*, by retreating behind the *fabula*, loses its spatial and temporal situatedness as an act of narration. This gives rise to the impression that, in some mysterious way, the *fabula* narrates itself (as if) by itself.

Narratologists have often cast doubt on Hamburger's theses about the timelessness of fiction. They have objected that the distinction between third-person and first-person narrative, so central for Hamburger, does not match up with the experience of reading in which there is no difference between fictitious and fictional sentences. For this reason, the past tense in fictional texts generally signifies the past—not only in first-person narrations (which Hamburger would not deny) but also in third-person narrations. Such objections, however, are based on a confusion of the form of time of narration, i.e., retrospection, with the extrafictional temporal meaning of the past tense. The claim that it is the past that is meant can obviously only refer to intrafictional temporal circumstances and not to fiction as a whole. What does not exist, and in that sense is fictive, cannot be past—although, within fiction, we can easily look back at a "yesterday" from a "today."

This is why Dorrit Cohn, in a modification of Hamburger's theorem, assigns temporal circumstances in narratives to the elementary category of "signposts of fictionality."[8] Cohn has shown that within fiction, narrative retrospectivity always includes the levels of *fabula* and *sujet*, which relate to each other as pastness and presentness. Cohn's remark that the pastness of a series of events cannot be established in relation to its narration by means of *fabula* and *sujet* alone leads us back to the question of fictionality. Fictional *fabulas* are always synchronous with their *sujets*: the *fabula* constructs itself at the same time as the *sujet*: the story constructs itself in the course of its narration. Even the indexicality of assigning dates falls victim to the logic of fiction, as Hamburger had already noted. A retrospection of the *sujet*—the past of the story in relation to the present of the act of narration—can only come about, as Cohn shows, by referring to a third level (alongside *fabula* and *sujet*) within narration, the level of reference.

Finally, we must mention the third and last of the markers of fiction Hamburger lists, the access to a third party's consciousness that, ever since psychonarration, comes with third-person narration as well.[9] This question, too, overlaps with that of the fictionality of third-person or first-person narration, namely insofar as access to consciousness in first-person narration loses its counterfactual character—everyone has access (however limited) to his or her own consciousness, but not to that of a third party. What is decisive here is the existence of an indirect relation to tense insofar as mental events can be synchronous both with the course of the plot and with processes of perception as well as of literary production and reception. The possibility of such synchrony will, above all in altermodernism, give rise to an abundance of new *sujets*, all of which seek to be synchronous with their *fabulas* (and often also with their reception) and are consequently written in the present tense.

In his 1964 study, *Tempus: Besprochene und erzählte Welt* (*Tense: Discussed World and Narrated World*), Harald Weinrich addresses the question of the temporal meaning of the past tense from the perspective of text linguistics and extends the question to tense in general. He comes to the astounding conclusion: that Käte Hamburger has not, as other critics have thought, gone too far ... she has not gone far enough. It is not just the "epic past tense," that is, the German tense *Präteritum* as it is used in poetic fiction, that has the properties described by Käte Hamburger; rather, all tenses have signaling functions that cannot be adequately described as information about time.[10]

Weinrich's pithy thesis, "Tense has nothing to do with time" (which he later wanted to be considered as no more than a historical provocation),[11] has given rise to a large number of linguistic studies devoted to the non-temporal meanings of tense.[12]

In Weinrich's own work, tense has the function of differentiating between the narrated world and the world discussed.[13] He divides the tenses into two groups: on the one hand those used to *discuss* [*besprechen*] (the present, present perfect, and future tenses) and, on the other, those used to *narrate* [*erzählen*] (the past, past perfect, and conditional tenses). It is, furthermore, possible to speak of the present tense in the discussed world and of the past tense in the narrated world "as zero-tenses, or as without attributes" because each leaves the relationship between the time of action and the time of speaking undetermined.[14] "The past tense is in particular a tense of the narrated world," it "signals ... the narrative situation as such."[15] Hence, for example, it is "characteristic of the formulaic opening of all fairy tales" to be written in the past tense ("Once upon a time there was ..."):

> This tense in the opening formula is a signal that says: Here begins the narrated world. All the tenses of fairy tale narration respond to this opening signal like a constant echo and remind us time and again that we find ourselves in an environment

that is different from the one that surrounds us in our everyday lives and makes claims on us. For a time, following the signal *Once upon a time there was*, only the world of the fairy tale endures.[16]

The end of the narrated world and the entry into the discussed world are equally marked by tenses, by formulations such as: "And if they haven't died, they are still alive today." With such a closing formula, the tenses of the narrated world are left behind and the tenses of the discussed world, here the present perfect and present tense, take their place. For with these tenses, the "real" world will make its claims in what follows as well.[17]

Among the most inspiring effects of Weinrich's analysis is that it moves narration into the realm of grammar. Narration does not so much appear as an action here, and it is not primarily taken to be a literary category. Rather, it is a serious attempt at putting the structuralist project of a "grammar of narration" (Todorov) into effect.[18] Following Weinrich's line of thought, we can see that the past tense not only performs a fictionalizing function, as we established with Hamburger, but a narrative one as well.

We read Weinrich's position as a "classical" position insofar as it shows itself to possess the greatest descriptive power when it comes to nineteenth-century classical narrated fiction. Just one example is the clear consciousness of literary norm presented to us by the realist[19] Wilhelm Raabe in the form of the caricature artist Strobel. This norm is not left without comment by Wacholder, the authorial character:

> "Hören Sie, Wachholder", sagte heute Strobel, mit den zusammengehefteten Bogen der Chronik aufs Knie schlagend, "wenn Ihnen einmal Freund Hein das Lebenslicht ausgeblasen hat, irgend jemand unter Ihrem Nachlaß diese Blätter aufwühlt und er sich die Mühe gibt, hineinzugucken, ehe er sie zu gemeinnützigen Zwecken verwendet, so wird er in demselben Fall sein wie der alte Albrecht Dürer, der ein Jagdbild lobte, aber sich zugleich beklagte, er könne nicht recht unterscheiden, was eigentlich die Hunde und was die Hasen sein sollten. Sie würfeln wirklich Traum und Historie, Vergangenheit und Gegenwart zu toll durcheinander, Teuerster; wer darüber nicht konfus wird, der ist es schon!" ...

Mit einem Kinderbaukasten verglich Strobel diese bunten Blätter ohne Zusammenhang? Gut, gut—mag es sein—ich werde weiter damit spielen, weiter luftige, tolle Gebäude damit bauen, da die fern sind welche mir die farbigsten Steine dazu lieferten! Ich werde von der Vergangenheit im Präsens und von der Gegenwart im Imperfektum sprechen, ich werde Märchen erzählen und daran glauben, Wahres zu einem Märchen machen und zuerst—die bekritzelten Blätter des Meisters Strobel der Chronik anheften!

"Listen, Wachholder," said Strobel today, with the sheets of the chronicle bound together lying on his knee, "when the angel of death snuffs out your life, and someone stirs up these papers among your things and makes the effort to look into them, before he uses them to charitable ends, he will then be in the same state as old Albrecht Dürer, who praised a hunting scene while at the same time complaining that he couldn't really decide what was supposed to be the hound and what the hare. You're really mixing up dream and history, past and present much too much, my dear; anybody would be confused by it!" ...

Was Strobel comparing these colorful pages without any context to children's building blocks? Well and good—that might be—I'll keep on playing with them, keep on building airy, fantastic buildings with them, since the ones that bring me the most colorful blocks, *they*'re far away! I will speak of the past in the present tense and the present in the imperfect, I will tell fairy tales and believe in the idea that I'm turning the real into a fairy tale and first of all—bind them together with the sheets scribbled up by Master Strobel![20]

The accusation here is that the different levels of reality, that is, "dream and history, past and present," are blended outside any narrative order. Successful novels, on the contrary, display the interweaving of narration and fiction typical of narrated fiction. Using Weinrich's theory of tense, it is possible to think through all the implications of the narratological function of both groups of tenses. This then makes it possible to spell out how tenses help to outline the scope of classical narrated fiction.

Bringing in the fiction-constituting function of the tenses we take from Hamburger makes the boundaries of the field of artistic prose up to and including the various avant-gardes visible. In Raabe, shreds of a mere chronicle, neither fictional nor narrative, blend with narration; the present tense, therefore, blends with the narrated world. Whereas the critic Strobel seems to advocate a kind of rule-based poetics of tense, which criticizes the blending of different types of text as a deviation from the canon, the author Wacholder interprets his *lapsus temporae* as a gesture that is documentary and alienating at the same time. This is how we understand Strobel's "scribblings" being bound together with the chronicle.

Such straddling of the limits between art and non-art will concern us again and again as we continue, especially because proclaiming the everyday to be art, and art to be sedimented high culture, was an important concern of the avant-gardes. The process of estrangement they make explicit can then also be traced in the use literary modernism makes of tenses. This, however, also raises a problem: at the very latest from this historical moment on, the use of tenses of the discussed world can in principle be read as an estrangement of the tenses of the narrated world or—completely desubstantializing the meaning of tense—the "switch itself" can be read as a "significant feature."[21] In this sense, the use of the present tense has also long been interpreted as an estrangement, which continues to presuppose the validity of the matrix of classical narrated fiction or, at the very least, to assume it as the background of this estrangement.

Particularly when starting from Weinrich's theoretical propositions, it seems appropriate to describe the development of the novel toward the widespread use of the present tense as a shift of dominants.[22] While in the classical matrix, the use of the past tense signals the narrated fiction and the use of the present tense indicates factual statements that do not claim to be art, the attribution of the present tense changes in the course of the twentieth century. The avant-garde reads the present tense's claim to be art only as an anti-narrative and anti-fictional estrangement. In altermodernism, however, the claim detaches from this horizon and becomes dominant. In the following section, we trace this historical movement by way of classical examples from the nineteenth century.

Classical examples

The novel *Oblomov* by Ivan Goncharov, first published in 1859, begins exactly as Käte Hamburger has described the entry into fiction:

> В гороховой улице, в одном из больших домов, народонаселения которого стало бы на целый уездный город, лежал утром в постели, на своей квартире Илья Ильич Обломов.

> One morning, in a flat in one of the great buildings in Gorokhovaia Street, the population of which was sufficient to constitute that of a provincial town, there was lying in bed a gentleman named Ilya Ilyitch Oblomov.[23]

The novel steps into fiction with its very opening sentence. There is no narrator as the subject of the proposition. The sentence is thus not anchored by any speaker at any particular place or at any particular time. Instead we enter without digression into the chronotopos of the fiction and stand at the main character's bedside. Furthermore, the opening sentence displays the irregularity of tense usage that Hamburger has called typical of fiction. The use of the progressive past tense "was lying" in connection with the temporal positioning "one morning" precisely does not make us imagine ourselves to be reading at noon that day or to be looking back from some other, later point in time to participate in past events: morning *is* now and Ilya Ilyitch *is lying* in his bed.

William Thackeray's *Vanity Fair or A Novel without a Hero* begins in a similar fashion:

> While the present century was in its teens, and on one sun-shiny morning in June, there drove up to the great iron gates of Miss Pinkerton's academy for young ladies, on Chiswick Mall, a large family coach with two fat horses in blazing harness, driven by a fat coachman in a three-cornered hat and wig, at the rate of four miles an hour. A black servant who reposed on the box beside the fat coachman, uncurled his bandy legs as soon as the equipage drew up opposite Miss Pinkerton's shining brass plate, and as he pulled the bell, at least a score of young heads were seen peering out of the narrow windows of the stately old brick

house,—nay the acute observer might have recognised the little red nose of good-natured Miss Jemima Pinkerton herself, rising over some geranium-pots in the windows of that lady's own drawing room.[24]

This episode also allows us to trace what Hamburger says about the temporal restitution of statements of date and time. Like historical dates, these lose their genuine temporal meaning. Although the first decades of the century are named as the chronotopos of Thackeray's text, it is in the fictional here and now that the young women are peering out of the window of their boarding school.

In the following example from the second half of the nineteenth century, the beginning of the fifth chapter of Émile Zola's naturalistic novel *Au Bonheur des Dames* [*The Ladies' Paradise*], we can trace the fluid character of the fictional present time, which always stays with the reader, even when there is a change in the characters the authorial perspective is oriented toward:

Le lendemain, Denise était descendue au rayon depuis une demi-heure à peine, lorsque Mme Aurélie lui dit de sa voix brève:

"Mademoiselle, on vous demande à la direction."

La jeune fille trouva Mouret seul, assis dans le grand cabinet tendu de reps vert. Il venait de se rappeler "la malpeignée," comme la nommait Bourdoncle; et lui qui répugnait d'ordinaire au rôle de gendarme, il avait eu l'idée de la faire comparaître pour la secouer un peu, si elle était toujours fagotée en provinciale. La veille, malgré sa plaisanterie, il avait éprouvé devant Mme Desforges, une contrariété d'amour-propre, en voyant discuter l'élégance d'une de ses vendeuses. C'était, chez lui, un sentiment confus, un mélange de sympathie et de colère.

"Mademoiselle," commença-t-il, "nous vous avions pris par égard pour votre oncle, et il ne faut pas nous mettre dans la triste nécessité …"

Mais il s'arrêta. En face de lui, de l'autre côté du bureau, Denise se tenait droite, sérieuse et pâle. Sa robe de soie n'était plus trop large, serrant sa taille ronde, moulant les lignes pures de ses épaules de vierge; et, si sa chevelure, nouée en grosses tresses, restait sauvage, elle tâchait du moins de se contenir. Après s'être endormie toute vêtue, les yeux épuisés de larmes, la jeune fille, en se réveillant vers quatre heures, avait eu honte de cette crise de sensibilité nerveuse. Et elle s'était mise immédiatement à rétrécir la robe, elle avait passé une heure devant l'étroit miroir, le peigne dans ses cheveux, sans pouvoir les réduire, comme elle l'aurait voulu.

The next day, Denise had scarce been in the department for half an hour when Madame Aurélie said to her in her sharp voice:

"Mademoiselle Baudu, you're wanted in the head office.

The girl found Mouret alone, sitting in the great office hung with green rep. He had just remembered the "unkempt girl," as Bourdoncle called her; and, although he was usually reluctant to play the policeman, he had had the idea of sending for her to give her a bit of a jolt, in case she was still looking dowdy like a girl from the provinces. The day before, in spite of the joke he had made, his vanity had been wounded when the smartness of one of his salesgirls had been discussed in front of Madame Desforges. His feelings were confused, a mixture of sympathy and anger.

"Mademoiselle Baudu," he began, "we took you on out of consideration for your uncle, and you must not put us to the painful necessity ..."

But he stopped. Opposite him, on the other side of the desk, Denise was standing erect, serious and pale. Her silk dress was no longer too big, but fitted tightly around her pretty figure, moulding the pure lines of her virgin shoulders; and if her hair, knotted in thick braids, remained untamed, she was at least trying to control it. She had fallen asleep fully clothed, all her tears spent, and when woke at about four o'clock she had felt ashamed of her attack of nervous sensibility. She had immediately set about taking in her dress, and had spent an hour in front of the narrow mirror, combing her hair, without being able to smooth it down as she would have liked.[25]

Mouret's gaze at the young girl is every bit as present [*gegenwärtig*] as Denise's lengthy gaze in the mirror, which precedes it by a few hours. The reconstruction of the narrative sequence of events, which can be accomplished here with no trouble, has no influence on the fictional equi-presentness of the two scenes. The scene introduced by the phrase "the next day" that features the paradoxical combination described by Hamburger of past tense and future time adverb is every bit as present as the scene in which the usage of the past perfect comes with the temporal specification "the evening before." This confirms Suzanne Fleischman's remarks on the use of the past perfect, whose function in narrated fiction is to signal the narrative antecedence of equally present events.[26]

In Walter Scott's *Ivanhoe*, on the contrary, we can track how across long passages the impression of the fictional here and now is precisely *not* produced because the narrator does not retreat behind what he is narrating. His narration thus reveals its retrospective character:

> Such being our chief scene, the date of our story refers to a period towards the end of the reign of Richard I, when his return from his long captivity had become an event rather wished than hoped for by his despairing subjects, who were in the meantime subjected to every species of subordinate oppression.[27]

In the presence of the narrator, this example also demonstrates the implicit present of the *sujet*, which here blocks the entry into fiction: Whenever narration displays its retrospective character so openly, it prevents the presentification of (implicitly) past events. These cannot transform into a fictional present because the *sujet* already presents itself as present. We will return at a later point to this ordering of time to be conceived within narration (that is, to the implicit present of the *sujet*, of narration, as opposed to the implicit pastness of the *fabula*, of the story narrated, in the matrix of classical narrated fiction) and to the problems connected to the temporal ordering of *fabula* and *sujet*. In classical narrated fiction, the present character of fiction (with its form of time, contemporaneity) and the retrospective character of narration (with its form of time, retrospection) merge into a synthetic form of time, the *figuration of time* that is presentification.[28]

Modernity: The emergence of the present-tense novel

Transition I: The break with fiction

Since modernism, we can observe a progressive distancing from the matrix of classical narrated fiction.[29] This change occurs on several levels. On the one hand, authors like Hamsun or Shklovsky write metafictional texts in which they experiment with the organon of existing procedures to expose the mechanisms of fictional construction or to break through to an imaginary basis for fiction.[30] While in this case, fiction remains reflective, there are, on the other hand, the declarations and manifestos of the avant-garde that are explicitly directed against fiction. The literary forms experimented with for this purpose are meant to avoid the "fiction effect" as much as possible.

Yet in that the texts of the Russian avant-garde (Sergei Tretyakov's, for example) avoid the past tense in favor of the present tense, they of course confirm the effect of the epic past tense in terms of fiction and narration as Hamburger and Weinrich describe it. First, avant-garde writers employ the present tense with a view to a "factography" (*literatura fakta*), which rules out the constitution of a fictional *fabula*. Second, the agitation against the fictional *fabula*[31] comes with a propagation of factual linguistic work on the *sujet*, which prevents the sujet from becoming "inconspicuous" (and thus a fundamental requirement for bringing about classical fiction is not met). The novel is to be replaced by operative sketches; the writer, from whose work only "paper people" are said to emerge, is to be replaced by the journalist, who is dealing with "living people":[32]

«Джонни»—зовут его близкие.

«Джонни»—зовут его совершенно незнакомые берлинские рабочие.

Он брат Виланда Герцфельде, директора-распорядителя радикального издательства «Малик Ферлаг», занявшего своими изданиями почетное место на гитлеровском костре …

Книжное дело за капиталистическим рубежом совсем не похоже на наше. Наша книжная витрина—это сотни, если не тысячи названий, на разные вкусы и темы. Там книжная витрина—одно-два, ну, много—пять названий. Книгоиздатель норовит выпустить такую книгу, чтобы она стала ‚шлягером‚—боевиком ...

И вот в кабинете этого солидного директора, где диктофон переливает в уши машинистки консервированную на восковом валике спокойную речь, где телефон с десятью кнопками для дачи приказаний во все отделы, где муштрованные секретари и механизированная наклейка марок на конверты, появляется Бэстер Кэйтон. Вы помните этого трагического комика американских экранов, никогда не улыбающегося, щуплого, одержимого.[33]

"Johnny" is what those close to him call him.

"Johnny" is what the Berlin workers call him who don't even know him.

He is the brother of Wieland Herzfeld, the executive director of the radical Malik Publishers, which was honored for its publications at Hitler's book burning ...

The book business in capitalist countries is in no way similar to ours. Our book displays—there are hundreds, even thousands of titles, works for the widest range of tastes and with the most varied topics. In the shop windows there, you see one, two titles, maybe five if it's a really big shop. The book publisher is therefore very keen to bring out a book that will become a "bestseller." ...

And there, in the workrooms, this respectable director appears, there where the Dictaphone trickles a calm speech recorder on a wax cylinder into the stenotypist's ears, where there's a telephone with ten buttons to give commands to all the departments, where there are drilled secretaries, and where envelopes are stamped by an automatic machine, a Buster Keaton. They are surely reminiscent of this tragic comedian of the American film, who never smiles, who is so lanky and obsessed.

Put in Weinrich's terms, Tretyakov presents us with a discussed world, a factual world, not a fictive world—and this he expresses by the use of the present tense. The people he describes are not the acting characters of a *fabula*, but writers, publishers, and journalists, that is, persons whose professional activity consists in producing (avant-garde) art. His factography refers to the act that constitutes works of art, and the factual reference thus acquires a self-referential character as well.

To clarify what level Tretyakov's facticity refers to, we must briefly explain the narratological distinction between *fabula* and *sujet*. We employ the original distinction articulated in Russian Formalism for methodological reasons but also for a reason that lies in the history of theory. We subscribe to Paul Ricœur's criticism of the transformation of narratological levels, that is, the transformation of temporal structures of story and plot into atemporal logical schemata. This transformation can be seen in French Structuralism (Todorov, Barthes, Greimas, Benveniste) and American neo-formalist film theory (Bordwell/Thompson, Chatman, Branigan). Yet when we go back to the formalist terminology of *fabula* and *sujet*, it becomes obvious that such detemporalizing schematization is due only to a style of structuralist theory. It is not prefigured in the narratological categories themselves. Quite to the contrary, Viktor Shklovsky[34] introduced the concept *sujet* in one of his first studies by means of the temporal dynamics ("temporal rearrangements" and "shift[s]") in Sterne's *Tristram Shandy*.[35]

Temporal relations between the two levels of narration are generally noticed only when one assumes a retrospectivity of narration, which makes it possible to look back at "past events" and thus to tell the story, to be self-evident. This understanding, however, obscures the proper (or genuine) temporalities both of the *fabula* and the *sujet*. *Fabula* and *sujet* are not transmutable one into the other, nor can they be derived one from the other, as is suggested, for example, by the terminology "narration" / "narrative." It makes sense, therefore, to stress the logic proper to each level in the terminology one employs as well.[36] Furthermore, there are no easy alternatives to be found for the term *sujet* (as is possible for "*fabula*") that could meet the following two requirements of our conceptual toolbox. The term "*sujet*" implies an openness to the reader[37] (which excludes all varieties of "narration," such as Genette's *récit*) and to the dimension of fictionality (which excludes the term *discours*). In addition, the terms should not already have a fixed meaning in narratology (as is the case with "narration" / "narrative," "*histoire*" / "*discours*," "story" / "plot") but rather allow for a differentiation in light of the questions raised by fiction theory.[38] The definition of the genuine temporality of both levels of narration in particular is dependent on the perspective one chooses: in narratology, the *sujet* is usually conceived of as present and the *fabula* as past; in fiction theory, in turn, the difference between *fabula* and *sujet* usually is such that the *fabula*—unlike the present *sujet*—appears as presentified.

We are using the terms "*fabula*" and "*sujet*" as fundamental categories to characterize two levels that differentiate out in all narrative texts, no matter whether they are described as the dualism of fiction and narration, of story and its rhetorical form, or of a text's reference and its literary materiality. The *sujet* is the constitutive act of the literary artifact (independently of whether this act is accomplished by the producer or the recipient) and all its variations; the place of literary and rhetorical technique; the archive of the artistic canon of forms; the voice of narration; the scene of writing. In the *fabula* of narrative texts an action acquires an unfathomable sense, a story takes a surprising course, the world changes for a character. Its fundamental operation is sequentialization. The *fabula* is the object of narrative texts, the object that is always ahead of the reader and that is (always) tracked by the reader. With the *fabula*, narrative texts aim for a reference, for a dynamic space into which actions can unfold, for persons whose subjectivity is formed in their (hi)story, and for a time that opens up to them. Such a pathos of the *fabula* could well be summarized by Theodor W. Adorno's formula: "History is the content of artworks."[39] This level is governed by the dynamic of the imaginary, of fiction, and of reference.

Let us return to Tretyakov's reflections and to his critique of the *fabula* in particular. The entanglement of *fabula* and *sujet* he criticizes in fiction, especially nineteenth-century fiction, can roughly be summarized as follows: *The factual* sujet *narrates the fictional* fabula. In factographies, the rejection of fiction in favor of fact is accompanied by a rejection of the *fabula*. This lack of *fabula*[40] is connected to the self-reflexivity of the process of literary communication, that is, to a self-awareness of the *sujet*, a critique of prior literary practice, and the demand for a new practice. Thus we read in Tretyakov's sketch about Brecht in the text already cited:

— Товарищ Берт Брехт, подымитесь с вашего низкого кресла на точных шарнирах коленных суставов. Перестаньте на секунду пить сгущенный ликер умозаключений. Почему эти люди здесь, а не в ячейках, не в гуле митингов безработных? Почему в здешнем дымословии и словодымии мне почудилось слово «штамтиш политик»?

В каждой пивнушке есть свои завсегдатаи. У этих завсегдатаев есть свой стол—«штамтиш». За этим столом они пьют пиво и разговаривают о политике. От пива наживают себе слоновью печень. От разговоров—полную отвычку от политического действия.

— Вы человек Советского Союза и прямого действия—отвечает Брехт.

Comrade Brecht, raise yourself up from the low armchair by the precisely functioning hinge of your knee. Leave behind for a moment the viscous liqueur of syllogism. Why are these people here and not in the party cells, why not in the bluster of the assemblies of the unemployed? Why is the word barroom politics pressing on me out of the clouds of smoke and the smoke of thoughts?

Every bar has its regulars. And these regulars have their table, indeed, the regulars' table. At this table they drink their beer and prattle on about politics. From the beer they get an inflamed liver, from their prattling they get abstinence from political activity. "You are a man of the Soviet Union and of immediate action," answers Brecht.[41]

The writer Bertolt Brecht, the liqueur of syllogisms, political babbling—all of this has a documentary character and refers to the conditions of literary communication (whose conventionality is attacked). Tretyakov casts his vote against an inventory of the business of literature and in favor of an operative literature. As became clear in his sketch of John Heartfield, when Tretyakov gives a speech to a literary figure, as he does here, he propagates the writer's intervention in reality, a factory of facts. At this point, a continuity between classical narrated fiction and early modern present-tense texts comes to the fore: even in modernity, whenever the present tense designates exclusively the process of narration, the classical tense system, in which the present tense has a documentary function, remains intact.

Seen from Weinrich's theoretical perspective, that is, from the perspective of the narrativity of literature, there is no break here; yet, with Hamburger, from the perspective of the fictionality of literature, we may diagnose a break. Roughly speaking: The present-tense literature of the first half of the twentieth century tends to neglect the fictional. We can distinguish two aspects of this neglect. On the one hand, we find a massive criticism of the fictional, in the factography movement in particular; on the other, there is a superabundance of narration. This narration is content with itself and frees itself from the service of the *fabula*. It no longer retreats behind the *fabula* or rejects it completely in a narration without *fabula*. In this way, it deliberately accepts (or attempts to ensure) that no fiction can arise. No (past) event is presentified, and the reader is not placed into the fictive here and now of a novel's events (to use Hamburger's terms). Thus we read in Vasily Rozanov's *Solitaria*, which Viktor Shklovsky celebrated as a new novel without a contrived story:

> Всякое движение души у меня сопровождается движением выговариванием. И всякое выговаривание я хочу непременно записать. Это—инстинкт. Не из такого ли инстинкта родилась литература (писменная)?
>
> Every impulse of the soul is for me accompanied by a *pronouncement*. And I would like promptly to *write down* every pronouncement. This is an instinct. Was it not from such an instinct that (written) literature was born? No thought comes from printing, and so Gutenberg came "afterward."[42]

If literature thematizes itself, speaks only about itself, then it documents and produces documents about both its emergence and, in the same breath, the tense it uses: present tense means present time and past tense means the past.

In terms of fiction theory, we could also speak of a break in a further sense, namely, where the switch to an (internally focalized) first-person narration is concerned. In accordance with Hamburger's assessment that first-person narratives are not fictional, Rozanov does not aim at any "timeless"[43] meaning of tense. Instead, the present tense aims for the present in quite a documentary sense.

From the point of view of literary history, it needs to be stressed that initially the tense switch from the past tense to the present does not involve a systematic break. Factographic texts do indeed avoid the (fictional) epic past tense and instead employ a documentary present tense. Yet they use this present tense precisely in the sense in which Weinrich defines its function, namely, to discuss and not to narrate. In avant-garde factographies, the documentary present tense retains its discussing function. The definition of the values of narratology and fiction theory that applied in the nineteenth century thus remains the same. Only their aesthetic value, the attribution of positive or negative value, changes.

Transition II: The break with narrativity

The problem of narration or of anti-narrativity in the transition to modernity is particularly evident in the work of Virginia Woolf. There is a noticeable detachment from classical narrated fiction, yet it takes a different form in Woolf than it does in the avant-gardes. This movement of detachment reveals the development of an explicit poetics of time since the end of the nineteenth century.[44] At first this is manifest only at the level of motifs, as it is in a number of well-known modern novels of time, for instance in James Joyce's *Ulysses*. Yet in Woolf, we also find compositional experiments with the temporal flow of the novel that eventually lead to a tense switch to the present tense.

Ann Banfield has focused on the interlude in *To the Lighthouse*. She uses the chapter to show how Virginia Woolf's conception of time follows from the ideas of contemporary Cambridge philosophers, above all those of Bertrand Russell, according to whom time appears as a discontinuous series of moments. The interlude, entitled "Time Passes," connects and disconnects two impressionistic narratives of particular moments.[45] These, in the manner of classical narrated fiction, are written predominantly in the past tense, while the interlude "Time Passes" presents certain programmatic forms of the present tense not only in its title.

Such a form of variable, internal focalization of the narration, that is, such a form of multiperspectivism,[46] in which all the characters in *To the Lighthouse* act as their own narrators, we already find in *Mrs. Dalloway*. What Woolf actualizes[47] at the level of a fictional motif is something that applies to fictional narration throughout: narrative, insofar as it is fictional, never exists prior to its communication or independent of the act of narration.[48] The journey of an ominous black car riding through the streets of London depicted in *Mrs. Dalloway* is consistently reproduced in the perception of narrator-characters, who are lined up as if for a relay race at the side of the road. The car is present only in each of the perceptions and, in conformity with Woolf's conception of time, is passed on momentarily and discontinuously from perception to perception, "handed off" from one narrating passerby to the next. The black car exists (as a fictional car) only so long as the chain of perceptions, which maintain its presentness, does not break and so long as the narrating characters pay (narrating) attention to it. The moment the onlookers' attention is distracted away from the car, it disappears.[49] Here we can recognize the temporal construction that is also actualized in the strokes of Big Ben (originally, the book was even supposed to be called *The Hours*): a flow of time is perceived in a series of discontinuous present points.

Mrs. Dalloway thus appears as a transitional text on the cusp of the modern present-tense novel. What we find developed here in motifs is explicitly actualized in the employment of tenses in *The Waves*. In this novel, written only a few years later, perceptible events are described synchronously with mental events—in the present tense. Description now is interrupted only by short sentences in the past tense, in which the perspective is transferred from one character to the next. The six characters have arranged to meet in a restaurant. While they wait for the main character, Percival, they are described one after another as they arrive:

> 'It is now five minutes to eight,' said Neville. 'I have come early …' The door opens, but he does not come. That is Louis hesitating there. That is his strange mixture of assurance and timidity.

The description of Louis continues in the present tense and then switches over to him:

> 'There is Susan,' said Louis. 'She does not see us.'

This is followed by the narration of Susan's path from the door to the table and the transfer of the perspective to Susan:

> 'There is Jinny,' said Susan. 'She stands in the door. Everything seems stayed. The waiter stops. The diners at the table by the door look ...'[50]

The development towards the present tense in Woolf's texts can thus be traced, using Hamburger and Weinrich's parameters, from the first motifs in *Mrs. Dalloway* (1925) via the compositional experimentation of *To the Lighthouse* (1927) to the switch of tenses in *The Waves* (1931). This development involves the narrator becoming a character; it also involves impressionistic discussion. What is doubtful is not the fictionality of this prose but its narrativity.

In this context, Dorrit Cohn has shown that narratology has been unable to harmonize its thesis of the past quality of narration—"narrative is past, always past"[51]—with the development of the modern present tense and therefore concludes that the present tense is intrinsically anti-narrative. The difference between a narrative and an anti-narrative interpretation of the text becomes clear in a comparison of the passage just quoted with the first draft, which often leaves out the single quotation marks that signal a character's monologue.[52]

The derivation of this present tense from a succession of interior monologues is evidence that its narrative character is not acknowledged; it is an attempt

> to understand the present tense ... as the normal tense of silently expressive self-communion, a language that emerges in a fictional mind without aiming at communicative narration or narrative communication.[53]

Cohn has the interior monologue emerge from the transparency of the characters to the narration. It thus arises from procedures of internal focalization, which loses its counterfactual character as it comes into widespread use in first-person present tense narratives. While access to the subjectivity of a third party—Hamburger's third criterion of fiction—is impossible and in this sense signals fictionality, the "fictional mimesis of mental life,"[54] as soliloquy, bears no trace of the impossibility of such mimesis. An analogous point can be made for reading the passage as dialogue; the character's parts can be put and have been put, implicitly and explicitly, in double quotation marks.[55]

In the interpretation of the passage as monologue or as dialogue, the implicit equi-presentness of an exterior event and its being communicated might appear odd, but it is possible in principle. If, however, we read the characters' passages in such a way that each narrator takes the relay of the previous narrator, we notice an aporia: in this case the narrator-characters would each have to experience and narrate at the same time. Later we will describe how it is precisely this aporia that promotes the fictionalization of the present tense.[56] In the meantime, let us note that at the threshold to modernity the problem of the present tense becomes more and more acute, especially in the first-person narrative. Modernity's first present-tense texts, such as interior monologues and early present-tense novels, are to be considered non-fictional (in Hamburger's sense) and anti-narrative (in Weinrich's sense).

The erosion of the matrix of narrated fiction

The avant-gardes adopted the matrix of classical narrated fiction and yet rejected it *in toto* as a "generator of fiction," and as literature develops in the twentieth century this matrix gradually loses its stability. This is evident in the disintegration of the matrix's three central dichotomies: *fabula/sujet*, fictional/factual, past tense/present tense. These couples no longer form the systematic and coherent whole that used to determine their position within the matrix.

In the classical system, each of the poles forms two series. Of the series *fabula*/fiction/past tense we can roughly say: The *fabula* (A) is conceived of as fictional (B) and past (C). For the series *sujet*/fact/present tense, the guideline is that the *sujet* (A) is said to be factual (B) and present (C). The coherence of the entire matrix, in which all categories smoothly interlock, follows from these equivalences: *the factual* sujet *presentifies the fictional* fabula.

In the earliest attempts to gain distance from this system, in Rozanov or in Woolf, for instance, the use of the present tense remains in conformity with the system and simply renounces all

Table 1.1 The matrix of narrated fiction

A	fabula	sujet
B	fiction	fact
C	past tense	present tense
D	she–he / I	I / you

those elements that might conflict with it. One result is that the present-tense texts of modernism can make use of only a small part of the possibilities available within the matrix of narrated fiction. This leads to a "short circuiting" of the remaining parameters, i.e., the factual, the *sujet*, the first person, and the present tense (for instance under the heading of the autobiographical).

The transition to the narrative present tense

Where, then, do the problems arise that lead to the dissolution of this matrix, which prevented a fictional *fabula* from being narrated in the present tense and allowed for a *sujet* to be thematized only as factual? Why and how does narration in the *present tense* come to be? The first problems appear in first-person narratives, and we have already mentioned that they constituted a hurdle for the elaboration of Hamburger's theory. Our concern, however, is not to ask whether her theory is restricted to third-person narratives or whether the mechanism of presentification is no longer effective in personal narration. We seek to differentiate the matrix of narrated fiction in terms of person and thereby understand the model in a purely heuristic way. The relations it presents are ideal and typical. It only presents a schema from which all concrete texts deviate and merely provides a point of reference and a background for estrangement.

In point D, the matrix of classical narrated fiction organizes the persons of the narrative and fictional levels as follows: I (narrator) hereby (*sujet*) tell you (dear reader) what once happened (*fabula*) to him–her (character/he–she). For modernism, the switch of persons at the level of the *fabula* is of particular significance. In the place of a third person as narrated character, we increasingly find the first person. To be sure, the first person can expand from the level of the *sujet* to that of the *fabula* within the matrix of narrated fiction as well, namely when a first-person narrator tells "the story of my life." In that case, however, the past tense still marks a temporal distinction between the first person at the level of the *sujet* and the "I who I once was" at the level of the *fabula*, such that the latter *I* can nonetheless be perceived as a fictional character (as a she–he). This "precarious" proximity of the implicitly factual first-person narrator and the implicitly past first-person character fuels a debate about the fictitious nature of first-person narratives (as opposed to the fictional nature of third-person narratives). Are first-person narratives classical narratives or ("merely fictitious") autobiographies? Does the (implicitly factual) first-person narrator narrate the story of a fictional character? Or does a narrator (invented by the author) narrate *his own* (implicitly factual) past? In every first-person narrative, the *I* is a fictional/factographic hybrid.

This shows that persons draw their fictionality from the organization of *fabula* and *sujet*. This organization endows each person with a different fictional status. *She–he* is fictional, because *she–he* is the subject of the fictional *fabula*; *I* is not fictional, because *I* is the subject of the implicitly factual (non-fictional) *sujet*. But why should the one be more fictional than the other? And what about present-tense texts in first-person form—is their *I* factual (as the subject of the *sujet*) or fictional (as the subject of the *fabula*)?

As long as we assume that every text should be examined as to who is speaking and that every *I* marks the position of the speaker (that it is the subject of the *sujet*), the answer must be: *I* is always factual. For a speaker cannot invent her- or himself *as speaker*; a narrator cannot narrate her- or himself *as narrating*. We will see that it is nonetheless possible to understand a first person in present-tense texts as fictional, that is, as a character's *I* [*Ich-Figur*], namely when the *you* of the reader becomes the subject of the *sujet*. In discussing the altermodern personnel policy in present-tense texts, we will see that the transfer of the present of the *sujet* to the reader, in particular, alters the temporal relations of *fabula* and *sujet*. The altermodern constellation of metafictional and imaginary narrativity results from the fact that the present of the *sujet* can be determined by the present of narration as well as by the present of the act of reading. This will remove one of the last obstacles to a global use of the present tense.

Within the matrix of narrated fiction, however, it is impossible *not* to think of the present of the *sujet* exclusively from out of the present of the narration process. Hence any first person must be the first person of the narrator, who (as the subject of the *sujet*) tells the story (that is, constitutes a *fabula*). While in narrated fiction, as we have said, an *additional* first person can nonetheless turn up at the level of the *fabula* (since the past tense marks the difference between first-person narrator and first-person character), this ought to be impossible in a present-tense text. For that would mean that the narrator synchronously experiences what she or he is narrating. Modern first-person narratives nonetheless attempt to confront this problem (which we will discuss later under the heading "aporia of synchrony").

But would these problems not simply have to disappear in present-tense texts in which no first person appears? If the narrator is not relating his own experiences but those of a (fictional) character in a novel, the problem seems to be resolved only at first glance: immediately, the already-mentioned breaking point in narrated fiction becomes noticeable. In narrated fiction, the past tense indicates that a narrator is looking back from his (implicit) present to (implicitly past) events thus presentified. In principle, then, there is no synchronous present [*Gleichgegenwart*] of *fabula* and *sujet* (within the matrix of narrated fiction): while the first-person narrator of a present-tense text has no time in which she could report on her synchronous experiences, the third-person narrator has no place from which he could narrate the experiences of a character.

And yet there are third-person narratives in the present tense that can be read and understood "through the lens of narrated fiction"—and that needs to be explained. In these third-person narratives, the contradiction between the present of experience and the present of narration becomes invisible thanks to procedures of fictionalization. There is no point at which the narrator reveals himself and his (paradoxical) present. How this is possible, what effect this creates, and what the limits of this process are can be seen in the example of John Updike's *Rabbit* novels.

Excursus: John Updike's notational present tense

Altogether unobtrusively or without too much poetological or aesthetic polemics, John Updike confidently describes his own employment of the present tense:

> *Rabbit* took off; as I sat at a little upright desk in a small corner room of the first house I owned, in Ipswich, Massachusetts, writing in soft pencil, the present-tense sentences accumulated and acquired momentum.[57]

The failure to treat of a historical topic links up with Updike's confession, or rather, his realization of being "too earthbound a realist or too tame a visionary for the vigorous fakery of a historical novel."[58] In any case, Harry Angstrom's very first appearance, at the beginning of the first *Rabbit* novel, already indicates Updike's capacity for graphic directness:

> Boys are playing basketball around a telephone pole with a backboard bolted to it. Legs, shouts. The scrape and snap of Keds on loose alley pebbles seems to catapult their voices high into the moist March air blue above the wires. Rabbit Angstrom, coming up the alley in a business suit, stops and watches, though he's twenty-six and six-three. So tall, he seems an unlikely rabbit ... His standing there makes the real boys feel strange. Eyeballs slide.[59]

We learn something about Updike's efforts to grasp his own present (in the sense of grasping the character of the times) and to write a contemporary novel in the present tense in one of his other, later descriptions of the process that gave rise to the novel:

> *Rabbit, Run* was written in 1959, in the present tense. The time of its writing contained the time of its action. The songs and news that Harry Angstrom hears on the car radio in his drive south, on the night before Spring arrives, were what came over my own, more northerly radio that very night. I fell behind in this synchronization, but still worked with such haste that I felt

impelled to rework all proofs heavily and, after the book was published, to make further revisions for the Penguin edition printed in England four years later.[60]

Yet Updike not only falls behind the events he wants to narrate; he achieves an approximate conformity to the events only because the *sujet*, just as in classical narrated fiction, retreats behind the *fabula*. Rabbit's story narrates itself in the manner of classical narrated fiction (as if) by itself. What Updike wants to synchronize is not so much *fabula* and *sujet* but the course of the *fabula* and the course of events.

In order not to squander time composing a *fabula*, Updike simply writes down the events in synchrony with their imagined (factual) course. In literary theory, Boris Uspensky stipulated that such a present tense has the correlating function of fixing the point of view "from which the narrative is carried out. Each time the present tense is used, the author's temporal position is synchronic—that is, it coincides with the temporal position of his characters."[61] A *fabula* that is synchronous with events lacks fictional traits at least from the perspective of temporality. The chronology of the course of the *fabula* corresponds to the course of events, and it does without condensing and grouping events together or providing compositional summaries. There is a similarity here to Tretyakov's factographies insofar as the *fabula* becomes a documentary.

The fiction of the documentary, however, does require that the *sujet* also take part in the process. The *sujet* may not get in the way of the chronological documentarism of the *fabula*. It may not counteract the *fabula* and must obediently assert that the notation of events is commensurate with their course. The documentary self-denial of the *sujet* goes so far that the sujet has to make itself disappear to avoid any contradictions. No one is allowed to ask who actually wrote down this story, where the narrator was standing in the picture, and above all when in the process of following the movements he wrote. This can only have occurred in the form of a fantastic stenography.

When the second volume of Updike's tetralogy is already stepping outside the synchrony of events time and again because memories have accumulated over a period of 10 years, this too is presumably conceived from the perspective of a *fabula* taken to be documentary, uncomposed, and ultimately causal. Ever more memories mix in with the events since the abundance of events becomes more and more complicated and no longer follows from the preceding moment but displays an increasing tendency to present itself as the sum of precedent moments. Yet this turns a pure and one-dimensional present tense into a problem.[62] If moments follow from a multitude of precedent moments, which one do you choose? Can several be included in the course of events at the same time? A parallel presentification of events would demand a multi-layered present tense and a new conception of the present. In such instances, however, Updike resorts to using the past tense.[63]

Updike's novel is thus located at one of the limits of classical narrated fiction. Its aspiration to present-tense narration wrests from the present tense the promise of presentness. This aspiration nonetheless takes a classical narrative form, in which the *sujet* renders itself invisible behind the *fabula* and the *fabula* narrates itself (as if) by itself. Updike, one might say, turns the *fabula* into a documentary. In such a linking of the levels A and B, problems arise the moment in which the present tense goes beyond the horizon of the present, that is, for instance, the moment it seeks to summarize what has happened between the first and the second volumes. It takes the altermodern novel to develop possibilities of solving this difficulty without (re)activating the matrix of narrated fiction.

There is a difference between the modern and the altermodern in relation to level C, which concerns the basic relation of the past tense and the present tense. In the texts in and around the *nouveau roman* movement,[64] the present tense acquires a counter-intuitive meaning. Since the 1960s, the present tense can also serve to narrate the past. It thus enters into a new relation to the past tense, and once again a correlative meaning of tenses arises. This is the point at which the asynchronous present tense refers to the presentifying past tense.

On level D as well, we will see commonalities arise between the altermodern present tense and the matrix of narrated fiction. In altermodern novels, the characters are not opaque to the narrator, as they usually are in the "canonical" *nouveaux romans*. Instead, there is a resumption of the third-person narrative. This, however, does not imply a return to authorial narration. Instead, it often serves to desynchronize the interior and exterior worlds. This desynchronization actualizes a latent delusion: even as characters are embedded in a present space, factual, past, and imaginary times pervade their consciousness.[65]

Yet the two levels that concern our central question—How does the present tense become a novelistic tense or how does narrated fiction in the present tense emerge?—are levels A (*fabula/sujet*) and B (fiction/fact). The question of the possibility of a narrative present tense can be posed in terms of (1) narratology and (2) fiction theory. The question in narratology is: How does the present tense gain access to the *fabula*? The question in fiction theory is: How does the present tense fictionalize itself?

How does the present tense gain access to the fabula?

To answer this question, we can begin by pointing out the second breaking point in the matrix of narrated fiction, the narratological breaking point. While the fictional breaking point refers to the coordination of the matrix's couples B and C (that is, to the linking up of fiction and the epic past tense that enables the presentification of implicitly past events), the narratological breaking point concerns the relation of couples A and C. Within the matrix, the *fabula* is conceivable only as implicitly past, the *sujet* as implicitly present— from the point of view of narratology, the present on the level of the *fabula* is a problem because it implies synchrony with the *sujet*.

We have already mentioned this aporia discussed by Dorrit Cohn and others, which we would like to call the aporia of synchrony: I cannot synchronously experience a story and narrate it.[66] It seems evident that this is a purely narratological problem. While in fiction theory it is possible to repudiate the *sujet*'s function of presentifying in favor of the *fabula*, that is, to invent the *fabula* synchronously with its being written down, narratology rules out such a synchrony. We will see that a series of altermodern present-tense texts can live with this aporia rather well. In accordance with Hamburger's theses on the tense-structured formation of fiction, these texts fictionalize *the sujet*, which uses a present tense "as if" it were a past tense.[67]

The reasons for treating this aporia as a "narratological breaking point" can be briefly addressed in terms of literary history as well. In the modern reflexive self-thematization of narration, the *sujet* no longer retreats behind the *fabula*; instead of an invisible third-person narrator we find a self-reflexive (first-person) narrator who thematizes her or his own narration. This does not yet lead to any break with traditional narration as long as the *fabula* remains untouched by it. As examples we cited Rozanov's novels without *fabula* and Tretyakov's factographies. To be sure, as soon as the threshold to present-tense narration is crossed and narration seeks to narrate more than just itself, that is, as soon as it seeks to narrate a *fabula*, it is confronted with the problem that there is no room, so to speak, for the narrated events in the present time of the process of narration. This present time is completely taken up by narration; fiction can, at most, accompany it.

Modernity tries hard to accommodate *fabula* and *sujet* in a single present time. This can be seen in attempts to synchronize the story and its narration, the *fabula* and the *sujet*. The problems that arise from this overlapping result in the specific options that literary history can detect in the various poetologies of modernity.[68] Two of these are: (a) *fabula* and *sujet* alternate in the foreground; (b) *fabula* and *sujet* overlap, and the *sujet* adopts the prospective contemporaneity[69] of the *fabula*.

(a) The attempt to synchronize fabula and sujet

In a narration in which the present *sujet* narrates a past *fabula*, *fabula* and *sujet* cannot be synchronous. One possibility of synchronizing them nonetheless is to let them alternate in the foreground. A passage from Peter Weiss's *The Shadow of the Body of the Coachman* may illustrate the procedure. While the first-person narrator writes down his text, the action must be suspended:

> Ich sehe ihn vor mir, wie er mit der einen erdigen, dickgeäderten, kurzfingrigen Hand das Holzstück auf dem Bock festhält ... Erst jetzt (eben schreit die Krähe noch einmal Harm) empfinde ich die Kälte an meinem entblößten Gesäß. Die Niederschrift meiner Beobachtungen hat mich davon abgehalten die Hose hinaufzuziehen und zuzuknöpfen ... Ich ziehe jetzt die Hose hinauf, knöpfe sie zu und schließe den Gürtel, ich nehme den hölzernen Deckel

> I see him in front of me holding the piece of wood on the jack with one earthy, thick-veined, short-fingered hand ... Only now (the crow is just crying harm again) I feel cold on my bare seat. Writing down my observations has kept me from pulling my pants up and buttoning them ... I now pull up my pants, button them and buckle the belt; I take the wooden lid[70]

Following this scene, the narrator continues to report the *fabula*, describes himself as he crosses the courtyard, walks through the rooms of the house, up the stairs, and reaches his room, where he sits down at the desk. At the margins of the action, writing stops are set up. The narrator can always only provide short pieces of the action, which must be interrupted to be written down. Neither a continuous flow of events nor an uninterrupted flow of narration can therefore come about. Because both the flow of events and the flow of narration obey the imperative that demands factuality, they are not (as they are, for instance, in Updike) synchronized inconspicuously, but are connected in series. The present-tense novel of the second half of the twentieth century transforms this model into a model of graduated time that employs the montage of temporal layers in the service of an archeological model of history. This is how Hubert Fichte clothes the altermodern plying of temporal layers in a poetological motif:

> Ich entschließe mich, während der Sturm den Schnee bis an das Bett treibt, mein schönes Buch zu schreiben, Gesichter zu vergrößern, Litaneien aufzuzeichnen—Schichten statt Geschichten, Kiesel, Zeitraffer, Zeitlupe, die Uhrzeit verlieren und auch die wiedergefundene Zeit wieder verlieren.

> I decide to write my fine book while the storm is driving the snow up to my bed, to enlarge faces, to record litanies—layers instead of stories, pebbles, time lapse, slow motion, losing the time of day and losing time again after having found it.[71]

(b) Fabula and sujet overlap

Already in modernism, we find Robert Walser using a narrative present tense in a way that quite simply abandons the claim that this tense cannot but be anti-fictional. The seemingly naïve objection is: What could be simpler than writing down a story while one is thinking it up?[72] Any story can be written down synchronously with its invention. Let us read Walser's "The Walk" in this sense:

> Ich wittere einen Buchladen samt Buchhändler, ebenso will bald, wie ich ahne und merke, eine Bäckerei mit Goldbuchstaben zur Geltung kommen. Vorher hätte ich aber einen Pfarrer zu erwähnen. Mit freundlichem Gesicht fährt ein radfahrender, fahrradelnder Stadtchemiker dicht am Spaziergänger vorüber, ebenso ein Stabs- oder Regimentsarzt. Nicht unaufgezeichnet darf bleiben ein bescheidener Fußgänger, nämlich ein reichgewordener Althändler und Lumpensammler. Zu beachten ist, wie Buben und Mädchen frei und ungezügelt im Sonnenlicht umherjagen.
>
> "Man lasse sie ruhig ungezügelt, denn das Alter wird sie leider Gottes einst noch früh genug schrecken und zügeln", denke ich.
>
> I catch a glimpse of a bookseller and of a bookshop; likewise soon, as I guess and observe, a bakery with braggart gold lettering comes in for mention and regard. But first I have a priest, or parson, to record. A bicycling town chemist cycles with kind and weighty face close by the walker, namely, myself, similarly, a regimental or staff doctor. An unassuming pedestrian should not remain unconsidered, or unrecorded; for he asks me politely to mention him. This is a bric-à-brac vendor and rag collector who has become rich. Young boys and girls race around in the sunlight, free and unrestrained.
>
> "Let them be unrestrained as they are," I mused. "Age one day will terrify and bridle them. Only too soon, alas!"[73]

Here we have a perfect superimposition of the present of the *fabula* and the present of the *sujet*. The synchronization of *fabula* and *sujet* is oriented prospectively: an absolute innovation of Walser's present-tense text over against traditional narration, in which the prospective progression is characteristic *only* of the *fabula*, while the *sujet* reconstructs the *fabula* retrospectively.[74] When an author narrates a text as she is thinking it up, and is thus herself interested in finding out what she will come up with next, fiction acquires a temporal connection with the present of the process of thinking and writing. This involves a peculiar fictionalization of the *sujet*.

How does the present tense fictionalize itself?

We also need to shed light on the possibility of present tense narration from the point of view of fiction theory. This will allow us to systematically summarize several aspects already discussed by way of addressing the question of how the present tense fictionalizes itself in turn from Hamburger's and from Weinrich's perspective.

Käte Hamburger provides a concise definition of the relation between the past tense and fiction, which we would like to apply to the relation of present tense and fiction and generalize to define the relation of tense and fiction. From her perspective, two things need clarification. The first is how the present tense loses its factographic reference to the present time; the second, how propositions are dissociated from the moment of their expression such that the narrator disappears from the text. The second point is easier to grasp than the first: altermodern present-tense fictions return to a heterodiegetic narration. Texts by Pynchon and Simon, for example, have third-person narrators.

Dorrit Cohn engages with the first and more difficult point and uses it as the basis for her understanding of the present tense in recent novels as a *fictional present*. This understanding has the advantage of dislocating the narrated text from a temporally fixed point of origin, much as Hamburger's interpretation of the past tense in third-person fiction detaches it from the obligatory retrospection it signifies in non-fictional discourse.[75]

The temporal aporia of synchronously experiencing and narrating is not resolved at all. Instead it is promoted and becomes an exclusive signal of fiction. Texts in which experience and narration are synchronous, the present of the *fabula* synchronized with the present of the *sujet*, are clearly to be identified as fictional.

From Weinrich's perspective, the question of how it is possible to fictionalize the present tense could be expressed in two ways: *How can one "narrate fiction"?* and *How can one "fictionalize narration"?* We have seen the second possibility, the attempt to "fictionalize narration," in the example of Peter Weiss's *The Shadow of the Body of the Coachman*, in which the process of narration occurs within the fiction itself.[76] The attempt "to narrate fiction" and narratively to illustrate the mental process that governs the genesis of the world of the text can be seen in Wolfgang Hildesheimer's *Tynset*. There, Hildesheimer demonstrates that fiction does not emerge from narration or, put differently, that one can narrate how a fiction does *not* come about. The dissolution of the classical matrix of narrated fiction renders visible the isolation of narration and fiction from one another. Narration and fiction are two independent principles of generating a text.[77] It is precisely in a failed fiction, "stuck" half-way, that we can recognize the process that produces it.

The novel begins, as does *Oblomov*, at the hero's bedside, who in this case is a first-person narrator:

> Ich liege in meinem Bett, in meinem Winterbett.
>
> Es ist Schlafenszeit. Aber wann wäre es das nicht? Es ist still, beinah still. Nachts weht hier meist ein Wind und es krähen ein oder zwei Hähne. Aber jetzt weht kein Wind und es kräht kein Hahn.
>
> I'm lying in my bed, in my winter bed.
>
> It is time to sleep. But when wouldn't it be? It is quiet, nearly quiet. Most nights, there's a wind blowing here, and a rooster crows or two. But now there is no wind blowing and no rooster crowing.[78]

The first thing that jumps out is the excessive nihilism that does not allow the narrator to let a single description stand without contestation. That it is time to sleep *now*, for example, does not tell us anything concrete about this now, for it is always time to sleep. Nor does the fact that it is quiet now, for it remains open *how* quiet it is. And the fact, finally, that the wind blows at night and a rooster (or perhaps another?) crows, may be true at night, but not now. *Not now* might even be the text's motto, a text that repudiates even its own metaphors. For the wind rises up after all a few lines later, yet only to immediately subside again and to take the fiction just beginning within the narration along with it:

> Plötzlich, zieht ein jäher Sog von Luft durch die Zimmer, Wind, ein Stoß geballter Zeit, er trägt einen Geruch oder auch nur die Idee eines Geruchs, als wolle er, unerwartet, eine Erinnerung

wecken, aber er will nichts dergleichen, ganz im Gegenteil, er bläst die Idee hinweg, bevor sie untergebracht ist, er löscht sie wieder aus, und das ist gut so.

Suddenly, abruptly an eddying current comes through the room, wind, a thrust of concentrated time, it carries a scent or only just the idea of a scent, as if it were seeking, unexpectedly, to awaken a memory, but it doesn't want to do anything of the kind, quite to the contrary, it blows the idea away before it can settle, it extinguishes it again, and that's quite alright.[79]

The poetological principle of immediately extinguishing every fiction that flares up is immediately extinguished in order to draw the image of a narrator lying in his bed. It is clad in the motif of a timetable lying next to the bed.[80] Soon, the narrator picks from this timetable the place Tynset, which gives the novel its name, in order to, again and again, attempt to imagine a journey there:

Jede Ankunftszeit und jede Abfahrtszeit steht für einen tatsächlichen, nachprüfbaren Vorgang: eine Ankunft, eine Abfahrt. Und mit jeder Zeile vergeht die Zeit, wechseln Zeit und Schauplatz des Geschehens. Und umgekehrt, jede Reise ist eine Bestätigung der relativen Verläßlichkeit dieses Buches, dem kein anderes Motiv zugrunde liegt als eben diese Verläßlichkeit, ohne die es, wie es sehr wohl weiß, sinnlos wäre—, aber im norwegischen Kursbuch steht mehr, wenn man es recht zu lesen versteht. Zwischen den Zeilen breiten sich die großen Entfernungen aus, weitet sich ein spröder, windiger Spielraum, den die Daten einer Ankunft oder einer Abfahrt nur ungefähr umreißen, ohne ihn zu nennen oder ihn zu erfahren; sie stecken nur die Grenzen ab zwischen diesem Ort, der im Nirgendwo liegt und dem anderen Ort, der ebenfalls im Nirgendwo liegt, aber in einem anderen Nirgendwo, in dem die Sage des ersten Ortes in einer Abwandlung erzählt, günstig dem zweiten Ort, dem ersten abträglich, und im dritten Ort, der wieder in einem anderen Nirgendwo liegt, ist eine andere Sage angesiedelt, die anderer Orte Sagen Lügen straft, und der vierte Ort ist Schnellzugstation, ihm ist die Sage schon lange abhanden gekommen.

Every time of arrival and every time of departure stands for an actual, verifiable occurrence: an arrival, a departure. And time passes with every line, the time and location of the event change. And in reverse, every journey is a confirmation of the relative reliability of this book, which is based on no other motive than this reliability, without which, as it well knows, it would be meaningless—but there is more in the Norwegian timetable, if you know how to read it right. Between the lines, large distances stretch out, a brittle, windy space opens up, which only approximately sketch out the dates of an arrival or a departure without naming it or experiencing it; they merely delimit the borders between a place that lies nowhere and that other place that also lies nowhere, but in another nowhere, in which the legend of the first place is narrated in modified form, favoring the second place and disadvantaging the first, and in the third place, which again lies in yet another nowhere, another legend has settled, which belies the legend of other places, and the fourth place is an express train station, it lost its legend a long time ago.[81]

Excessive repudiation leads to the edge of the narration's self-annihilation and concerns not only the present of narration but also its topology. The story of one place annihilates the story of the next place, which in turn annihilates the story of the place after that, and so all the way to the place that lost the story by itself. In lieu of a fictional here and now, the text posits a negative chronotopos: no now, nowhere.

In Walser's "The Walk" (1917), too, we can observe a fictionalization of the present tense, in which the present tense is "detemporalized" in the way Hamburger described. Nonetheless, this fiction remains closely coupled with the imagination and achieves no narrative stability. The present is made inactual and indistinguishable from the fiction. We can no longer say whether we are dealing with an author in the here and now who is sitting at his desk and imagining a walk, or with a walker who is imagining himself narrating his impressions. The author is embroiled in a process in which the activity of imagining develops an uncontrollable dynamic, a process in which we can no longer distinguish between fiction and hallucination.

The "relapses" into the past tense in Walser's text indicate that, although the narrative present indicates an inactualization, the fiction is still based on the model of tense structure of presentification. The inactuality of a "present of things present" (*praesens de praesentibus*) in Augustine's sense[82] thus functions less as an indication of fiction than as an indicator of a loss of the real.[83] This is true especially when the imagination conquers a field that can no longer be restricted to the level of the *sujet*, when it is presented as something imagined not only synchronous with narration, but synchronous with experience as well. Such a fabular present tense stands in need of very specific *fabulas*, in which the synchrony of imagination and experience is either motivated or suspended by a new meaning of the present tense.[84] Only when the present tense of the altermodern novel grants access to the past does a new matrix of fictional narration stabilize.

Before we turn to altermodernism, we should briefly summarize some developments in modernity. It seems central that over the course of the twentieth century the present tense spreads into areas where it comes into conflict with the matrix of narrated fiction (and its operational couples fiction/fact, *fabula*/*sujet*, present/past tense). We can then identify the erosion of the matrix of narrated fiction but also the transformations that lead from fiction in the epic past tense to fictional narration in the present tense. This development involves, on the one hand, narrativizing the present tense and, on the other, fictionalizing it, that is, in terms of fiction theory, rendering its tense meaning inactual. In both cases, however, problems emerge. In Hildesheimer, a pronounced fictional nihilism comes to light, and the fictionalization of the present tense (in the case of Walser) has no way of staving off a loss of the real.

The narrativization of the present tense comes up against the aporia of the synchronous present of *fabula* and *sujet*. The fact that one cannot experience and narrate at the same time leads to attempts to synchronize *fabula* and *sujet*—either by alternating them in the foreground (as in Weiss), or by superimposing them (as in Walser). What we need to explain next is how the narrativization of the present tense is accomplished. Once this narrativization is possible, we have reached the (narratological-fictional) breaking point in classical narration: the synchronous present of *fabula* and *sujet* no longer represents an aporia and the past no longer has to be fictionally presentified. Its being-past can instead be *narrated* as such.

From the perspective of narratology, one might of course suspect that the meaning of being past thus taken on by the present tense is only a relic or shadow of the traditional principle of retrospectivity.

Could it be that all that is left of the old *fabula—sujet* relation is its retrospective moment? We will see that this is not the case. To be sure, the meaning of being present of the present tense is indeed *de-actualized*, but not because of any pressure from a narrative retrospection. On the contrary, the overbearance of narration is reduced. Altermodern fictionalization applies leverage to the form of time of retrospectivity in order to bring out the principle of anteriority. Anteriority can only arise in the present tense and appears in the present tense as asynchrony within the horizon of the present.

The function of narrating the past taken on by the present tense cannot be explained solely from a narratological perspective, nor can it be understood as exclusively a result of fictionalization. Because continuously fictional narration has come back, we should refrain from such an opposition of fiction and narration and instead describe how they condition one another. In particular, the altermodern present tense should not be regarded as totalizing a historical present tense, such as we encounter it under the aegis of traditional narration.

The linguistics of the (historical) present tense

Die Sonne war untergegangen, und es dämmerte schon und duftete feucht um den See. Ottilie stand verwirrt und bewegt; sie sah nach dem Berghause hinüber und glaubte Charlottens weißes Kleid auf dem Altan zu sehen. Der Umweg war groß am See hin; sie kannte Charlottens ungeduldiges Harren nach dem Kinde. Die Platanen sieht sie gegen sich über, nur ein Wasserraum trennt sie von dem Pfade, der sogleich zu dem Gebäude hinaufführt. Mit Gedanken ist sie schon drüben wie mit den Augen. Die Bedenklichkeit, mit dem Kinde sich aufs Wasser zu wagen, verschwindet in diesem Drange. Sie eilt nach dem Kahn, sie fühlt nicht, daß ihr Herz pocht, daß ihre Füße schwanken, daß ihr die Sinne zu vergehen drohn.

Sie springt in den Kahn, ergreift das Ruder und stößt ab.

The sun had set, and already twilight and mist were settling on the lake. Ottilie stood agitated and confused; she gazed over to the pavilion on the hill and thought she saw Charlotte's white dress on the balcony. The way back around the lake was long; she knew Charlotte would be waiting impatiently for the child. She sees the plane-trees standing on the other side of the lake; only a sheet of water divides her from the path leading straight up to the pavilion. As with her eyes, so in her mind she has already reached it. The doubtfulness of venturing on to the water with the child is forgotten in this sense of urgency. She hurries to the boat, she pays no heed to her beating heart, to her trembling feet, to the signs that she is near to swooning. She leaps into the boat, seizes the oar, and pushes off from the shore.[85]

Passages like this have provided the basis for understanding the historical present tense in Goethe's *Elective Affinities* as a "demonic present tense" or as a tense of "demonic events."[86] Along with sentences that are paratactic, jotted down hastily and put into sequence without connection, with sentences meant to evoke extreme agitation, such passages, according to Hennig Brinkmann, form an entire layer of the (narrative) events of Goethe's novel. Käte Hamburger shares this reading of the historical present tense and sees in it a rhetorical stylistic device for enhancing the dramatic effect of events or for making them more vivid. Within fictional texts, according to her, the historical present tense serves "neither a temporal nor a fictionalizing" function; it can therefore "always be replaced with the past tense."[87]

We can see the narratological tension particular to the concept "historical present tense" already in 1924, that is, at the very moment in which modernist present-tense texts first emerge. Otto Jespersen's attempt to conceptualize the historical present tense is thus part of a much larger discourse. He writes:

> Among expressions for the simple past we must here also mention the so-called historic present, which it would be better to call the unhistoric present, or, taking a hint thrown out by Brugmann, the *dramatic present*. The speaker in using it steps outside the frame of history, visualizing and representing what happened in the past as if it were present before his eyes.[88]

This present tense is "unhistoric" because it is tied to processes of fictional presentification; in turn, it is "historic" because it operates under the aegis of narrative retrospection, that is, of narration (in the past tense). This present tense is turned into a stylistic contrast, a "subjective stylistic device,"[89] a literary procedure of placing what is described or what is past in general "*in a vivid way* before the reader's eyes"[90] and presentifying it.

This is the state of literary theory at the time the present-tense novel is constituted. Later, beginning at mid-century, many of the attempts to define the historical present tense can also be read as explicit or implicit engagements with Hamburger's ideas about how tenses participate in the emergence of fiction. Starting from narratological positions (usually Franz Stanzel's), these attempts are also directed against the reductionist tendencies of earlier definitions of the (historical) present tense we just discussed, and they continue to attempt to characterize its narrative function. Aiming to obtain a more precise assessment of the narrative impact of using the present tense, Udo Fries (1970) and Christian Paul Casparis (1975), among others, raise substantial objections. Although Casparis uses Weinrich as a "working basis"[91] for his argument, he suggests "narrativity" as a criterion for defining the historical present tense to counter rhetorical "vividness" and fictional "presentness"[92] and links the search for an external schema of narrative techniques to an "elimination of the time factor."[93] Much like Casparis, and taking up the arguments narratology directed at Hamburger mentioned earlier, Fries, too, argues against conceiving of the historical present tense merely as sporadic vividness and presentification.[94]

> In the novel, the past tense is the narrative tense par excellence ... stylistically "without characteristics." In contrast, every present tense used as a narrative tense in a novel is stylistically "characteristic." The expressions "epic present tense" [in German] or "narrative present" for the present tense as a narrative tense can be conceived in this general sense.[95]

In our objection to the endeavor to define the narrative present tense on the basis of the historical present tense, we assume comprehensive transformations of entire systems: from fiction, which takes the form of time of retrospection and is dominated by narration, to narration, which takes the form of time of contemporaneity and is dominated by fiction. For this reason, we believe that there is no uniform definition of the present tense that would be valid for both the nineteenth and the twentieth century. Insofar as the shift of dominants we are interested in is concerned, we can take Weinrich as our starting point, according to whom the narrating tenses are predominant only in the epic genres, while biographical essay, poetry, and drama clearly incline toward the discussing tenses.[96]

The systemic shift to a present tense that is both fictional and narrative, which we describe in contrast to Weinrich's and Hamburger's theoretical models, could be overlooked for so long not least because the presence of the (allegedly "non-epic") present tense in narrative texts could be "explained" as a poetic or dramatic element. From a certain point in the history of literary theory and ideology onward, this explanation is to be provided by the concept "historical present," a concept that was also always brought up in objections to Hamburger and Weinrich's theoretical model (at least in the time after the emergence of the present-tense novel). On the one hand, there is a tendency to interpret the historical present tense only in terms of its reference. It is understood only as referring to the present of a past. This entails losing sight both of its fictionality and of its narrative complexity (its relation to at least two narrative levels, that is, the *fabula* and/or the *sujet*, and the compositional virtuosity that follows from this possible dual relation). On the other hand, there is a theoretical short circuit that mistakes the present-tense novel for a hyperextension of the historical present tense.

Picking up on Harald Weinrich's thesis of the non-temporal meaning of tenses, we also have to address a linguistic line of argumentation among discussions of the historical present tense that disavows any temporality of tenses. If only because of the wide variety of cases in which the present tense in literary texts has a (temporal) meaning, we cite theories that understand the present tense per se as "timeless and semantically unmarked"[97] only by way of contrast. On the basis of Weinrich's *textual*-linguistic argumentation against the temporality of the tenses Manfred Markus, for instance, makes a lexicological argument against a "semantic substance of the various tense forms." Against the "idea that tense function can be defined absolutely," he objects that the present tense can even refer to the future.[98] We do not wish to discuss in detail the multiple, negative strands of argumentation that deny temporal meaning to the present tense but only mention them as background for the debate about the temporality of the present tense.

In her *Die Verbalkategorien des Deutschen* [*The Verbal Categories of German*], Elisabeth Leiss gives an account of how the designation of the present tense as "atemporalis" arises from efforts to provide *uniform* definition for the *contradictory* meanings of the present tense.[99] Her definition of the present tense as "pre-tense" (*Prätempus*) accounts for these contradictions in that it specifies what both the temporal and the atemporal dimensions of the present tense consist in. The present tense is temporal because it points to a temporal *placement* [*Lagerung*] of perspective; it is atemporal because it does not accomplish any temporal *displacement* [*Verlagerung*] of perspective. The present tense is characterized by the simultaneity of the time of acting, the time of observing, and the time of speaking. Leiss then interprets the historical present tense as a present tense in a past context, a context in which it tends to synchronize the time of acting, observing, and speaking and thus to produce once more a simultaneity between them:

> This is how the actualizing meaning of the historical present tense comes about. The historical present tense does not set the observer back in time, but transports historical or narrated events into the present.[100]

Understood this way, the historical present tense is a presentifying present tense in which time is figured in the same way as in the epic past tense. We have to read Käte Hamburger's point about the fictional quality of the presentifying effect of the historical present tense in this sense as well. "The historical present tense here does not fulfill a function of temporal presentification but rather one of fictional presentification."[101] Yet what is decisive here is a negative consequence: the suggestion that the present-tense novel over the course of the twentieth century develops from the historical present tense and is to be understood as its merely quantitative extension to a whole text is tempting but misleading. For if the altermodern novel of the past were in fact only a variant of the traditional presentifying novel—a variant written entirely in the historical present tense that establishes the past context necessary for this present tense through the use of adverbs such as "yesterday" ("yesterday is Christmas") or dates, historical settings, and persons—then the present tense in the altermodern novel would serve the same stylistic function as the historical present does in the traditional history novel, namely "to restore ... the unity of the time of speaking, the time of observing, and the time of acting, as it is normatively given in the present tense."[102] But the asynchronous present tense, which we include in our account of altermodernism, is distinct precisely because the times of acting, observing, and speaking are desynchronized.[103] In contrast, the present tense as a pre-tense has only a quasi-spatial function, namely to signal or to produce by means of synchronization the simultaneity of the moments of acting, observing, and speaking. The presentification achieved by the historical present remains a dependent temporality that restores the initial state of synchrony between the times of acting, observing, and speaking against the temporal background of the (displacing) past tense. The "narrative tense present tense," however, initiates a temporal displacement. This is where its enormous poetological potential lies, and not in an alleged capacity to bring events into presence.

Thus, on the one hand, there is the accomplishment of synchronization of the historical present tense active in the figuration of time that is presentification, and, on the other, there is the figuration of time that is asynchrony thanks to which the present tense gains something impossible within the framework of grammar: in literature, the present tense acquires the significance of a full-fledged tense.

Altermodernism: The shift to the present tense of the past

Earlier, we defined a motto for narrated fiction: "I tell you what once happened to him–her." Such novels conceive of narration according to the model of historical narration, in which the author/historian paints the most "vivid image" possible of historical events in order for the past to open up to readers as if it were their present. Such historical novels implement the focus of a historiography determined by events in the arrangement of the *fabula*.

Claiming to capture the true moment of a history, their authors use documents and sources, even visit archives, yet the process of artificial construction used to extract history from these documents is carefully concealed, always with the goal of seizing the true moment of the story. The method of the altermodern novel is the exact reverse. By analyzing the processes readers use to construct the course of the *fabula* from the *sujet*, it focuses on the possibility of inventing (hi)stories. In this sense, the altermodern novel of the past can be conceived as the reinvention of the history novel as a time novel (*Zeitroman*). Following Heidegger, we can also say that the "*Dasein*" of the altermodern novel "does not first become historical in retrieve, but rather because as temporal it is historical, it can take itself over in its history, retrieving itself."[104] The altermodern history novel starts with the *equi-presentness of all pasts*[105] to the reader expressed by the present tense. In the asynchrony of the present-tense novel, the reader not only actualizes a present but at the same time its immanent other temporal pole, that of the past.

We are also using the concept of an "altermodern narration" in order to emphasize and generalize a particular aspect of the spectrum of so-called postmodernism. In its undercutting of (modernist) narrative strategies, altermodernism is not content with mere textual games. Its reinterpretation of the reference to history follows from an act of re-evaluating documents. The recovery of the factual through such a retro-referentiality itself institutes a form of historicity. We will see that in altermodern narration, reference does not simply join *fabula* and *sujet* as a third level of the model of historical narration. In altermodernism, attempts at historical narration as well as attempts at factographic reporting are sublated in another significance.[106]

Fictional present tense

I. The past meaning of the present tense

From the perspective of altermodernism, that is, having traced the developments, narrow paths, and impasses of modernity, we see once more that the conversion of the meaning of the past tense into the fictional here and now has basically blocked access to the past—contrary to what might seem to be the most fundamental intentions of the past-tense paradigm.[107]

What we mean by the transition from a historical novel to a temporally determinate altermodern novel of the past can be clarified by critically distinguishing it from Paul Ricœur's reflections on narrativity and temporality.[108] Ricœur reduces Heidegger's three ("ecstasies" of) time(s) in a one-sided approach clearly directed toward a philosophy of history. He eliminates the anticipatory dimension of the future and thus conjures Heidegger's fundamental experience of temporality in the "anticipation of death."[109] The corresponding concept of the past as a living tradition he then projects onto the *fabula—sujet* distinction (Ricœur uses the terms *story* and *plot*). In retrospection, prospective action or events of the *fabula* acquire a teleology. Strictly speaking, though, retrospection in Ricœur is less a *retro*spection (onto the past in its difference and, in the end, its irrecoverability) than it is a catalyst for sense and teleology. The story (*fabula*) is thus situated ambivalently. Initially it looks as if the story were happening (as unforeseeable) in the (imperfect) present. Yet if it becomes clear within the story that it is produced by a plot (a *sujet*), the story suddenly seems to lie in the past. Correspondingly, it would only be the plot's retrospection that produces the teleology of the *fabula*; this, too, is a moment in which the plot initiates a past action in the first place because it is the plot that creates the teleology.

Considering the altermodern novel of the past, we see that such a mechanism follows from a narratological decision made in advance that has immediate consequences on the level of the theory of history (and of the historical novel). The difference between a presentifying novel in narrated fiction and a novel of the past in altermodernism also becomes clear when we determine which of the two narrative levels, *fabula* or *sujet*, is perceived to be fundamental to the constitution of historicity. For Ricœur, it is the story (the *fabula*), that is, an (implicitly past and implicitly factual) action conceived as historical. This action is presentified (as a historical event is presentified by historiography)[110]—the past is retrieved. Ricœur thus adheres to the narratological dogma (in narrated fiction) of the retrospectivity of narration, which the present-tense novel dismisses. Ricœur's theoretical approach, then, cannot account for how it becomes possible to abandon the epic past tense or what narration in the present tense is able to accomplish. To bring it to a point, Ricœur—like all presentifying, historical narration—presupposes that every past present has factual existence, namely *as a present which was once present to itself*. In contrast, altermodernism insists on an "unconscious past,"[111] on the fact that no present is completely present to itself and that the only thing that can be narrated of a past present is what is never present [*Nie-Gegenwärtige*]. This is why in the altermodern novel of the past a past present does not appear as *presentified* past, but precisely *as a past* past. The novels narrate in full awareness of the impossibility of narrating the past present *as present*. The "inherent latency of the event," which "paradoxically explains the peculiar, temporal structure, the belatedness of historical experience," according to Cathy Caruth, can also be seen in a "latency within the experience itself"[112] and appeals to a fictionalizing moment in narration.

II. Altermodern fiction, or the loss of the documentary character of the present tense

In the previous section, we discussed the fictionalization of a present tense that, in terms of tense structure, no longer refers to the present. We must now address another aspect, which we can define, in general terms, as the dedocumentarization of the documentary or, in concrete terms, as the de-actualization of the present tense. The present tense of altermodern novels of the past distinguishes them both from postmodern metafictional historiographies[113] and from the memory novels of classical modernity. The primary concern of altermodern novels of the past is not to reconstruct personal experiences. Thus the discovery of the past, for instance, develops from the interpretation of documents, that is, from what has actually happened or is at least factually verifiable. The category of the documentary is therefore doubly relevant for defining the once-factographic present tense. On the one hand, the status of the documentary changes; on the other, the present tense changes: it is henceforth a *narrative* tense. There is a double dedocumentarization taking place: (1) that of realities and, more importantly, (2) that of the present tense itself.

(1) The altermodern imaginative vivification of the documentary radicalizes the postmodern thesis that, put simply, fiction or imagining is constitutive of reality and of understanding it. In view of such a panfictionalism, to which correspond the procedures of

historiographic metafictionality, altermodernism develops a new form of reflexive fiction (previously metafiction) that can be analyzed in terms of a different temporal orientation. In the words of Quentin Meillassoux, "the past, as one says, is unpredictable."[114] Since time is not only unknown in the direction of the future but also in the direction of the past, there is nothing "given" that could serve as the starting point for metafictional stratification. As an alternative to the postmodern reflexive option of piling meta upon meta in the direction of the future, there is the option of taking the present moment, and thus the self-reflexive circle, as a starting point, and of going into the past as deeply as one likes. A literary example clarifies how every viewpoint, due to its self-reflexivity, founds itself in fiction.

In his novels, Claude Simon often depicts a scene only to show us that the protagonist holds or has held in his hands a film reel or a (historical) document. What we observe here is a re-motivation of the present tense. What can at first only be read as the present tense of the events of the *fabula* develops in the course of reading into the present of the literary process of presentification or narration. But Simon is not content just to expose fiction by a metafictional procedure. He presents these documents to us as the fiction's point of departure. This is done programmatically in the prologue of *The Georgics*, in which Simon reads a sketch:

> De même que les corps nus sont dessinés avec une froideur délibérée détaillant des anatomies stéréotypées apprises sur l'antique, les objets qui les entourent, la pièce où se tiennent les deux personnages, sont figurés avec cette sècheresse qui préside à l'exécution des projets d'architectes proposant aux regards non pas des monuments déjà existants mais des combinaisons et des assemblages de formes nés de leur imagination, ne renvoyant qu'à eux-mêmes.
>
> Just as the naked bodies are drawn with conscious detachment, in the manner of stereotyped anatomical drawings based on classical models, the objects surrounding them, the room in which the two figures stand, are depicted with the lack of emotion associated with the execution of architectural projects, which similarly offer the spectator not existing monuments but combinations and collections of forms that are purely imaginary, referring only to themselves.[115]

With the altermodern novel, we also begin to see reading as a constituent part of fiction. For the experience of fiction does not consist in registering the signals of fictionality (which guards us against potentially wrong conclusions). Rather, fiction is a form of experience of its own. It has variously been described as identification with the hero, then as co-authorship of the text by filling in places of indeterminacy, and in recent years increasingly as a phenomenon of immersion. To be sure, many authors target their readers, which includes playing with their power over them, for instance, in attempts to wrest the text out of their reading readers' hands in Kafka's "Wish to Become an Indian" or in Kharms' "On Phenomena and Existences." But rarely is the conclusion drawn from the equi-originarity of reading and writing. In Simon, however, this becomes part of the poetics of the novel, a poetics that can be paraphrased as "imagine me reading as you are reading." While the novel *The Georgics* presents itself throughout as a heterodiegetic third-person narrative, this third person is retrospectively shown to be the narrator himself. The retroactive effect of reading is thus an autodiegetic effect; the story narrated is the story of a first-person narrator. In the case of Simon's novel, the story narrated is likely to have been that of the actual author Simon, with the material of his ancestors and his own readings and experiences worked in. It is according to this principle that Simon constructs the fiction in his novel of the past. The narrator does not narrate the story, he reads it (as his own) from historical documents and images, and he always shows us the hand that is holding them as he reads.[116] The appeal to the reader is not to listen to him or to the narration, but to imagine the author's reading as one's own, according to the maxim: "Imagine me reading as you are reading" or even "Imagine I am reading along."

The altermodern novel of the past no longer needs to make the detour via the presentification of events. The reader is not to imagine being (or having been) there, as if something were happening presently before his eyes. At no point in time does the historical in this altermodern novel arise from events themselves. It results from the construction of a historical consciousness on the level of the *sujet*, of a reading consciousness that emerges from the double inheritance of the traditional historical novel and the modern novel of consciousness. Such construction includes, for example, producing linear events from the succession of the following sentences:

Il a cinquante ans. Il est général en chef de l'artillerie de l'armée d'Italie. Il réside à Milan. Il porte une tunique au col et au plastron brodés de dorures. Il a soixante ans. Il surveille les travaux d'achèvement de la terrasse de son château. Il est frileusement enveloppé d'une vielle houppelande militaire. Il voit des points noirs. Le soir il sera mort. Il a trente ans. Il est capitaine. Il va à l'opéra. Il porte un tricorne, une tunique bleu pincée à la taille et une épée de salon.

He is fifty. He is the general in overall command of the artillery with the French army in Italy. His residence is at Milan. He wears a high-collared tunic with a front embroidered in gold. He is sixty. He oversees the completion of the terrace of his chateau. He is shivering, wrapped in an old military cloak. He sees black spots. By evening he will be dead. He is thirty. He is a captain. He goes to the opera. He wears a three-cornered hat, a blue tunic gathered in at the waist, and a dress sword.[117]

It is highly unlikely that anyone reading this passage would think of it as a crude back and forth, as magical rejuvenation and rapid aging. Instead, such a passage can be taken as evidence that the order of the *fabula* is anchored in the consciousness of the reader. Whatever order the *sujet* places before readers' eyes, they will first of all bring chronological order to the *fabula*.[118] Simon's text tries with all available devices to undermine the canonical order of retrospective *sujet* and chronological *fabula*. The manipulated *sujet* shows how a chronological course of the *fabula* is constructed from a text; at the same time, the text makes it possible to experience one's own operation of reading. It is typical for an altermodern text that it does not proceed by reducing the number of conceivable *fabulas* but by multiplying it. What remains, however, is the attempt, already familiar from modernism, to dissolve (the chronology of) the *fabula*. It does not suffice to bring the *sujet* into temporal disorder and to string together digressions (as Shklovsky describes in Sterne's *Tristram Shandy*), that is, to attempt a purely narrative subversion of the *fabula*'s chronology. As we will elaborate in the fourth chapter, the tense system of language institutes an order of time; only when this order is suspended—and this is the function of the present tense in Simon— do readers no longer succeed in actualizing a chronological order of the *fabula*. Only in altermodernism's asynchronous present tense can the experience of history that is the experience of the twentieth century be narrated: history is out of joint.

(2) To explain the second dedocumentarization, that of the present tense itself (which subsequently is able to appear as a narrative tense on a par with the epic past tense), we can pick up on our earlier analyses of the documentary present tense. Here, the contrast is not with postmodern theories of narration and history, but with the traditional as well as modernist approaches that preceded them (e.g., factographic approaches, in which a present tense that insists on reference to the present obeys antifictional and anti-narrative tendencies). For altermodern narration refers to the already-discussed breaking point that arises under the aegis of classical fiction. Because of the epic past tense's presentifying effect, the past could not appear as such. Instead, the automatism of fiction always causes (past) events to convert into the fictional here and now. Although narration conceives of itself as retrospection, the story it tells is necessarily presentified. Contradicting both the classical presupposition (*the past can be narrated*) and the modernist one (*the past cannot be narrated*), the altermodern present novel tries to narrate the past as such, that is, *as non-present*. To do so, it is necessary to understand the past as a (co-present) form of time, entirely in line with the paradoxes of the past established by Gilles Deleuze in *Difference and Repetition*: "Each past is synchronous with the present it was, and the whole past coexists with the present in relation to which it is past, but the pure element of the past in general pre-exists the passing present."[119]

The asynchronous present tense of altermodernism operates the inverse of the presentifying function of the epic past tense, where presentification constitutes a fictional (contemporaneously past) present. Asynchrony, in contrast, constitutes a fictional (non-contemporaneously present) past.[120] This runs parallel to doubts about the facticity of history and to attempts to define history's form of existence differently.[121] Even in historical narration, doubts arise about whether the past that a text creates can be anything but fictional. In order to specify this for the literary process that interests us here, we speak of dedocumentarization.

The fictional narrative present tense thus establishes a relation to classical narrated fiction. Yet instead of just using it for postmodern variations, altermodern narration finds its own solutions and, fully aware of the achievements of modernist narrative procedures, proposes an alternative to the modernist understanding of the present tense. The establishment of the present tense as a continuously employed tense of fictional narration also entails that it changes its meaning and opens up to the past.

Narrative present tense

Above, we portrayed the transition to present tense narration by means of a multi-level structure (cf. *The matrix of narrated fiction*). The shifts presented there from the perspectives of narratology and fiction theory have an analogue in the altermodern expansion of the present tense. In relation to the *fabula* and the *sujet*, the altermodern present tense acquires narrative functions that rely on modernist devices and yet avoid the aporias associated with them.

Although we assume a basic parallelism between the two levels of *fabula* and *sujet*, it still makes sense to discuss them separately once more, if only because, within the matrix of narrated fiction, the *sujet* is to be thought as present and the *fabula* as past. It follows that, as *sujet* and *fabula* leave the matrix, they must overcome different problems. When we look at the level of the *sujet*, the main focus is to determine which *sujets* make it possible for an equipresentness of *sujet* and *fabula* to be unproblematic. At the level of the *fabula*, which we will analyze first, the most significant aspect for our inquiry is the basic establishment of a *fabular present tense*.

I. The fabular present tense

From the perspective of narratology, there are at least two innovations thanks to which present-tense *fabulas* transgress the boundaries set for them within the matrix of narrated fiction. They counter the persistent prejudice according to which the return of the *fabula* is nothing more than a remnant of pre-modern narrated fiction. First, new patterns of *fabulas* arise and, second, a fabular present tense develops (already in modernity). It is in the second change that a fundamental shift of dominants, that is, a new balance of forces in the relationship between narration and fiction, becomes manifest.

Since modernism, which was (almost exclusively) oriented toward narrative innovation, any narration constituted by a *fabula* has been considered obsolete, and most prose has been structured, as we saw, by excessive and purely self-satisfying *sujets*. Yet the reprise of the *fabula* in altermodernism does not represent any kind of regression (as it did, for instance, in Stalinist realism, where the *fabula* reenters narratives) but instead follows a new mode of criticism. Altermodernism deliberately sets itself apart from the nihilistic reductionism of avant-garde modernity by overfulfilling the very norms it scrutinizes. This endows modernity's representificational techniques with new potential. It would thus be wrong to judge the return of the *fabula* to be a regressive moment. (Such accusations were made against Simon on the basis of orthodox theories of the *nouveau roman* such as Ricardou's.) Rather, the return of the *fabula* opens up a field of innovation.

Regardless of modernism's systematic contempt for the *fabula*, new types of *fabulas* arise at the same time. These proliferate mostly in mass culture. Mysteries, detective stories, and thrillers, for example, are constructed according to a new principle, which Hitchcock has termed *McGuffin*.[122] The control of recipients' interest by withholding information at the level of the *sujet* and the construction of a *fabula* by means of a logic of suspense were unfamiliar to the avant-gardes and to other authors devoted to modernism. The impetus of the present tense for narrative technique can also be seen in the devices by which the altermodern novel picks up on and integrates elements rejected by modernism, thereby ennobling them and acknowledging the artistic merit of popular *fabula*-genres. Peter Handke's *Der Hausierer* [*The Peddler*] is a good example:

> Wie alle andern Geschichten beginnt auch die Mordgeschichte mit den bestimmenden Artikeln ... Das Treiben ringsherum muß ihn derart verwundern, daß die Geschichte entsteht: er wird aufmerksam. Er sieht viel, kennt aber niemanden. Er unterscheidet sich von anderen schon durch äußere Merkmale. Sein Gehaben, seine Blicke, sein Auftreten, sein Gang müssen so sein, daß sie geeignet sind, später Verdacht zu erregen. Er muß auffallen, um eine Beschreibung seiner selbst zu rechtfertigen. In der Regel beschreibt er sich selber, wie er sich in einem Spiegel sieht.

> Er trägt staubige Schuhe, wenn alle anderen saubere Schuhe tragen.
>
> Like all other stories, the murder story, too, begins with definite articles ... The commotion all around must astonish him so much that the story emerges: he begins to pay attention. He sees a lot, yet doesn't know anyone. He is different from others already on the outside. His comportment, his gazes, his demeanor, his gait must be such that they lend themselves to arousing suspicion later. He has to stick out in order to justify description of himself. As a rule he describes himself as he sees himself in a mirror.
>
> He wears dusty shoes when everyone else wears clean shoes.[123]

The self-reflexivity of the *sujet*, the commentary, and the emotional qualities of the sentences evoke a mystery novel, although no action ever appears in the text. Insofar as the *sujet* evokes an "empty *fabula* structure" but no *fabula*, we may speak of narration without a *fabula*. The sentences recall a mystery novel, the descriptions give rise to horror at a murder, and in the speculations that follow one can sense the anxiety of growing suspicion. All of this, however, does not take place in any *fabula*, but, as the secret of the text, is completely immured in its style. The self-reflexivity and reductionist rejection of the *fabula* are clearly modern textual gestures, whereas the usage of the new *fabula* structure (of the mystery novel) as well as the overfulfillment of the norms inherent to the genre (the exposure of the gears of its affect machinery) are the altermodern traits of Handke's text.

Even more important than the deployment and transvaluation of existing types and structures of *fabulas*, which we nevertheless consider important indicators of the fundamentally new meaning of the present tense in altermodernism, is the emergence of a fabular present tense. It requires quite particular *fabulas* for their present tense to function, otherwise there is the danger that a hallucinatory loss of touch with reality befalls all events. The synchronous overlapping of imagination and experience, in particular, creates difficulties (as we saw in the example of Walser's "The Walk"). It must therefore either be motivated or resolved by a particular model of *fabula*, i.e., a present-tense *fabula*. In pathographies of fiction the danger becomes apparent. There, fiction transgresses the bounds of unreality, beyond which it can no longer be distinguished from hallucination. There too, however, the basis of an imaginary present tense in classical narrated fiction is exposed.

In Thomas Pynchon's novel *Gravity's Rainbow*, the present tense is motivated by a *fabula* in which the present curiously precedes itself (and which thus makes visible precisely those non-present elements that are also constitutive of pastness as such). The "Ends of the Parabola" (so the title of German translation) emblematically stand in for the flight trajectory of a V2 missile. This projectile, traveling at supersonic speed, hits its target before its screaming sound can be heard. This is precisely what the horror of the V2 consisted in: the direction of cause and effect seems to be reversed, and this turns the perception of time "upside down" as well. The rocket is, so to speak, the rescindment of the familiar orientation of time in the shape of a missile. While the tense system of language suggests that time springs from the past and opens up to the future by traveling through the present,[124] the irregular asynchronous present tense, directed as if systematically against the tense system, weakens this linguistically stabilized order. If the novel also cloaks this in a motif such as the V2[125] and furthermore elaborates the story of the agent Slothrop, whose desire has a reversed temporal structure (the possible time and place of future V2 attacks might possibly be forecast by his erections), then a new order of time is established at the level of the characters, the *fabula* narrated, and the tenses used.

Already the novel's first sentences contain this effect in all of its violence, which, however, completely unfolds for readers only after a delay, for they have to grasp the central significance of the V2 motif:

> A screaming comes across the sky. It has happened before, but there is nothing to compare it to now.
>
> It is too late. The Evacuation still proceeds, but it's all theatre.[126]

The third sentence is the decisive one for interpreting the present tense. It *is* too late. This sentence projects a present that is contemporaneous with its past. The present tense develops a temporal bipolarity, that is, a very specific double reference that calls up an anteriority at the same time as it calls up the present that the present tense passes through: the double reference actualizes asynchrony. At this point we rejoin one of our central hypotheses about the meaning of the present tense in the altermodern novel. For it is not simply too late for something here, as if the right moment for something had passed: it is too late for a *now*. Neither is there a *here* from which some *I* might be able to experience or narrate something—there where the screaming of the V2 missile is approaching, it has already struck, and there where it has struck, no one can hear its screaming anymore. The reality system put in place by the subjective interconnection of I, here, and now is unhinged.

How is it that such a sentence, inconspicuous in itself, can count as the icon of an altermodern present tense? Could it not also be found in a classic author, in Charles Dickens, say? One could imagine, for example, that David Copperfield, when he is haunted by the memory of the moment he became aware of the inevitability of his beloved Dora's death, thinks to himself: *it is too late*. But, on the one hand, in *David Copperfield* there is no present-tense *fabula* that would unsettle the order of time and, on the other, the present tense would operate within the classical matrix of narrated fiction at the level of the *sujet*. In such a context, the present tense of this sentence would always remain with the narrator. It would be a present tense of the *sujet*, not a fabular present tense. In Dickens, *fabula* and *sujet* would not be synchronous, the *fabula* would, as past, be presentified. In Pynchon's present-tense *fabula*, in turn, the present tense is *pastified*.

The altermodern novel circumvents the aporia of the synchrony of the present of the *fabula* and a present of the *sujet* by means of an asynchronous present tense, and runs the risk of losing its relation to the real by projecting a present non-synchronous with itself. Even if Tyron Slothrop is committed for experiments to a psychiatric clinic, where psychologists schooled in Pavlov's methods ponder their patient's libidinous time shift, he as a character evades the loss of the real because the tense and the organization of time in the *fabula* support his version of the time of the world.

From a systematic point of view, we can state that the aporia according to which an event cannot be synchronous with its narration is motivated in present-tense *fabulas* like *Gravity's Rainbow*'s by an organization of time that finds a parallel to the passing of time in narration. The present tense thus takes on a past meaning, or the past at least becomes semantically accessible to the present tense. In our view, this distantiation of the tense from the meaning of tense proper—a distantiation that takes place quite unlike the present-ification of the past tense—is responsible for the fact that the altermodern present tense develops the same "power of fictionalization" as does the epic past tense.

A further example of how an altermodern present-tense *fabula* is constructed is Hans-Joachim Schädlich's novel *Tallhover*, which tells the story of a secret agent. The *fabula* is motivated by a Janus-faced main character who relates asynchronously to himself, his observations, and the report about them:

> Wie einer, das ist Tallhover, hinter einem hergeht, das ist einer, den Tallhover nicht kennt, aber er geht hinter ihm her in der Sehgier, in der Hörgier, Tallhover hört den Atem des Gehenden, also nah ist er, er hört die Schritte, er sieht unbedeckten Kopf, das Haar dunkel, Tallhover schätzt ein Alter, die Halshaut zwar straff, die Schultern aber, Schmalheit beiseite, fallen vornüber ... der Rauch vorbei zu Seiten des Kopfes in das Gesicht von Tallhover, der Lust hat auf die Zigarette im Mund dessen und sein will der, der vor ihm geht, dass er hinter sich herginge in seiner Sehgier, in seiner Hörgier, sich selber im Auge, wie er vor sich herginge, wer Tallhover sei, wie er atme und gehe, welchen Anblick sein Kopf und Kopfhaar biete, die Halshaut, Schultern, Rücken, Beine, Füße, Hände, beschäftigt in der Lust auf den Rauch der Zigarette und eins wäre das Gesehene und der Sehende, gleicher Bewegung, gleichen Gedankens, nicht mehr geteilt nach Anblick und Blick, so sich zu beruhigen.

> Just as someone, that is Tallhover, trails behind someone, that is someone whom Tallhover doesn't know, but he trails him greedily seeing, greedily hearing, Tallhover hears the breathing of the one walking, so he's close, he hears the steps, he sees a head uncovered, hair dark, Tallhover guesses at age, the skin of his throat is taut, but the shoulders, beside being narrow, are hunched over ... the smoke past the side of the head into the face of Tallhover, who would like to smoke the cigarette in the mouth of the one whom and would like to be the one walking in front of him, so that he would trail behind himself greedily seeing, greedily hearing, eyes on himself he would be walking in front

of himself, who may be Tallhover, as he may breathe and walk, what look his head and the hair on his head may offer, the skin of the throat, shoulders, back, legs, feet, hands, occupied in the desire for the smoke of the cigarette and one would be the seen and the one seeing, of the same movement, of the same thought, no longer divided into view and gaze, thus to calm down.[127]

The novel motivates the hero's split from himself by a corrosion of reality through subverted references that is typical of the world of intelligence services. Secret agents who trail informants and pass on information usually have to be monitored by their own organizations because spreading falsehoods and counter-information is just as much part of their behavior as repeatedly switching sides is. In the end, no one knows anymore who is on whose side, or whether it is not one and the same person on both sides, or, rather, whether they still *are* one and the same person:

> Das bin nicht ich, das nicht, schreit Tallhover, das ist, was wer sich ausdenkt gegen mich, das nimmt die Freude, da hört, was ich tue, auf, meine Sache ist Arbeit, die getan werden muss in meinem Kopf bin *ich*, der andere ist in seinem. Jetzt schreit Tallhover nicht mehr, er beruhigt sich, dass gilt, was er sagt, und dass es gesagt ist, genügt, da soll gedacht werden, was will, oder geschrien, wenn nur geschrien ist, was Tallhover schreit, oder sagt, aber dessen muss er sicher sein, das ist *er*.

> That's not me, not that, Tallhover screams, that's what someone is thinking up against me, that takes away the joy, that's where what I'm doing ends, my thing is work that has to be done in my head *I* am, the other is in his. Now Tallhover is not longer screaming, he calms down, that counts, what he says, and it's enough that it's said, think what one will, or scream what one will as long as what is screamed is what Tallhover screams, or says, but of that he must be sure, that *he* is.[128]

In retrospect, it becomes clear that a split of identities defines Tallhover's story from the beginning. His first mission consists in traveling to Cologne in September 1842, where he is to learn the basics of his profession from the experienced agent Friedrich

Goldheim. When he meets Goldheim, "in whom, as a confidant of Herr Police Inspector Hofrichter, he has confidence," for the first time, he immediately "draws up a profile of his interlocutor in his mind, as has been his habit for a while already."[129] But "Goldheim does not let Tallhover in on the surveillance of suspect persons, such that Tallhover has to see to himself."[130] Left entirely to himself, he fosters not only resentment for Goldheim (barely perceptible through the masterfully bureaucratic style of the text), but also develops, in the shortest of times, those extraordinary intelligence skills that will make him indispensable to his superiors. In December 1842 already, his superior ("who is interested in Tallhover's interest in surveillance and wants to advance Tallhover")[131] consults with him about how to proceed in the case of Georg Herwegh:

> Wer überwacht Herwegh?
>
> Ab Berlin Herr Goldheim.
>
> Tallhover verbringt den Vormittag im Polizei-Präsidium unruhig. Goldheim! Wann werde ich eingesetzt?
>
> Who's watching Herwegh?
>
> From Berlin on, Herr Goldheim.
>
> Tallhover spends the morning at police headquarters, anxious. Goldheim! When will I be deployed?[132]

Soon thereafter—a few pages later—ten years have passed, and Tallhover has an opportunity to take Goldheim's place without becoming active in his place:

> Tallhover, aber unter dem Namen Goldheim, Friedrich, trifft am Freitag, dem neunundzwanzigsten Oktober Achtzehnhundertzweiundfünfzig in London ein. Polizeileutnant Friedrich Goldheim ist unter anderem Namen in Deutschland unterwegs.
>
> Tallhover, but using the name Goldheim, Friedrich, arrives in London on Friday, the twenty-ninth of October eighteen hundred and fifty-two. Police lieutenant Friedrich Goldheim is travelling in Germany under a different name.[133]

When one of the London informants refuses to come to Cologne under a false name to swear to the authenticity of a forgery of his, Tallhover does not know "whether he should not also wish" for the plan to fail because if it were exposed, "he, Tallhover, would be incriminated as an instigator, albeit under the name of Goldheim."[134]

The *fabula* spells out the possibilities open to a narrative personnel policy to occupy the place of an ambiguous I—as narrator of an intelligence service story, as agent of this story, or as counteragent of its narrator. Betrayal, as a pattern of behavior of the secret agent, a type of acquiring information and subverted communication, also has a very specific event character. As Eva Horn has shown in reference to Borges:

> Betrayal is the event par excellence, a caesura at which history bifurcates, the moment in which one possible course of events is enacted while many others are discarded. It is the starting point of a narrative that will present this particular course *and not other* as true, necessary, and above all *noncontingent*, thus elevating the chosen story to the status of *history*. But if this particular story-as-history is tied to the implicitly suppressed version, it can be recognized as something manufactured and artificially created—as fiction.[135]

Over the course of reading, the dating of the documents lets readers notice that Tallhover reaches an inexplicable age and remains in active political service for almost two hundred years. In the 1890s he takes part in the persecution of the writer Peter Hille, in 1917 he organizes a collective transport of Russian revolutionaries (including Lenin) through Germany. At this point, the dialectic of the intelligence services' way of proceeding— the principle of supporting revolutionaries for the purposes of conservative provocation and of identifying political opponents— is already in effect. It transforms into an absolute ambiguity of political history when Tallhover, now a GDR agent, is punished by being transferred to the archives because he takes the liberty of pointing out that parts of the services—namely a certain Lieutenant General Müller—are seeking to dissimulate their fascist past and thus act to their own advantage as persons and to their disadvantage as employees of the State Security Service.

With Tallhover in the archive, one would expect him to have arrived at the level of historiography and to be able to adopt the retrospective perspective on documents characteristic of the *sujet*. But in this secret service plot, the logic of the synchronicity of intelligence acquisition and political action continues to hold sway. The hero, transferred to the state archive, acts within the past horizon of his documents, whose information he both processes and collects on his own initiative. A schizophrenic situation, which in many narrated fictions appears as the inner boundary of fictions, is thus motivated in a present-tense *fabula*, and its pathological character is repealed by the forms developed by altermodernism.

The emergence and possibility of a fabular present tense is an incisive phenomenon in the history of the present-tense novel. It is the point within the logic of the system at which the dominant reverses from narration to fiction. Within the matrix of classical narrated fiction, the *fabula*, narrated in the past tense, is always (implicitly or explicitly) located in the past, and since *sujet* and *fabula* are, in terms of fiction, present, an (implicitly) past *fabula* is presentified. With the emergence of the fabular present tense, however, we see the emergence of a *narrative* present, without there being any need for presentification. Present *fabula* and present *sujet* are synchronous; fictional present and narrative present are indistinguishable.

We thus localize in the emergence of the fabular present tense the point of a *reversal* of the dominants narration and fiction, the hypostasized moment of their equilibrium. Starting with the possibility of a fictional (asynchronous) present tense, we accordingly have to speak of a *switch* of dominants. A fictional fabular present tense creates the figuration of time that is asynchrony; an openness to the future as the horizon of possibility of the present determines the conception of the present and at the same time extends to the *fabula*. The contingency of the *fabula* is no longer interpreted after the fact by the *sujet* as teleology but maintained in its potentiality. A fictional fabular present tense implies a poetology of an incomplete past in which, despite its being past, acting is still possible.

Discussions of alternate histories indicate a situation that intersects with our reflections in a number of ways. The various designations alone—*alternative histories*,[136] *counterfactuals*, or *what-if-novels*—indicate that in counterfactual plots, narration and fiction enter into a new, irregular, or as-yet-unintelligible relationship. Alternate histories—as we would like to call them—are conspicuous in that they do not simply narrate an (implicitly fictional) *fabula*. Rather, it is the process of fictionalization that comes to light at the level of the *fabula*. The story narrated quite obviously deviates from the history transmitted by tradition. Every *alternative history* shows the extent to which the world is historical and (since it is dependent on history) could therefore also look different. Counterfactual histories thus stand out against any understanding of fictionality according to which fiction creates possible worlds. Narration does not narrate (implicitly) factual (hi)stories; instead, *fabulas* emerge only in the cooperation of narration and fiction. Whether and under which circumstances this can be seen as constitutive of worlds is another question. In this sense, the writing of history, too, does not create anything other than *fabulas*. The decision whether and under what circumstances they are to be understood as narrations of an (explicitly) factual past or not, the decision, that is, how strong the story aspect of history is, then depends in each case on the relationship between fiction and narration.

Counterfactuals confound the classical order according to which (hi)stories are narrated and worlds invented. What is invented is not a world but history. Counterfactuals emphasize the cooperation of narration and fiction in a new way. This cooperation, furthermore, displays the same shift of dominants from narrated fiction to fictional narration that we have described for the change from an epic past tense to a narrative present tense. Counterfactuals do not tacitly invent a world in the service of narration; instead, fiction produces history. For the narratological question of how a *fabula* creates a logic of decision[137] or how the decision in favor of a story is made, it does not matter whether an alternative history is to be judged as better or worse than the traditional history. What is important in the context of a conception of "altermodernism" is that it is no longer a teleological understanding of the *fabula* that prevails. The contingent present of the *fabula* appears as a moment of branching. Understanding alternative histories as histories characterized by a "bifurcation or branching of narrative paths" (Hilary Dannenberg)[138] also clarifies the relation between history and its temporality, which is obviously related to the reinvention of the history novel as a time novel. Altermodern *what-if-novels*[139] not only alter (on the level of story) our view of the past or[140] (on the level of the plot) the past itself. They do not only pose the question of how to access the past. They also alter the much more fundamental question of the formation of time, including the past.[141]

II. New sujets

The emergence of a fabular present tense already belongs to the innovations of the altermodern usage of the present tense. The power it develops in the history of literature, however, only becomes recognizable in the transformation of old *sujet* forms that make the narrative present tense possible (which is related, in part, to their retroactively becoming visible in modernity or in the genesis of new *sujet*s). On the level of the *fabula*, the important thing is not the discovery of new types of *fabulas* but the invention of a fabular present tense. On the level of the *sujet*, the opposite is the case: what is new here is not the present tense but a whole series of *sujets*.

Generally, the innovative force of altermodern *sujets* lies in their ability to elude the modernist aporia of synchrony. In these *sujets*, it is quite possible to synchronously remember, imagine, read (write), and experience. The equi-presentness of *fabula* and *sujet*, where modernist narration reached its limits, is not a problem for the altermodern *sujets*. We have discussed one modernist approach to overcoming the aporia of synchrony in the writings of Robert Walser. His "Walk" deals with the aporia of the synchrony of narration and narrative by reintroducing an ontological difference. According to the principle, "I am telling you what happens to come to my mind," the experience itself is fictionalized, that is, it is no longer conceived of as the (implicitly factual) experience of an (implicitly factual) narrator.

What, then, are the new *sujets* that elude Cohn's aporia of synchrony? There are memory-*sujets* and imagination-/fiction-*sujets* as well as reading-*sujets*; there are, finally, mental-reception-*sujets*, which combine and synthesize the latter two. All these *sujets* can be divided into two groups.

(1) What distinguishes the first group is that it restructures previously known classical and modernist *sujets*. Altermodern narration demonstrates that the elaboration of the level of the *sujet*, that is, the literary text's level of communication, can take more varied forms than previously possible.

In classical narrated fiction, the level of the *sujet* is understood primarily to be narrative—it emphasizes narration. Earlier, we defined its motto as "I am telling you, dear reader." The memory-*sujet* (1a) to be mentioned now, whose motto can be defined as "I remember," is an implicitly first-person narrative already known to modernists, Proust, for example. The reason for the narrative complications of this memory-*sujet* has turned out to be the implicit hierarchization of narrator and character.[142] When a first-person narrator remembers a first-person character, he retreats (almost programmatically) into the background in order to allow for the presentification of an (implicitly) past first-person character. Yet where memory signifies the power of what is remembered over the (implicit) present of the first-person narrator, the hierarchy of character and narrator ought to be reversed. And indeed, such a reversal can be identified already in pre-modernist texts, and there already it involves the consistent use of the present tense. Chapter LIII ("Another Retrospect") from Charles Dickens' *David Copperfield* (1849–50), written entirely in the present tense, is one example.[143] It begins:

> I must pause yet once again. Oh, my child-wife, there is a figure in the moving crowd before my memory, quiet and still, saying in its innocent love and childish beauty, Stop to think of me—turn to look upon the Little Blossom, as it flutters to the ground!
>
> I do. All else grows dim, and fades away. I am again with Dora, in our cottage. I do not know how long she has been ill. I am so used to it in feeling, that I cannot count the time. It is not really long, in weeks or months; but, in my usage and experience, it is a weary, weary while.[144]

The painful memories Copperfield is exposed to as the (implicitly factual) narrator of his (past) life story render him temporarily unable to narrate. The narrative afflicts him and assumes power over the process of narration. What is remembered dominates the present like the former first person dominates today's, and the character becomes the narrator. Here, too, the *sujet* becomes in a sense invisible, but it does not retreat behind the *fabula* (as if obligingly) in order to presentify it. Instead, it is usurped, so to speak, by the *fabula*. Here, Franz Stanzel's thesis about personal narration's affinity for the present tense is particularly tangible.[145] His assumption that limited narrative distance is responsible for this affinity can even be radicalized: The present of the *fabula* or, rather, the synchrony of the *fabula* with the present of the *sujet* follows from the leveling of the difference between *fabula* and *sujet*.

What, in classical narrated fiction, requires extraordinary motivation is generalized in the altermodern present tense. Here, the remembered and memory are within the same temporal horizon; narration and narrative are synchronized; narrator and characters can stand side by side, on equal footing and synchronously. Yet unlike in *David Copperfield*—where the first-person narrator loses control over the narration for only a few pages before the temporal relationship of retrospective (implicitly present) *sujet* and prospective (implicitly past) *fabula* is stabilized again—the altermodern present tense no longer has any "Archimedean point" in the present of the *sujet*. There no longer exists any point around which the chronotopos of the text is structured and from which a retrospection at the level of the *sujet* and a prospection on the level of the *fabula* could support one another.

We have also already encountered the imagination-*sujet* (1b) with its motto "I imagine," namely in Hildesheimer's *Tynset* and (albeit in a conflicted sense) in Walser's "The Walk." While memory tends toward the facticisms of modernism (insofar as remembering presupposes the implicit factuality of a past experience that is remembered), imagination tends toward the fictionalizations of altermodernism. This fictionalization of the *sujet* is, strictly speaking, not to be confused with a *re*fictionalization. Instead, the level of the *sujet* is explicitly fictionalized for the first time. Implicit fictionalizations in which, as in Walser's walk, an (implicitly) past *fabula* transforms into an (implicitly) present imagination are generally motivated by a pathology,[146] in which the equi-present of narration and experiencing (or of *fabula* and *sujet*), as we have mentioned, can be explained by a de-actualization. If the narrator in his (implicitly factual) present thinks he is experiencing something that he is synchronously narrating, then this experience can only be a hallucination, a delusion, or some other way of losing touch with reality.[147] If, however, it is no longer the (implicitly factual) present of the *sujet* that structures temporal relations within the text but the present of the reader, for whom *fabula* and *sujet* are situated on one and the same level of fiction anyway, then it is no longer necessary to motivate the imagination-*sujet* by a pathology.

(2) Among the new *sujets*, too, there seem to be forms that are significant either for narratology or for fiction theory. They share a peculiar new orientation of the *sujet* toward the reader. We can define them as new because a certain knowledge from (modernist) narratology and fiction theory has now reached the level of the *sujet* itself. We can trace this in the modernist narratological insight that the *fabula* is a mental construct. In altermodernism, this insight determines no longer just the aesthetics of reception but also the poetics of production, namely insofar as authorship itself features a reading aspect: authorship bears an affinity to reading. Writing, that is, is affected by the questions of narratology and fiction theory discussed above, for example the question of how implicit assumptions about fictionality and factuality are distributed in relation to individual narrative levels.

The reading-*sujet* (2a) is at first announced in the motto "I am reading (while you are reading)" or "I/you/we are reading." We find it at the beginning of many of Borges' narratives, in which, for instance, encyclopedias (usually unauthorized editions) are browsed or apocryphal writings are to be deciphered. The reading-*sujet* conceives of the reader more and more as the co-producer of the narration, instead of merely its recipient. To some extent, this co-producing, too, already refers to fiction, since the reader is implicitly invited to take part in it ("Imagine").

A synthesis of the *sujets* already mentioned can be found, for instance, in Simon's (2b) reader-*sujet* with its inherent motto "Imagine me reading as you are reading." The fictionalization of reading actualizes *sujets*' narratological knowledge and in so doing offers a new variation of an old insight of narratology—that it is the reader who mentally constructs the *fabula*. For the *sujet* is now conceived of as that level of communication that makes it possible to construct the *fabula* in the first place. Since the author, too, can only do this by means of the *sujet*, he is as involved in this communicative process as is the reader. In altermodernism, the author himself is (has become) a reader, and the reader—who is instructed to imagine the author reading—an author.[148]

This example of a sujet is one of many self-reflexive modernist procedures the altermodern novel deploys in new ways. In altermodernism, it becomes possible to fictionalize mediality itself, that is, to fictionalize reading (or hearing). This fictionalization of the *sujet* (understood as the material or discursive level of communication) thus takes part in the generalization of the present tense.

To conclude, we now have to look into the narratological differentiations that come with the changes described so far.

III. Personnel policies (I/you/she)

Why does the return of the third person in altermodern novelistic practice seem like a move back toward the matrix of classical narrated fiction? This, at least, is the way it might appear from the perspective of modernism's first-person narrative practice. This practice saw the two-person schema of classical narrated fiction, in which there are only "I" and "she–he," as inescapable. Viewed from this perspective, any resurfacing of narration in the third-person must indeed appear as a regression. That is why the innovation of altermodern narration in the third person has to be placed in the context of a larger question. This is the horizon we touched on in our discussion of the debates concerning the non-fictionality of first-person narration. We now suggest the name "personnel policies" for this larger question.

As we have done throughout this chapter, we do not argue against Hamburger here, but merely extend her theories by distinguishing between *fabula* and *sujet*; hence the reformulation: For the impression to arise that a story narrates itself (as if) by itself, the *sujet* must retreat behind the *fabula*; if it remains in the foreground, no fiction can be constituted. Yet in the case of the *sujet*, too, we have to account for signals of fiction, and this includes the temporal structures of fiction. Dorrit Cohn points out a particular mechanism of fictionalization of the *sujet*: "homodiegetic fiction signals itself solely by way of fictional identity of the narrator."[149] Cohn thus refers to a characteristic of fiction that starts from the personality of narration.[150]

In contrast to third-person narrations, homodiegetic first-person narration is not necessarily fictional, nor need it contain any fiction signals. In first-person narrations, the counterfactual access to a third party's consciousness can become the documentation of an access to one's own consciousness. To be sure, it would be paradoxical if a first-person character thus documented were to invent him- or herself.[151] It is hence silently presupposed that the narrator-first-person in first-person narrations homodiegetically narrates something *about himself*. Yet it could also be assumed that this *I* is no (implicitly factual) first-person narrator at all but a first-person character, who, exactly like the *fabula* in the classical system of narrated fiction, narrates himself (as if) by himself.

The (implicit or explicit) use of the second person in novels of the second half of the twentieth century restructures the relationship between narrator and reader. It manifests an imbalance of power that previously existed only latently. Insofar as the elements of consciousness that emerge in the course of reading are controlled by the author, the author retains (in relation to the reader) the sovereignty over the text. The author's power over the reader derives from those elements of consciousness that are necessarily produced in the process of reading. One should not, incidentally, have all too many illusions about developing other options, a harmonious balance, say, that would put author and reader on an equal footing. Even the author's granting the reader access to the narrator's consciousness need not be a sign of authorial pacifism. Quite the contrary: the narratological peacefulness that seems to characterize the procedure is to be found precisely in those late modernist authors who experimented with strategies of, to put it drastically, mind-fucking—Robbe-Grillet in *The Secret Room*, for instance, or Bret Easton Ellis in *American Psycho*. Both live-murder texts use the present tense in which they are written to force the perpetrator's perspective onto the reader. The reader is not released from his participation in the text. Only one last option remains open to him: to stop reading. In some authors, even this violent act of authorial extremism is integrated into a kind of educational agenda, an agenda, for example, of overcoming an addiction to reading,[152] of providing insights into the moments of literature that induce addiction, or of criticizing the use of literary modes of making sense to fashion images of oneself and projects for one's life.

Monika Schmitz-Emans has observed that the text of the so-called "postmodern" novel (Borges and, especially, Italo Calvino's *If on a Winter's Night a Traveler*) is deictic. This means that "as a text about a reader-you,"[153] it is gestural because the novel is present both within and outside the text (in the real hands of the reader). That is why books constitute "a hinge between the imaginary world and the so-called real world."[154] Already in Calvino, the first-person present tense narration is interrupted by direct addresses to a reader-you. In the context of second-person narrations generally, narratology has diagnosed a breakdown of the distinction between reality and fiction[155] or between story and discourse.[156] Monika Fludernik ascribes this breakdown to a contradiction within the *you*. The *you* is, on the one hand, the addressee (implicitly apparently the addressee *of the narration*) and, on the other hand, a character. But it cannot be both at the same time. Already in modernism, there are texts that employ the ambiguity characteristic of the personnel policy of the *you*, namely, to be situated in the middle between *I* and *he* and thus to have an affinity to both *fabula and sujet*, to circumnavigate the narrative breaking point of synchronous narration. This is what Georges Perec, for example, does in *Un homme qui dort* [*Man Who Sleeps*].[157] In altermodernism, though, we can detect two forms of fictional second-person narration in which such a contradiction does not even appear any more.

The relation of *fabula* and *sujet* changes to the extent to which the reader of altermodern novels is a co-producer of the world of the text. As soon as there is no longer any narrator (transmitter, deployed by the author), who from out of his (implicitly factual) present tells the reader (addressee) a story and has to be assumed as the *sujet*'s subject, the reader takes over both functions *synchronously*. Not only does he construct the *fabula*, he is also the subject of the *sujet*. It should be clear by now that this renders the synchrony of *fabula* and *sujet* unproblematic.[158] Yet the contradiction cited by Fludernik is resolved as well: the reader is not *addressed* by a subject on the level of the *sujet* but instead *takes over* the function of this subject.

A second variant of non-contradictory second-person narration simply actualizes once more the traditional thesis about the emergence of fiction according to which a reader identifies with a story's heroes: The reader who "puts himself in a character's place" is synchronously reader and character. This synchrony, called immersion, does not break through the boundary between fact and fiction. Indeed, it is typical of the reception of fictional texts. From the point of view of fiction-narratological poetics, which focuses on a dimension of experience unavoidable in any literary text, this means that the identity of character and reader is typical even and precisely of the level of reception, that is, typical of how a fictional text addresses its reader.

Up until modernism, narrations' constellations of persons are obviously quite restrictive. They identify the first person with the subject of the narration and the third person with the character of the *fabula*, while the second person as it were stands alongside the events of the text. In other words, they reduce the three persons to their deictic positions: addressee (you), speaker (I), and the person discussed (she–he).

An altermodern perspective makes the contingency of these restrictions apparent. They might be canonical, but they are by no means compulsory. Both the subject of the *fabula* and the subject of the *sujet* show themselves to be free: they can be occupied by all three persons singular. Altermodernism abandons the one-dimensional allocation of the first person to the narrator and the third person to the character. The narrator suddenly finds himself among the characters and is treated as a character; an *I* turns out not to be the narrator but a first-person character; and a *she* or a *he* can take over the role of the narrator. The following table shows the changes that have taken place.

In these four modes, we initially only see the person (first- or third-person singular) and the tense in each case. As we have just indicated, however, these personal tenses do not lie on the same narratological levels. The altermodern, in particular, leaves open on what level the fourth sentence (*He goes*) is to be situated, on

Table 1.2 Overview of the personnel policy

	Person-tense allocation	**Narratological allocation** (*fabula/sujet*)
classical narrated fiction	He *went*.	character of the *fabula*
classical narration / reminiscing autobiography	I *went*.	subject of the *sujet* (narrated by the subject of the *fabula*)
modernism	I *go*.	subject of the *sujet*
altermodernism	He *goes*.	character of the *sujet*

the level of the *fabula* or that of the *sujet*. Put another way, if we read the altermodern third person only as a character (that is, if we assume that it is to be located on the level of the *fabula*), we would probably also speak of a return of third-person narration in the service of establishing the present tense. For the third person in this case resolves the first-person narration's problematic synchronous present of *fabula* and *sujet* and allows for the use of a narrative present tense. (We discussed such an option in the example of Updike's *Rabbit* novels.) Yet the fictionalization of the altermodern present tense, as we have mentioned, is not simply acquired at the cost of reactivating third-person narration. Instead, the ostensible return to classical narrated fiction comes with a reflection on the personality of narration, that is, on the subjects of the *fabula* and the *sujet*. As a consequence, we find numerous narrators among contemporary third-person characters. In this sense, personality in these novels reveals itself to be altermodern as well. That is why these novels' third persons cannot simply be identified with characters of novels from classical narrated fiction. Recent present-tense novels rather fathom an empty space that comes to light in an irregularity of the allocations of person and tense: Both the past tense *I (went)* (B) and the present *I (go)* (C) are subjects of the *sujet*. With *I went*, we have no trouble locating the *I* on the level of the *fabula*, namely as an "additional" first-person character. *I go*, however, involves the aporia of synchrony, which makes such a location impossible as long as the first person is conceived of initially and primarily as the subject of *sujets*.[159] Within the matrix of narrated fiction, therefore, only three of the four possible person—tense points are occupied; one marked here by an asterisk, must remain empty:

Table 1.3

[I went]	(level of the *sujet*)
[I went]	(level of the *sujet* + level of the *fabula*)
[I go]	(level of the *sujet*)
*[I go]	(level of the *sujet* + level of the *fabula*)

If the level of the *sujet* and that of the *fabula* lie within the same present, the first person cannot be the subject of the *sujet* and character of the *fabula* at the same time, for in that case, the first person would have to shift *itself* onto the level of the *fabula* and thus invent *itself*. (We have described such a case in Walser's "The Walk," which, nonetheless, is to be interpreted only as a loss of touch with reality.) The reader, however, can indeed shift the first person onto the level of the *fabula*, namely when he becomes the subject of the *sujet*.

To illustrate this, we can once again bring in Dickens' *David Copperfield*. With Copperfield himself as the narrator of his life, the novel is an excessive first-person narration. He narrates the story of his life in the past tense, in the mode *I went* (B). If we read the novel as a classic narration, then the first person is both the subject of the *sujet* (as a first-person narrator) as well as a character of the *fabula* (as a first-person character). The narrative is presentified no differently from how it is in a third-person narration in the mode *He went* (A). A narrator looks back at what a (fictive) character has experienced in *his* present, and this story in the *epic* past tense narrated itself (as if) by itself.[160]

Things change as soon as we conceive of the novel as a reminiscing (even if "fictitious") autobiography. The past tense then indicates that a first person is looking back from his present to experiences in *his* (implicitly factual) past. What Dorrit Cohn has noted for the temporal relations between *fabula* and *sujet* also applies to the characters. In fiction, the character of the first person is synchronous with the events—only when a level of reference is introduced does it suddenly appear in the narrator's past.

In the passage from the chapter "Another Retrospect" cited above, we saw how the (implicitly past) first-person character briefly usurped the level of the *sujet*. This, however, requires the cooperation of the first-person narrator who withdraws step by step from the *sujet* ("I must pause yet once again" / "there is a figure in the moving crowd before my memory" / "All else grows dim, and fades away")[161] for the first-person character to be able to appear both on the level of *fabula* and the level of *sujet*. Here, then, the possibility flares up of *synchronously* locating the *same* first person on the level of *fabula* and of *sujet*. We said that this is generalized in the altermodern present tense; now we can be more precise and add the following: in the altermodern novel, (1) there is no longer any need (as there is in *David Copperfield*) for the cooperation of a narrator who first has to let a fictitious character emerge as a narration to whom he then relinquishes the field of the *sujet*; (2) it does not necessarily have to be first-person characters who act on the level of the *fabula* of a present-tense narrative, because (3) it is the reader who becomes the subject of the *sujet* and thereby produces on the level of the *fabula* a fictive character *as a character*.

The altermodern novel restructures the hierarchy of persons that exists within the matrix of classical narrated fiction accordingly: in contrast to first-person narration, third-person narration has no specific temporality and thus is similarly unspecific temporally as is the present tense. With the reintroduction of heterodiegetic third-person narrations, the aporia of synchrony dissolves as if by itself and becomes a genuine characteristic of fiction.

The synchronous present of an event and its narration shows that this event occurs within the consciousness of a fiction-producing reader, that it thus is a fictive event. In the reader's psyche, the *fabula* is equi-present with the *sujet*, because it is the *sujet* that generates the *fabula* in the first place. Only when we assume a third level of external reference does the *fabula* precede the *sujet* (*ex post*).[162] *Fabula* and *sujet* are synchronous as well for a concept of fiction based on a phenomenology of reading (which starts with a reader conceived of as the producer of fiction). In that the reader is included in the constellation of persons in altermodern novels, the inner logic of the order of *fabula—sujet* reference shifts. The impossibility, from the point of view of narration, of synchronously experiencing and narrating does not apply in the reader's consciousness. Here, the narration of the story and the experience of the story build up synchronously.[163] The fictive event is always synchronous with the idea (reception) of a fictive event, because otherwise it does not exist at all.

We can now reformulate one last time the question raised at the beginning about whether first-person narratives are fictional *or* fictive. Käte Hamburger assumes that fictionality can be described only by looking at the act of producing a text—for her, it goes without saying that it is the author who synchronously with producing a fictional text produces the fiction *as such*.[164] Yet according to Hamburger, for this production to succeed the text must not contain any subject of statement. A first-person narration can thus only be fictitious. It has been objected that such a distinction between fictive third-person narration and fictitious first-person narration is inexplicable from a reader's viewpoint.[165] Those who raise this objection, however, overlook that the very objection already contains the decisive argument for solving the problem. What is needed is "merely" a rigorous change of perspective to the recipient. As soon as the reader is understood as the producer of the fiction, the first person is fictionalized as well.

Hamburger is nonetheless correct in saying that a fictional text must not contain any subject of statement. For a subject of statement marks the position of the speaker. And where a speaker is positioned in time and space over against an addressee, it is indeed impossible for fiction to arise. Yet for Hamburger it is also the case that any first person in a text can only be understood as a position or positioning of a speaker (thanks to which it implicitly refers to a second person, that of the reader). More traditional narrated fiction becomes problematic, however, when a first-person position begins to form on the level of the *fabula*. This position is the fictive *origo* of a reader, not (as Hamburger's holds) the fictitious *origo* of a speaker.

We can thus summarily state the main effects of the new allocations that result from the new personnel policy: in modernism, the "present" was seen exclusively as the unavoidable present of the process of narration and not as the unavoidable present of reading. We now see the degree to which Updike's present-tense novel, analyzed above, already contains an altermodern insight: to organize the time of the *fabula* from out of the time of reading.[166] Modernist novels know the present of the story exclusively as the present of narration. Altermodern narration in turn knows: The present of the story as a story that is read is the present of reading (at best, it is the presence of narration, but never its present). From this perspective, the time of narration no longer appears as present, but as timelessly non-contemporaneous, and consequently as eminently fictive. It can only ever be made contemporaneous by the reader. The altermodern present tense in its entirety is thus to be thought from the present of reading and not (as in modernism) from the implicit present of narration.

The history of the theory of the altermodern present tense we have traced shows: The present of reading implies the present of the reader.[167]

You know it.

2
Readings in methodology

As we have shown, the use of the present tense in the novel is not an exception, nor does it mark an estrangement from a universally valid rule. Instead, the development of the present-tense novel represents a literary epistemological process that goes beyond current narratological knowledge and, therefore, calls for a revised methodology. This is true in particular for the shift of dominants from narrated fiction to fictional narration we discussed. Narration no longer simply gains full access to the past through a past tense, but does so through a non-contemporaneous present tense.

It takes the development of a *fiction-narratological* approach to fully appreciate the poetological insights afforded by the altermodern novel into how narration and fiction interact.[1] The problems the present-tense novel confronts cannot adequately be grasped from either a purely narratological perspective or from a purely fiction-theoretical one. For this reason, to put it succinctly, our poetics of tense follows the methods provided by the present-tense novel itself, or rather, it follows the insights of the present-tense novel into how narration and fiction are constituted. Only a *fiction-narratological* approach can shed light on the *interaction* of fiction and narration. Without explaining this relation, we cannot understand how narrative literature functions as *fiction*.

From our point of view, the deficits of narratology in terms of a theory of time and of a theory of fiction appear in a different light because narratology insufficiently accounts for the temporal deformation of fictionality.[2] The novel, always determined by both the contradiction and the collaboration between narration and fiction, is also governed by the conflict between each of its forms of time.[3] Narration and fiction always stand in a tenuous relation. They never coincide—either (retrospective) narration is dominant or (contemporaneous) fiction is. In classical narrated fiction, retrospective narration dominates: the figuration of time *presentification* names the retrieval of a past present.[4] In fictional narration, contemporaneous fiction dominates: the figuration of time *asynchrony* already indicates that the tension between past and present is to be discussed as a split in the present itself. Asynchrony brings out the necessity of an understanding of narration and fiction that includes the possibility that the two do not merely form a unity by addition but mutually contain and comprehend one another: the past (non-present) moment of the present is conceived of as part of the present.

Drawing on these two figurations of time, presentification and asynchrony, we can finally grasp the function of the tenses past tense and present tense. They serve as linguistic construction material, determine the aesthetic surface, and mark the literary texture—no novel can get around the decision about its own tense. The friction between the time-forms fiction and narration is manifest in the novel's tense texture as well, and it is often spelled out explicitly in authors' own poetologies. This friction cannot be dialectically sublated; one of the two time-forms will always be dominant.

The reason why these connections (and thus also the historical shift of dominants from presentifying narrated fiction in the past tense to asynchronous fictional narration in the present tense) could so far not have come into view can be explained by the history of theory. The dominance of narration in the history of literature (in classical narration fiction) has a correlate in the dominance of narratology in the history of literary scholarship. Since, in narrated fiction, it is in fact narration that constitutes fiction, the impression arose that fiction as such is an effect of narrative procedures and consequently an epiphenomenon of certain narratives. Under these circumstances, the task of fiction theory seemed to consist in investigating whether a given form of narration is able to produce fiction. In turn, there has been little reflection on the perspective in which narration itself is to be traced back to feigning.[5]

The collaboration of the two forms of time of fiction and narration that characterizes narrative literature and literary narration as such is thematized in this chapter on three different, but systematically connected, levels of argumentation and observation.

(1) At first, we pick up on the findings of phenomenological inquiries into literature from the previous chapter. There, we were able to describe two forms in which the altermodern present tense appears, namely a non-synchronous present or "asynchrony" (seen exemplarily in Thomas Pynchon's *Gravity's Rainbow*) and a synchronous progression or staggering of multiple presents in a "synchronous succession" (seen exemplarily in Claude Simon's *Les Géorgiques*). Contrasting Uri Margolin's theorems in the narratology of time on narrative temporal shiftings and Seymour Chatman's theories about the extreme poles of narrational speed we will show why up until now it was not possible to include the temporal phenomenality of recent present-tense novels in the explanatory schemata of narratology.

(2) These reflections will be followed by a revision of the approaches of narratology and fiction theory. In a critical re-reading of Gérard Genette we will show how narratology's forgetting of time arises from its forgetting of fiction. We will also see why the structure-forming functions of the literary tenses were so often overlooked. In reverse, a reading of Käte Hamburger will show how a concentration on the past tense and on the timelessness of the fictional present led to a skewed definition of forms of time.

However, we are not discussing Genette and Hamburger to criticize them, nor do we wish to take individual concepts from their theories to syncretically construct a new theory. Rather, we are looking for the points of connection that enable us to bring together both methods *as such*, that is, we want to find points from which both their positions can be assumed. The fiction-narratology we describe is thus tasked with describing both the narrational *and* the fictional dimensions of a text as well as the relation of dominance between fiction and narration within it.

(3) In the third section we introduce deictic shift theories (the doctrine of a threefold shifting of space, time, and person) and outline how they facilitate an integration of narratology and fiction theory. Theories of deixis systematically interweave the question of tense with that of fiction. They do so from a strongly linguistic perspective, which sets them apart from all those approaches that argue on the basis of morphology and either assume no temporal meaning of tense at all or hold it to be determinable only through context.[6] Furthermore, we can observe in recent deictic shift theories an increased interest in the systematic connection of

questions of narratology and fiction theory—"The language of narration," Mary Galbraith, for example, writes, "is the mode of being of the fiction."[7]

Thanks to the linguistic impulses of deictic shift theories, theories of narrativity find a new foundation in language theory. At the same time, deictic shift theories' interest in the cognitive processing of narratives provides an opening for questions of reception. In addition, the shifting of parameters from tense to space, time, and person described by deictic shift theories allows for a comprehensive inscription of narrated fiction within the dual mediality of film (space) and literature (time) as well as for an elucidation of the connections between production, figuration (of time), and reception. Going back to the conceptual origin of the term *shift* in the procedures of shifting practiced by the avant-garde and formalism, the genuinely aesthetic and literary moment of the shift emerges in clear outline. By way of conclusion, we will use this insight to systematically outline the spectrum of possible dynamics of shifting in fictional texts.

Findings from the phenomenology of literature

The genuinely altermodern literary figurations of time, i.e., (a) asynchronous anteriority (Pynchon) and (b) synchronous succession (Simon), are only insufficiently captured by "classical" narratological terms such as relative duration and speed, frequency, or prolepsis and analepsis. One step toward understanding their poetological goal consists in conceiving of these novels' temporality as a whole starting with their usage of tense. Yet tenses can only be related to the narrativity of literary texts by taking into account these texts' fictionality. If the systematic relation of narration and fiction is not taken into account, it is also impossible to clarify the (temporal) meaning of the tenses. In that case, there is a tendency to interpret the contradictions that emerge from a one-sided consideration of the semantics of tense—that is, the semantic interpretation of the present tense as a noun signifying "present"—in such a way as to claim that we have to assume an atemporal meaning of the tenses.

According to Uri Margolin, it is only a "subset of present-tense literary narratives that can be meaningfully recuperated as creating the illusion of concurrent narration." He concludes that there is no "full overlap between grammatical and semantic features."[8] What are the consequences of applying this thesis of an idiosyncratic deformation of tense in literary narration to the present-tense novels of Simon and Pynchon? Since the present tense in these novels does not signify any present, we as readers would have but two choices. Either we assign an agrammatical present meaning to the present tense or we assume a grammar of tense that is devoid of sense. We described the extent to which one can recognize the effect of fiction in the distancing from a semantic meaning of tense in the previous chapter. Now we would like to show, on another (methodological) level, why neglecting fiction necessarily leads to a false interpretation of the relation between tense and narration.

Non-synchronous present or narration of the future

The very first sentences of Pynchon's *Gravity's Rainbow* actualize the central motif of a present that is non-synchronous (with itself):

> A screaming comes across the sky. It has happened before, but there is nothing to compare it to now.
>
> It is too late. The Evacuation still proceeds, but it's all theatre.[9]

In its temporal meaning, the "It is too late" traverses the present. But it does not designate itself as present tense. Rather, the present tense is an asynchronous one, in accordance with that peculiar figure according to which the present precedes itself or, in relation to itself, comes too late.

At first glance, it would seem that we are dealing here with the narration of the future sought but not found by Uri Margolin. From a strict narratological point of view, however, such a narration cannot exist.[10] Narrating the present as future would correspond to a shift of narrated time and narrating time in which the narrative would lie in the future of narration (or, in Genette's terms, of the narrator). Margolin's persistent and unrewarded search for a paradoxical narration of the future—"Present as future: No example found,"[11] he states succinctly—brings out a persistent inconsistency in the interweaving of purely narratological approaches with temporal questions.

In order to explain this in more detail, let us go to the starting point and opening sentence of Margolin's essay "Shifted (Displaced) Temporal Perspective in Narrative":

> Any narrative involves essentially two time spans: that of the events or actions being reported, and that of the act(ivity) of narrating them. Normally, the tense in which a narrative is told (past, present, or future) indicates the temporal relation between the time of narration and that of narrated events.[12]

What is problematic is not the fact of drawing on three tenses—for we do in fact encounter forms of the past, present, and future[13] (and their tenses) in literary texts—but the projection of tenses onto the narratological distinction between narrating time and narrated time. Margolin attempts to accommodate more than two times (past, present, *and* future) between the two narratological times (time spans) of narration and narrative. This hopeless endeavor has a correlate in his necessarily unsuccessful search for a narration of the future. Margolin's postulate of future-related forms of narration merely fills in an empty linguistic schema of language set out by the three tenses. In the grammatical system of tenses, a future does indeed exist, but narrating the future is linguistically impossible.[14] Whenever there seems to be a case of narration of the future, it can be shown that with regard to narrativity, its temporal relations are identical with those of retrospective narration. Science fiction novels, whose stories take place in the future, are written in the past tense just as classical historical novels are. Everywhere, narration (or the narrator) looks back on the narrative.

If we look more closely at the temporal relations between reported events and narrative activity, it is striking that Margolin seems not to notice the fundamental temporal difference between the two. His elaboration of the shifting of temporal perspectives is based on the assumption that "narrated and narration" relate to one another the same way utterance and uttering [*Aussage und Aussageakt*] do. Margolin accordingly assumes that (under normal circumstances, as it were) they would temporally coincide in time and that it is only through tense that, by means of a shift, a temporal relation between the two is produced. But it is precisely such a coincidence that is extremely problematic if we take it to be the temporal relation between *fabula* and *sujet*. We have already discussed in detail the aporetic or anti-narrative effects that can arise from attempts to synchronize *fabula* and *sujet*. In the case of narrations of the future, the situation is even clearer. There cannot be a *fabula* not yet narrated that awaits its future narration, for in what form would it exist or preserve itself until it could be narrated in the future? It might be easy to imagine an experience that is recorded only in the future, but this case of a "future narration" is in no way different from the kind of (retrospective) narration to be found in any autobiography or memoir. The fact that Margolin considers narration of the future to be possible at all (or at least considers it possible to think such narration) can only be explained by the fact that, in concentrating on the utterance and its temporal semantics, he does not consider the temporal differentiation between *fabula* and *sujet*, which is the fundamental determination of all narratological reflection.[15]

We are now in a position to answer the question of why there is neither narration of the future in *Gravity's Rainbow* nor an unsystematic usage of tense. This is particularly conspicuous in the temporal interferences between *fabula*, *sujet*, and tense in Pynchon's novel, which in the V2 missile finds a motive for this principle of temporal interference on the level of the *fabula* and thereby *actualizes* its procedure of metanarrative asynchrony.[16] Pynchon's present-tense novel renders visible the participation of the temporal relation between *fabula* and *sujet* in the constitution of the time of the novel. The search for a narration of the future actually placed in the future, not just narrated in the future, the search for a fictional (hi)story that already has a present before it is narrated in the future regarding that present can only seem plausible if one overlooks this systematic narratological connection.

Tense usage in altermodern present-tense novels, however, provides evidence not just to show why the search for a narration of the future is meaningless. Because Margolin conceives of narrative relations on the basis of a coincidence of utterance and uttering, his argument also suffers from his neglecting the function temporal shifting performs in the constitution of fiction.[17] He sidelines the deictic quality of tense usage in narrated fiction, i.e., the dependence of anteriority and posteriority on the temporal *origo* of a narrator or a character.

What does the dependence of tense usage on temporal horizons of *sujet* and *fabula* mean for the usage of the future tense? Since narrations are always oriented retrospectively, the events they narrate that lie between the temporal horizon of the (implicitly past) *fabula* and that of the (implicitly present) *sujet* can be viewed from two temporal perspectives. From the point of view of the *sujet* they are to be classified as past, while from the point of view of the *fabula*'s fictional present they appear to be futural. Since classical narrated fiction privileges the temporal horizon of the *sujet*, it works with the past perfect, which is to mark a temporal difference from the *fabula* (we saw this in the scene from Zola's *Au Bonheur des Dames*). Altermodernism, in turn, prefers the temporal horizon of fictional events and therefore uses the future tense, as does, for example, Marcel Beyer in his present-tense novel *Kaltenburg*:

> Nach einer Phase der Ernüchterung, in der Martin sich jede dialektale Einfärbung schroff mit gestochenem Hochdeutsch vom Leib zu halten versucht, wird er sich mit wachsender Neugier hineinhören, sich des Sächsischen nach und nach bemächtigen, ohne es allerdings je ganz anzunehmen.

> After a period of disenchantment, while Martin tries to ward off any taint of dialect by employing a harshly correct High German, his growing curiosity will lead him to become more accustomed to it, and he will gradually acquire a command of Saxon, though without ever accepting it completely.[18]

This is not a "looking ahead that is certain about the future." Here, too, the "fact" that Martin adopts a Saxon dialect is already past from the point of view of the *sujet* because it is located between the two poles of the present of the *sujet* and the past of the *fabula*. Another passage from Beyer's novel reads like a homage to Robert Walser's fictionalized *sujet*, which acquired its flexibility from the fact that Walser's fiction meditatively nestles up against the course of a prospectively oriented *fabula*. Walser's imagination accompanies the course of the *fabula*, makes suggestions (Do you want me to narrate you like this? Will we come across a bakery?), and runs ahead of the *fabula*—on the wings of a fictional *sujet*. A few decades later we read in Beyer:

> Bald wird uns, wie damals dem Professor, ein Kiefernwäldchen in den Blick geraten, wir werden das helle, gleichmäßige Rauschen in den Bäumen hören, der Wind, der eine endlos weite Landschaft zu durchwehen scheint, wo immer ein paar Kiefern beieinanderstehen, und dann tauchen zwischen den Kronen auch die Gebäude des früheren sowjetischen Armeelazaretts auf. Soweit ich mich erinnere, hat Kaltenburg dort gleich nach seiner Ankunft, noch ehe die Klinik an die Kasernierte Volkspolizei übergeben wurde, im Speisesaal ein riesiges Aquarium eingerichtet.

> Soon we will see, as the professor did, a little stand of pines, we will hear that high-pitched, even rush of wind in the trees, the wind that seems to be sweeping through a vast expanse of landscape wherever a few pines cluster together, and then the buildings of the former Soviet field hospital appear between the treetops. As far as I recall, this is where, soon after his arrival and before the medical facility was transferred to the Garrison People's Police, Kaltenburg has installed a huge aquarium.[19]

Despite the objections raised above, we will take up Margolin's ideas of a temporal shift in connection with our detailed analysis of deixis, that is, our reflections on the dependence of linguistic meanings on personal, spatial, and temporal *origines* or reference points. We will see that narration and fiction are mediated by a deixis, or, more precisely, by deictic shifts. This will also clarify why the temporal shifts that Margolin understands to be merely unsystematic deformations of tense are relevant to fiction theory. These shifts can indeed be grasped in all their stringency. They can be traced back to interferences generated in the projection of personal, spatial, and temporal deixis onto narrative differentiations of precisely these spatial (e.g., in focus), temporal (e.g., in aspect), and personal (characters, narrators) moments. Accordingly, Pynchon's V2 motif is not to be read simply as a post-modern author's capricious deformation of time, but as the actualization of complex temporal differences in which the forms of time of narration, fiction, and tense participate.

Staggered past or zero poles

Claude Simon's *Les Géorgiques* connects episodes from before and after the French Revolution with episodes from both World Wars and the Spanish Civil War. Yet it does not constitute any relation between these different, even disparate moments that one could call a "course"—even if, from a purely narratological perspective, it is difficult to say at first what else such a connection could be other than a course:[20]

> Il loge avec son état-major au château de Mittelhagen. Il couche dans des palais. Il couche dans des étables. Il couche dans les bois. Il couche sous la tente. Il couche dans une église incendiée. Il couche dans un terrain vague, dissimulé par les hautes herbes, dans un chantier abandonné, recroquevillé dans l'escalier d'un abri anti-aérien au fond rempli d'eau croupie. Pendant la journée il échappe à ses poursuivants en fréquentant les restaurants de luxe et les bains publics. Il couche à même le sol enveloppé dans son manteau. Quand il ouvre les yeux au réveil ils sont obstrués par une matière grenue, scintillante, d'un blanc grisâtre et opaque. Son visage et son manteau de cavalerie sont couverts de neige. Il recommande que l'on prenne soin de son matelas de campagne en peau de mouton de Barbarie.
>
> He is billeted with his general staff at Mittelhagen castle. He sleeps in palaces. He sleeps in cowsheds. He sleeps in woods. He sleeps in tents. He sleeps in a gutted church. He sleeps on waste ground, hidden by high weeds, on a derelict building site, curled up on the stairs of an air-raid shelter, its bottom awash with stagnant water. During the daytime he evades his pursuers by frequenting expensive restaurants and the public baths. He sleeps on the bare ground wrapped up in his greatcoat. When he opens his eyes at dawn they are clogged with a gritty, crystalline, off-white, opaque substance. His face and cavalry greatcoat are covered in snow. He recommends that particular care be taken with his campaign mattress in Barbary sheepskin.[21]

While at first it may seem as if the various overnight stays constituted stations within a continuous action (of the Napoleonic Wars, for example), it quickly becomes clear that sleep itself travels through time. Sleeping takes place in all times, or more precisely, through(out) all times. For the individual (sleep) stages to develop their full narrative [*erzähltechnische*] effect, it is not necessary for the reader to know or to reconstruct which concrete strand of narration they belong to. The only essential thing is that they are (can be) in principle ascribed synchronously to different times or slices of time. If we say that these stages operatively connect the stages of the (hi)story that come before and after them, this is not to be taken in the narrative sense of linking them up in a course. In the "sleeping" that traverses the centuries, the (hi)story seems to synchronously pause and elliptically to evade all narratability.

We can outline and illustrate this phenomenon with more precision with critical reference to Seymour Chatman's reflections on pause and ellipsis. For Chatman, pauses and ellipses are the extremes of an order that is thought in terms of different relations of speed between narrated content (story) and formal expression (discourse). In the passage above, we are not dealing with any sleep stretched out over two centuries or a summarized "sleep of history." In Simon's novel, pauses and ellipses are no longer conceived of as opposites that necessarily exclude one another. In altermodernism, they turn out not to be the extreme poles of the two speeds of the course of the story and the course of discourse (*fabula* and *sujet*) defined in relation to one another. For Chatman, though, pause and ellipsis are extreme forms of *summary* and *stretch*, and he invokes narratological reflections (such as Günther Müller's distinction between narrated time and narrating time)[22] and Genette's differentiation of narrative speeds. Yet these narratological prejudices imply the sidelining of fictionality.

Chatman presupposes the existence of a scalable relation between a *story-time* (narrated time) and a *discourse-time* (time of narration or reading). As long as *fabula* and *sujet* relate to one another the way they do in traditional narration, it is in fact unproblematic to presume such a relation and to interpret the "difference in speeds" as stretch or summary.[23] This changes, however, as soon as there is an ellipsis or a pause. Ellipsis and pause cannot be understood, as Chatman proposes, as a merely quantitative exaggeration of stretch and summary. We are dealing with a qualitative difference because what is set to zero is story-time in the one case and discourse-time in the other.[24] Both cases are only conceivable at all if we think of the story as existing independently of its narration, that is, if we ignore the fictionality of the narration and the fact that the *fabula* is constituted by the *sujet*. For his explanation of ellipsis, Chatman must presume that events unfold independently of whether they are narrated. And in the end we can only assume that there is a pause if we presume that the story is narrated as if by itself. Both gestures are typical of the classical narrated fiction. And to a certain degree, this is also why this approach to how narrative fictions constitute time is so productive. The self-reflective narrative poetics of classical modernism, like the rigorous avant-garde's facticism so critical of fiction, can still be understood thanks to this matrix and be described as being without *fabula* and *sujet*. In Pynchon and Simon's altermodern fictional narrations, however, this is no longer possible, for the reasons spelled out in the previous chapter. The narrations practiced by altermodern present-tense novels thus require a revision of narratological theory.

Revising the approach to time in narratology and fiction theory

Now that we have discussed two theorists who build on Genette's narratological typology, Margolin and Chatman, we would now like to consider this typology itself in order to get to the cooperation of tense, fiction, and narration we are looking for. Is it possible to find a point within narratology from which we could open up narratology to questions of fiction theory? In our view, the distinction between a perceiver and a speaker in the narrative text, for which Genette coins the concept of "focalization," is one such point. Genette himself recognized that the difference between "Who is speaking?" and "Who is seeing?" is relevant not just in narratology. This recognition has (rightly) established itself within the field: "Only in fictional texts can a perceiving perspective be differentiated from the speaking perspective."[25] The fact that only fictional texts are focalized makes "focalization" one of the points of connection between fiction theory and narratology.

Narratological revisions: Gérard Genette

A series of problems in Genette's theory results from the fact that he did not develop his categories strictly from out of an analysis of fictional narrations and their narration but evidently also from out of an engagement with the debates about literary showing and telling. Since he superimposes the question of the fictionality of narratives onto the question of their mediality, it looks to Genette as if medial illusionism already were to be identified with fiction. For him, this also implies that the explanation of the genuine narrativity of literature over against the spatial, visual, and indicative arts has to lie in its character as an art of time.

From Henry James to Percy Lubbock, *telling* and *showing* have been defined as two different modes of narration.[26] Prior to film studies' participation in narratological research, narratology considers any *showing* to be a narrative illusion. But once neo-formalists like David Bordwell, Seymour Chatman, and Kristin Thompson define showing as neither metaphoric nor illusionary but as a genuinely medial mode of filmic narration (as factual showing in narrative film), showing loses the status of being illusionistic, i.e., of being counter-factual in principle, that it previously had in an exclusively literary narratological cosmos. And this means that narratology loses its central explanation for the fictionality of narratives.

Genette's lack of an explanation for the significance of fiction and the ensuing incapacity to understand the significance of temporality results in a distortion of individual narratological categories of analysis. All of Genette's conceptual organon is affected by a time-theoretical ambiguity and the basic distinction imported from the showing/telling debate. Time and again, Genette immediately applies the medial distinction showing—telling to narratological categories. In his commentary on narrative distance, for instance, he points out that Plato is the first to encounter the problem of distance, namely when he distinguishes two narrative modes, diegesis and mimesis, "according to whether the poet 'himself is the speaker and does not even attempt to suggest to us that anyone but himself is speaking' (this is what Plato calls *pure narrative*), or whether, on the other hand, the poet 'delivers a speech as if he were someone else.'"[27] Genette then immediately turns to a discussion of the opposition between showing and telling to short-circuit this opposition with that between mimesis and diegesis. He thus regards every *showing* in literary texts as illusory and as standing in direct opposition to a quasi-natural *telling* (as if a voice in a text were less illusory than a gaze). Genette understands telling in the (written) text to be a mimesis of narration, and accordingly understands the relationship between image and text to be an illusion created by showing. In this sense, then, he writes:

> that the very idea of *showing*, like that of imitation or narrative representation (and even more so, because of its naively visual character), is completely illusory: in contrast to dramatic representation, no narrative can "show" or "imitate" the story it tells. All it can do is tell it in a manner which is detailed, precise, "alive," and in that way give more or less the *illusion of mimesis*—which is the only narrative mimesis, for this single and sufficient reason: that narration, oral or written, is a fact of language, and language signifies without imitating.[28]

But this last point precisely does not apply: not all narration is linguistic in character. Genette's exclusion of the large number of existing filmic narrations indicates how much his understanding of narrative mimesis and illusion is shaped by the basic assumption that narration is linguistic in nature. Without taking recourse to reflections on the mediality of language and images, however, there is little hope of grasping the fictionality of narration beyond its distortion in an inquiry into "voices" resounding or "gazes" appearing in a text. As an alternative, we propose a concept of a medial difference that does not inscribe an illusionary dimension in the narrative text but a potential for fiction into the medium. Fiction is triggered by a paradox particular to each medium of narration. In order to establish a definition within fiction-narratology that corresponds to this insight, we read Genette not only as a narratologist, but also as someone who provides cues for fiction theory.

As a media purist and a modernist proponent of a linguistic self-reflexivity of literature, Genette advocates a concept of medial embedding in the literary text (for instance, of orality in writing). For him, illusions emerge wherever there is a medial difference instead of medial embeddedness. What Genette denounces as pure media illusionism in *Narrative Discourse* in the 1970s has retained its negative connotations when, 20 years later, he is interested in the genuinely fictional aspects of narration. In *Fiction and Diction*, the narrative process of "focalization" (previously examined in purely narratological terms) appears as an exclusive criterion of fiction.[29] Focalization is not chosen by chance. As a determination of perception, it recalls narrative showing and the media illusionism of narration. Genette is interested in medial differences only insofar as he can understand them as instituting illusion. Only then does he draw on them to explain fiction in narrative texts. His fixation on media illusionism thus affords him insight into focalization's potential for fiction (since it operates with media illusion) and at the same time prevents him from recognizing the participation of tense and temporal structure in the constitution of fiction. Since tense and temporal structure in the literary text do not possess an illusionary quality, Genette considers them to be irrelevant.

One of the most serious conceptual distortions to arise from Genette's media-theoretical presumptions is the introduction of an additional third level, that of *narration*[30] (the act of narrating), with which Genette believes to have to supplement his distinction between *histoire* (*fabula*) and *récit* (*sujet*). We consider it to be not only unnecessary but misleading. For when Genette defines *narration* as an additional differentiation between the medium (*récit*) and structure (*histoire*) of narration, he overlooks the fact that *récit* already implies a media structure, that is, the oral. One could go even further and say that the concept *récit* one-sidedly reduces the concept of the *sujet*, which is open to medial differentiations, to an oral structure.

The allegedly additional category of *narration* can be traced back to the structural differences between oral and written narration. It is not by chance that the neo-formalists of the Wisconsin group go back to the bipolar formalist distinction between *fabula* and *sujet* at the very moment in which their (film-) theoretical acknowledgment of an actual showing in narrative film has determined its medial status. For our explanation of fiction in narrative texts as the form of their organization of time, too, the use of a bipolar distinction is sufficient and more consistent.

What Genette is really reacting to with his attempt at an (allegedly typological) distinction is narration that, in terms of media, is more complex. Oral narration is embedded in the written text as a fiction reduced to medial illusion. His assumption of three narrative levels arises only because he misunderstands a medial differentiation (that is, a medial stratification or staggering in narrative texts) to be a narratological distinction. For instance, if the form of oral narration (medium 1) is embedded in a written text (medium 2), there will be medial interferences because the form of oral narration is superimposed on the mediality of the written text.

The question of the relation between media and narrative levels comes up in analogous manner for the relation between the medium of film and narrative levels. Film and literature are two primary media that differ and oppose one another while they both participate in narrative (chronotopos) and narration (spatial and temporal deixis).[31] It is thus not enough to define fiction as embedded medial mimesis or medial illusion. Instead, what should be emphasized is *medial difference*. This would explain how filmic *and* literary narration relate and react differently to the medial differences that are relevant for them. There would be no need to assume either an (as yet underdeveloped) film language[32] or an (as yet concealed) kinesthesia[33] of literary narration. Film language and literary kinesthesia are to be counted among the media aesthetics of narration, and they may be in fashion in various styles. They nonetheless do not belong to the fundamental narrative distinctions. Instead of introducing a third category of *narration*, it makes more sense methodologically to understand *narration* as one more difference within a series of distinctions that remain bipolar. We thus assume a constitutive differential or dual mediality, for example, linguistic—filmic in the twentieth century, oral—written in early stories-within-stories or so-called Chinese-boxes- or Matryoshka-doll-narratives. Genette's system of categories, however, makes it impossible to understand the phenomenon that has been foregrounded by present-tense narration since the middle of the twentieth century: the interplay of temporality and fiction in the narrative text is rendered invisible.

A similar categorical distortion becomes apparent when we go through Genette's categories of time: order, duration, and frequency. The fact alone that Genette mostly develops his fundamental narratological categories by way of Proust's classic-modernist exemplary *A la Recherche du temps perdu* explains the ubiquity of temporal questions. These are, however, systematically subsumed under the questions "Who is seeing?" (mode) and "Who is speaking?" (voice). The "time of narration," for instance, is discussed under the category "voice"—narratologically, "time" turns up at the most surprising places. It neither has its own systematicity nor does it take the tense system in language into account. If, therefore, we forego Genette's distinction between mode and voice, we do not do so simply out of a kind of conceptual purism but with the goal of methodically returning to that point in Genette's system at which he makes this categorial distinction. There he claims to have derived its systematicity from the grammar of verbs:

> Since any narrative, even one as extensive and complex as the *Recherche du temps perdu*, is a linguistic production undertaking to tell of one or several events, it is perhaps legitimate to treat it as the development ... given to a *verbal* form, in the grammatical sense of the term: the expansion of a verb. *I walk, Pierre has come* are for me minimal forms of narrative.[34]

We share Genette's view that literary narration must be understood as an extension of the categories of verbs. But he lives up to his own demand, "to organize, or at any rate to formulate, the problems of analyzing narrative discourse according to categories borrowed from the grammar of verbs,"[35] only in a very limited sense. In the case of tense, too, a very promising announcement is all there is. Genette does place "the problems" that belong to the "temporal relations between narrative and story ... under the heading of tense,"[36] but in his later writings he no longer ascribes any systematic significance to the tenses.[37] What is more, in one of the few later instances in which he mentions tense, in the *Nouveaux discours du récit* (1983), he even contests such significance. He criticizes Hamburger's definition of the epic past tense for being merely a special case to which Hamburger attributed too much significance. Genette mentions the presentifying effect of the epic past tense but at the same time insists that this effect is limited exclusively to third-person narration and dissipates in the switch to first-person narration. Even in the historical novel, he maintains, the principle of presentification is ineffective. Instead, the retrospectivity of the past tense remains intact. According to Genette, "there is no need to say that virtually all classical novels, from *La princesse de*

Clèves to *Les Géorgiques*, are included in the group."[38] The fact that even and especially the historical novel deals with the form of time of fiction (with contemporaneity), we said in the first chapter, serves as a poetological springboard for altermodern narration. We described how the novel of the past is formed over the course of the twentieth century and—precisely to signal the fictiveness of its past—develops a fictional present tense. In this context, it may not be superfluous to mention that Genette's own example contradicts his thesis (and confirms Hamburger's): *Les Géorgiques* is indeed a historical novel—but it is not written in the past tense (as Genette claims) but in the present tense. It can even be considered one of the most exceptional present-tense novels written so far.

We have seen that the blindness to fiction of Genette's narratology comes with a blindness to time. We can, however, take some elements from his analyses and use them in our later systematic elaboration. What we gain from Genette's discussion of telling and showing in the literary text is the importance of the medium—but precisely not just for narration but also for the question of creating literary fictions. We will explain our thesis, according to which fiction is to be understood in terms of medial difference, in more detail when we discuss the deictic shift later in this chapter. For now, suffice it to say that we assume that a medial difference is always the trigger for shifts within a deictic triad *space–time–person* and that fiction emerges in these shifts.

We have gone back to that point in Genette's theory of narration at which we think it can link up with a theory of fiction, or more precisely: to that point at which Genette understands narration as an extension of the categories of the verb. In order to make good on his narratological claim to derive the essential determinations of narration from the grammar of verbs, we would like to start not with the distinction between "mode" and "voice" that is only allegedly grounded in the grammar of verbs but with a properly linguistic argumentation.

It is here, too, that we find one of the points at which the approaches of narratology and fiction theory can link up. Tense, as Käte Hamburger's fiction theory systematizes it, is one of the morphological categories of the verb. Our methodological approach of a fiction-narratology, too, starts with tense and its meaning for fiction and narration. While we adopt the *narratological* indication of focus (as a *characteristic* of fiction) from Genette, we owe to

Hamburger the *fiction-theoretical* discovery of the fiction-*constituting* meaning of tense. We thus establish a context that brings tense and focus together with a dual mediality of narrated fictions and fictional narrations. This also names the second motivation for a comprehensive fiction-narratological approach: in the end, we take our characteristics of fiction from narratology and the form of time of narration (retrospection) from fiction-theoretical approaches.

Our fiction-narratological dual perspective thus also requires revising Hamburger's theory of fiction. Once again, it takes a detour through a critique of theory to find the connecting points with narration and to discover theories and partial objects. Having gone through narratology, however, we already suspect some narratological points of connection, namely the phenomenon of focalization and the form of time of retrospection. What is still lacking are their correlates in fiction theory. We thus have to join narratological arguments to those arguments from fiction theory that take the tenses of verbs as their central object. We will therefore briefly explain Käte Hamburger's approach to this question before we extend it and take it in a new direction.

Fiction-theoretical revisions: Käte Hamburger

In her approach, which is to understand fiction by way of how tenses are organized in texts, Käte Hamburger makes use of Karl Bühler's *origo*-model with its "basic deictic words *here*, *now*, *I* in their absolute function, so to speak, as a local mark, a temporal mark, an individual mark."[39] Among Bühler's three basic categories of personal, spatial, and temporal deixis, it is primarily the last that provides the linguistic background for what Hamburger calls (deictic) shifting. For her, this is a "shifting of the spatio-temporal system of reference, i.e., of the orientational system of reality, into a fictive one, the replacement of a real I-Origo, which anyone doing the telling in a reality-report represents, by the fictive I-Origines of the figures in the novel."[40] The fiction effect that arises in this shifting is characterized by the amalgamation—triggered by a paradox of tense structure—of the reader-*origo* with the fictive *I–here–now* points (the *origines*) of the characters.

Strictly speaking, Hamburger provides a theoretical foundation for only one of the three characteristics of fiction she names, namely for the epic past tense. The argument concerning person (the combination of third-person narrative plus verbs of inner processes places the origo of the reader into another I) is only partially articulated, that is, justified only in terms of tense structure but not in terms of spatial deixis or in relation to person, for instance by an othering constitutive of an ego. The disappearance of the narrator, her third criterion, is a collateral or subsequent result of the de-actualization of the narrative tense past tense we have previously analyzed: when the narrator drops out as the subject of the utterance, so does the spatial and temporal connection of the narrative utterances. According to Hamburger, this decoupling allows for the fictionalizing relocalization of the deicitic field, which is thought in the terms of Bühler's model. In losing its "grammatical function of designating the past,"[41] the past also loses its deictic character. This makes it possible to enter into the timelessness of the fiction. As proof of this, Hamburger cites the combination of past tense and time adverbs that contradict the literal tense meaning of the past tense—she considers the connection of "was" with "tomorrow" in a single sentence to be a sufficient indication of fictionality.

Linguists have raised a fundamental objection to Hamburger's assumption that in fiction, tenses lose their deictic quality. According to Gisa Rauh, the contradiction in temporal orientation mentioned by Hamburger is not to be understood as a loss of the deictic quality of the tense (the past tense), but can be explained by the fact that events appear synchronously from two different temporal perspectives. There are two deixes *at the same time*: the deixis of a narrator and that of a character.[42] From the perspective of the narrator, the events take place in the past; from that of the character they are still to come. In this interpretation, of course, the fictional character of contradictory deixis vanishes and only its narrative character remains. In contrast, Monika Fludernik stresses that the contradictory temporal deixis of fiction (which she refers to as "odd") cannot simply be dissolved in a dual perspective (focalization). Instead, it has an effect on the spatial and temporal situatedness of events as a whole. It is located in a "temporal nowhere."[43] While we subscribe to Fludernik's observation that a contradictory temporality can be described in terms of spatio-temporal indeterminacy (that is, as a chronotopos of the Hildesheimerian "no now, nowhere"), we will nonetheless, within the framework of an engagement with deictic shift theory, combine this thesis with Rauh's diagnosis of a dual personality. This will present us with all three parameters of deixis (space/time/person), and we will see that the deictic shift, which creates the fiction effect, concerns all three.

An observation that pertains to both literary theory and literary history reveals a further point of connection of Hamburger's fiction theory and narratological discussions. Her argument about the persons of fiction, according to which fiction is the only place where "the I-originarity (or subjectivity) of a third-person *qua* third-person can be portrayed,"[44] can be accounted for by narratology. On the new narrative terrain opened up by narrated monologue in the nineteenth century, a claim to interiority familiar from expressive literature narrated in the first person (epistolary novels, autobiographies) lives on a higher narrative level and develops a calculus of fiction. Dorrit Cohn locates the point at which this migratory movement traverses a boundary at one of the highpoints of the matrix of narrated fiction.[45] Flaubert's virtuoso use of focus shows in a particularly vivid way that fictions narrated in the third person need not necessarily be understood in terms of a retreat of the narrator. Rather, the dual time perspective of prospection within a retrospection indicates that there are still two perspectives, that of the character *and* that of the narrator. The narrator thus does not disappear in fictional third-person narratives, as Hamburger thought—rather he enters into the character:

> She was about fed up with both of them, father and daughter. Above all, she was sick and tired of hearing him mourn about his poor child. His poor child this, his poor child that: enough already! Yes, she could hear his poor child crying now.[46]

A two-in-one is thus responsible for the paradoxical temporal structure of the epic past tense. This two-in-one attests to the participation of a personal and a spatial moment in the shifting of the tense structure. The peculiarity of the tense does not arise from the temporal structure as such (that is, not from a quality of literature as pure time-art) but goes back to the two-in-one perspective of focalization. This confirms our assumption that the existence of a medial difference is a necessary condition for fiction to come about.

Furthermore, the personal dynamic of the two-in-one personality throws new light on the cooperation of the *origines* of reader, narrator, and character described by Hamburger. Obviously Hamburger thinks that whenever fiction is triggered, the triad I/here/now is shifted to another point. The I-*origo* of the reader amalgamates with that of the characters, and the reader is displaced from his (actual) here and now into the characters' (fictional) here and now. In order for this to happen, no narrator is required; on the contrary, a narrator would make it impossible for the reader to place himself in the character's situation. If we start from a two-in-one, however, the mechanism appears differently: when fiction begins, the narrator does not disappear in order to make room for the amalgamation of the I-*origo* of the reader with the I-*origo* of the character. Instead, the *origo* of the reader follows the perspectival shift of a narrator who settles in the character.

For the new systematic approach we propose in the next section, we thus need to extend Hamburger's model. While Hamburger reduces the shifting dynamic to an *amalgamation* of the I-*origo* of the reader with that of the character, we want to conceptualize the shift as a *dissociation*. We consider the three deictic categories of space, time, and person to be relevant on the level of the work itself, not only on the level of the reader's experience (or on the level of production). In our view, the *origo* becomes dissociated in the shifting process. And the fiction effect arises from shifts within the (spatio-temporal-personal) deictic system of actuality, shifts within which one of the three categories usually serves as a trigger for shifting the other two.

The fact that Hamburger conceives of deictic shifts only in terms of amalgamation is surely grounded in her literary historical perspective, which is mainly oriented toward classical narrated fiction. Another reason is that she primarily looks at the entry into fiction, which only opens the temporal space of fiction. She does not pursue the narration's dynamic of shifting that sets in with this entry. If we nonetheless follow narrated fictions (and even more, literary texts that aesthetically oppose them) in their movement and take their poetologies seriously, we see that they often resist an amalgamation of the three deictic parameters. This is most obvious in avant-garde texts, which systematically make it impossible to constitute any coherent fiction at all. Kharms' "On Phenomena and Existences" is one example:

Представьте себе, Николай Иванович заглядывает во внутрь бутылки со спиртуозом, потом подносит ее к губам, запрокидывает бутылку донышком вверх и выпивает, представьте себе, весь спиртуоз.

Вот ловко! Николай Иванович выпил спиртуоз и похлопал глазами.

Вот ловко! Как это он!

А мы теперь должны сказать вот что: собственно говоря, не только за спиной Николая Ивановича, или спереди и вокруг только, а также и внутри Николая Ивановича ничего не было, ничего не существовало.

Оно, конечно, могло быть так, как мы только что сказали, а сам Николай Иванович мог при этом восхитительно существовать. Это, конечно, верно. Но, откровенно говоря, вся штука в том, что Николай Иванович не существовал и не существует. Вот в чем штука-то. Вы спросите: «А как же бутылка со спиртуозом? Особенно, куда вот делся спиртуоз, если его выпил несуществующий Николай Иванович? Бутылка, скажем, осталась, а где же спиртуоз? Только что был, а вдруг его и нет. Ведь Николай Иванович не существует, говорите вы. Вот как же это так?»

Just imagine. Nikolay Ivanovich peers into the bottle of vodka, then he puts it to his lips, tips back the bottle bottom end up, and knocks it back—just imagine it, the whole bottle.

Nifty! Nikolay Ivanovich knocked back his vodka and looked blank.

Nifty, all right! How could he?

And now this is what we have to say: as a matter of fact, not only behind Nikolay Ivanovich's back, nor merely in front and all around him, but also even inside Nikolay Ivanovich there was nothing, nothing existed.

Of course, it could all be as we have just said, and yet Nikolay Ivanovich himself could in these circumstances still be in a delightful state of existence. This is, of course, true. But, as a matter of fact, the whole thing is that Nikolay Ivanovich didn't exist and doesn't exist. That's exactly the whole thing. You may ask: And what about the bottle of vodka? In particular, where did the vodka go, if a non-existent Nikolay Ivanovich drank it? Let's say that the bottle remained. Where, then, is the vodka? There it was and, suddenly, there it isn't. We know Nikolay Ivanovich doesn't exist, you say. So what's the explanation?[47]

One by one, Kharms' text calls up the parameters relevant for the emergence of fiction. Sometimes he offers a *now* and then rejects the *I* that belongs to it; sometimes he calls on a character but only systematically to clear out the space that belongs to it, right before the reader's eyes. The conditions under which fiction is constituted are presented one by one in isolation, and do not come together in a fiction effect. Kharms' text is thus meta-fictional in the full sense of the word, that is, not only in the sense of an anti-illusionist parekbasis. The text does not simply deny the existence of a textual Nikolay Ivanovich or of his surroundings. It is meta-fictional because it constructs a *fabula* over the course of which the non-existence of Nikolay Ivanovich confirms the existence of the liquor he has finished off.

Once modern meta-fictional texts conspicuously place the conditions of their constitution right before the reader's eyes and celebrate a dislocation of space, time, and person, a similar dynamic of shifting becomes legible even in older texts of narrated fiction. Such is the case for Adalbert Stifter's *Hochwald*, which, on Hamburger's reading, splits into fictional and non-fictional components.[48] Whether such texts are more modern in the differentiation of space, time, and person than the matrix of narrated fiction that they belong to is a question that can hardly be answered. At least, however, it can be claimed—by means of a deconstructive gesture against the alleged indivisibility of the (spatial-temporal-personal) deictic triad—that a (fictional) dislocation of the parameters of space, time, and person by literary texts cannot be separated from their aesthetic reactualization by a present reader and is therefore also part of a history of reading.

The asymmetry of space, time, and person is at the same time responsible for their dynamics and thus for their mobility, openness, and vitality. This leads to the question:

> [W]hat is more immersive: the form of expression that gives us a complete but temporary relocation to the narrative scene and

jogs us in and out of this focal point, or the one that maintains a constant position halfway between a narrator's and the character's spatio-temporal location?[49]

Like Marie-Laure Ryan, we suspect that temporary total identifications (with a fixed I–here–now-*origo* as described by Hamburger) are less immersive than the squinting of a person who focalizes, one of whose eyes belongs to the narrator and the other to the character.

A complete amalgamation with the perspective of a character necessitates repeated switching of perspective. Because it is necessary to narrate over and again, the perspectives alternate or interrupt one another in the text. The same can be said for the perspectival relations (of focalization) of narrator and character. The focalizing attempt simultaneously to present the perspectives of both narrator and character corresponds to temporal attempts to synchronize *fabula* and *sujet*. In modernism, the presents of experience and of narration constantly have to alternate over the course of the text in order for a successive synchrony to emerge.[50] Only the asynchronous present tense in altermodernism makes it possible to join both presents together. This connection can also be formulated at the level of characters, namely with regard to the relationship between character-I, character-here, and character-now. Or, framing it as a question: Does it make any difference whether the reader-*origo amalgamates* with the *origo* of a character and whether this protagonist-*origo* constantly changes location over the course of the fiction (this seems to be the case for the adventure novel)? Or whether the reader finds no consistent, only a dissociated protagonist-*origo*, that is, a character whose spatio-temporal positioning is unclear? Putting it this way is to transfer Marie-Laure Ryan's question—whether it is more plausible to understand personal relations as jogging in and out of a temporal identity or as a *constant being-in-between*—onto the notion of a personal deixis.[51]

In modern pathographies of fiction, the dissociation of the three parameters of space, time, and person in fiction is particularly evident. But even independently of any aesthetic expressionism we have to assume a fundamental asymmetry of the three deictic parameters. One of the consequences of our fiction-narratological reflections with regard to the basic assumptions of deixis is the hypothesis that the three parameters always split apart (dissociation), always remain connected (continuity), and are never equivalent (asymmetry).

We have now found and discussed all the parameters relevant to fiction-narratology. In Hamburger, these parameters are—under a temporal dominant—space, time, and person (dislocation of the reader-*origo*/presentification/experience of the subjectivity of a third party), which are, however, not systematically tied to narratological categories. As if it were a mirror-image, only one category relevant to fiction theory flashed up in Genette's narratological reflections: focalization. Yet this category is capable of combining the two criteria of fiction neglected by Hamburger, namely the retreat of the narrator and the verbs of internal processes. For a fiction-narratological systematization of otherwise particular phenomena, this means that in each case, the trigger of fictionality is a media structure bound up in a paradox. An epic past tense can answer for this as much as focalization can in narrated fiction or simultaneous narration can in fictional narration. The following systematization of a *fiction-narratological* theory will further clarify these connections.

Deixis

Theories of deixis, that is, of interpreting a series of linguistic expressions depending on points of orientation, operate with the categories of space, time, and person. Karl Bühler assumes a central point of orientation, an I–here–now-*origo*, from out of which spatial, temporal, and personal reference unfolds. Käte Hamburger, as we saw above, adopts Bühler's model for her own reflections in fiction theory. Harald Weinrich, with regard to an "interpersonal deixis," objects that language cannot meaningfully be thought when one starts with a single personal *I*. Behind such an idea, the "'egocentric fallacy' of many linguistic reflections on deixis" is said to become visible. The *origo* of linguistic communication is rather a "communicative diad" of *you* and *I*, and in written language we must take a there and a then into account, that is, communication over spatial and temporal distance.[52]

The criticism of the linguist Gisa Rauh, too, focuses on just this hypostacized point of unity in Hamburger. Rauh points out that space, time, and person can in some forms of deixis be posited arbitrarily.[53] We showed what this might mean in the phenomenon of the two-in-one and pointed out that it is a dynamic of shifting that is in effect.

In order to understand what happens in such a shift, we have to be aware that space, time, and person are the three dimensions of the deictic system of actuality they set up. In every non-fictional context, this system of actuality is organized from out of a singular I–here–now point, in which the three axes intersect. This both constitutes actuality and "positions" a subject within it. Fiction, however (and only fiction), modifies the arrangement of the system of actuality. While in every non-fictional context the system is referred to an undivided I–here–now, fiction effects a shift within the three deictic dimensions. They can be addressed independently of one another, but there is always an interplay between them. The personal, local, and temporal axes do not coincide in a single point. Since no such point is given, the reader of a fictional text can also not step into it in order to view (for example, through the eyes of a character) the system of actuality *as a world* or *as actuality* from that position. In other words, he cannot displace his I-*origo into* the fiction, or rather: In following the deictic shifts of the text, his unified *I–here–now* is dissociated (in the experience of fiction). This experience of dissociation is what fiction consists in.

What this means in concrete terms and how such a shift unfolds has to be explained in more detail.

Dynamics of spatial deixis and temporal deixis

First we will look at a sentence often cited as an example in research on the theory of deixis:[54]

(1) Caesar marched into Rome. There, a strong faction had formed around Pompey.

In this sentence, a historian is reporting on Caesar's march to Rome and the conspiracy that formed before his arrival. In Hamburger's parlance we could say: The reader-*origo* is neither with Caesar nor with the conspirators, but with the subject of the utterance. The *origo* of the reader does not shift but we, along with the historian, "observe" events from a secure spatio-temporal distance, and it makes little difference whether events took place only a few decades ago (as they did for an ancient historian) or two millennia (as they do for the contemporary reader). Things are different in the following example:

(2) Caesar marched into Rome. *Here*, a strong faction had formed around Pompey.

Lexically, this sentence differs from example (1) only in its spatial deixis. "Here" and "there" are the only differences manifest in the text, and they seem to affect exclusively the spatial points of orientation, once within and once outside of Rome. We will see, however, that the *here* necessarily implies a shift of the temporal deixis of *had* and that the personal deixis is affected as well. The spatial deixis also shifts the temporal and personal deixes. This is "simply" the effect of entering into fiction, which we described in Hamburger (although fiction-narratology still requires a further differentiation of Hamburger's theorem of a fiction-triggering deictic shift).

The deictic coordinates of both examples can be spelled out as follows: In the construction, "Caesar marched into Rome," it is still undecidable whether this is a past tense that refers to a past only from the narrator's or historian's perspective or an epic past tense in which events at the same time appear as present (from the perspective of the characters). In example (1) the "there" makes it perfectly clear that the reader can no longer assume Caesar's perspective. From Caesar's perspective, Rome is *here* (where he has already arrived), and the same can be said of the conspirators, from whose viewpoint, too, the faction was formed *here* in Rome. Their perspective also cannot be assumed. Example (1) is thus unambiguously a historical utterance: what is under discussion are historical persons and events that have occurred in the past in the city of Rome.[55] We perceive them from the standpoint of a historical narrator who portrays them from his I–here–now.

The deictic relations are quite different in example (2). The "here" already makes it clear that it is not a historian-*origo* from whose position spatio-temporally distant events are being viewed. "Here" rather refers first of all to Caesar's perspective: We attend his arrival *here* in Rome. And thus the deictic structure slowly starts to fan out. For the past tense indicates that there is not only Caesar's perspective, who from his viewpoint has just *now* come to Rome. Already through the combination of *marched* with *here*, a fiction effect arises—the past tense has become a presentifying epic past tense.

Up to this point, matters can still be described using Hamburger's concepts. A first deviation, however, arises already from the fact that it is not a *tomorrow* but a *here* that brings about the presentification. Compared to (the purely temporal constellation) *tomorrow/was*, a temporal shift catalyzed by *moved/here* is the more complicated or circuitous result of a spatial deixis. This yields a first preliminary result of our work with theories of deixis: fictionality is not induced solely by temporal shifts but also by spatial shifts.

At first glance, this result seems to confirm Hamburger's assumption that a deictic shift implies the reader's placing-himself-into the (undivided) *origo* of a character. For only by placing ourselves in the perspective of Caesar's *I–here–now* does a spatial deixis result in a temporal one, a *here* in a *now*. But besides the phenomenon of the two-in-one already mentioned, which explains the effect of the epic past tense as a synchronous temporal perspective of narrator *and* character, there is another deictic shift in example (2). Let us look at the function of the tenses in the two examples.

In general, the past perfect indexes a relation of anteriority to the past tense. In example (1), in which the event is portrayed from the perspective of the historian, this means: The conspiracy has been formed *before* Caesar's arrival. In example (2), the case is more complicated. The *here* does not only refer to Caesar's viewpoint, but also to the perspective of the conspirators gathered around Pompey, for they, too, are *here* in Rome. It would thus be possible to assume their position as well. In that case, however, a different temporal deixis is associated with this *here*. While Caesar on his arrival is confronted with a conspiracy existing *now*, his arrival is still to come from the perspective of the conspirators *now* gathering around Pompey. Even if the spatial adverb "here," unlike Hamburger's temporal adverb "tomorrow," does not directly interact with the narrative tense, it nonetheless has a (fictional) effect, namely by way of the anteriority (Benveniste) the past perfect attributes to it as background.[56] The crossing of narrative tenses and (in this case spatial) transverse adverbs then leads to a fictional synchronization of two different personal chronotopoi.

Now it is also possible to make the third deictic parameter, namely that of person, more concrete, even if it is not explicitly thematized in our example sentences but is merely present in its position within the deictic grouping. As a reminder: In a purely tense-structured example such as "tomorrow was still far off"[57] from Dostoevsky's *The Adolescent*, the temporal contradiction between past and future can be explained by assuming two overlapping temporal perspectives, those of narrator and character. The "tomorrow" already past from the narrator's viewpoint is still to come from the character's perspective. The reader enters into this deictic network and synchronizes. In our (spatio-temporal) example (marched/here/had formed), an additional fictional intervention takes place between the two chronotopoi of Caesar and the conspirators. Thus, both a spatial deixis and a temporal one are in effect, the positing of a "here" together with a synchronicity and an anteriority. Spatial and temporal deictics once again do not coincide in a single point but influence one another.

Deixis and tense

Understanding tenses to be deictic means viewing them not as references to past, present, or future points in time, but as an effective connection of the deictic dimension of time with the two other dimensions (space and person). What consequences does this have for our reflections on the present tense? Linguist Elisabeth Leiss, as we have mentioned, goes so far as to say that the present tense, by localizing a "now" in relation to space and person, can only be considered a "pre-tense" because it always runs the great danger of tautologically referring to itself as a point in time. She suggests "dismissing the conception of the present tense as a point or moment in time." The "image of the temporal space" is a means to a more appropriate interpretation of the present tense.[58] Leiss consequently defines the characteristics of tenses by way of the other two parameters of deixis—space and person—and not in regard to temporal semantics or reference. In the present tense, "speaker, viewer, and verbal situation are localized in the *same* space. The temporal space is the surroundings of the one speaking."[59] In addition to the definition of tense by its relation to the spatial component[60] of deixis, there is the definition in relation to the personal components, the I-*origo*: "Properly speaking, the present tense is a synonym for the anthropocentric field of showing."[61] The grammatical function of the tenses is said to consist in allowing for anaphorics or cataphorics (that is, references forward or back and shifts in the relation to space and speaker), in which the "function of phorics" would be "to dislocate deixis."[62]

One advantage of Leiss's approach is that the meaning of tense can be defined by way of its grammatical function. Such a grammatical determination of the function of tense, which she shares with Gustave Guillaume and Roman Jakobson, is different from many other linguistic attempts to explain tense, which argue primarily semantically or semiotically. This also clarifies why explanations of tenses by means of their semantics or reference always lead to the thesis of an "atemporality of the present tense." On the one hand, the present tense appears in a large number of linguistic studies[63] as the tense that does not refer to time at all because it is used in utterances, descriptions, and all those contexts that have no temporal reference; on the other, its temporal meaning appears to be random because in everyday communication the present tense often also refers to points in time that lie in the past ("Yesterday, I'm sitting on my balcony when suddenly it starts raining"). What many theorists and linguists, working with a grammar of meaning, consider an argument against or difficulty for a description of the meaning of the present tense turns out to be a precise observation of its function in terms of functional grammar. Present-tense utterances localize their speaker in the utterance's field of showing. The present is not lacking any temporal "location," but the capacity to effect the "temporal dislocation of an event."[64] The pre-tense present tense only has the effect of localizing, whereas the achievement proper of the "absolute tenses" of past tense and future lies in a translocation. They enable a speaker to abandon his standpoint and allow him a "mental mobility that overcomes the spatial."[65]

These grammatical reflections on deixis are close to our tense-poetic definition of fiction as a shift within a deictic triad in two respects: first in that Elisabeth Leiss describes the deictic functioning of tenses generally in great detail, and second in that she defines the deictic or shifting character as the central characteristic of tenses. Given this proximity, however, a certain delimitation is necessary as well to avoid blurring the line between poetics and linguistics. Why is language not fictional as such (as Roland Barthes, for instance, claims)?[66] What distinguishes the poetic or fictional use of language from its everyday use? And with regard to the distinction between fiction-narratology and linguistics: At what point does a poetics of tense go beyond a grammar of tense?

On the one hand, we assume that grammatical structures play a part in the constitution of fiction; on the other, grammar is not fictional as such. Within the framework of a deixis theory, the reason can be stated quite precisely: triggering a shift by grammatical tense alone is insufficient. Fiction must also involve space and person, that is, parameters that cannot be shifted in grammar itself but only in the text or in the experience of reading. Temporally induced fictionality is thus distinct from the pure grammatical function that tenses perform in a non-fictional context, a function Elisabeth Leiss states succinctly: "Tenses are to be understood as directives to fictively seek out the present at other points (earlier or later)."[67]

What is decisive for a *literary* interpretation of the tenses is the moment Leiss calls dislocation. From her definitions of "dislocation" and our descriptions of "shift," it is clear how reductive it is to define tense generally and the present tense in particular only as localizing. Looking back at our Caesar examples, this also elucidates the question of the relationship between reference and deixis. In the presentification that is activated by a "here" in example (2), we have found a *temporal translocation*. At the same time, we have seen that in this no longer localizing, but *trans*localizing moment of tense-dislocation, it is always the entire deictic triad that is at work. This is the procedural level of fiction. The reason for this is precisely the (deictic) shifts operating in fiction, which will also guide our definition of the relationship between fiction and reference.

Deictic shifts

In our discussion of Genette's narratological approach, we saw that (literary) fiction cannot be interpreted as the (quasi-pictorial or proto-filmic) illusionism of a narration unaware of its own mediality. The central point of our critique of Genette was that fiction can hardly be understood from the perspective of a monomedial text theory. To understand fiction, we need to understand the differentiality of media. The narratological perspective established the necessity of a fiction-constituting difference, but in our earlier discussion, we could not yet precisely account for why a medial difference should produce anything more than an aesthetic extension. The pathos of the media aesthetics of avant-garde modernism (think, for example, of collages made of contrasting materials and of contrapuntal montages of sounds and images) is explained precisely by the possibility of aesthetically staging the differences between materials in order to experience the material as such. At the same time, however, the avant-gardes, convinced of the linguistic materiality of the present tense, are certain that they could thus prevent fictionality. They believe, that is, that they have cast out aesthetics with aisthetics—an opposition that does not arise within the framework of a deictic (shift) theory of fiction.

Why, then, does the "materiality of signifiers" not merely unfold in an avant-garde material aesthetics or a modernist self-reference of literary texts? Why does it instead provide the basis for narrated fictions? From the perspective of a deictic shift theory, it is clear that fiction cannot be grasped either with arbitrary semantic attributions[68] (which can be imagined independent of the media by which they are constituted) nor by mere "reality effects" of medial subterfuge.

In narrated fiction as we reconstruct it from the perspective of linguistic tense, a primary shift conveys to a reader an aesthetic sensation of difference. A passage from Tolstoy's *War and Peace* often used in the secondary literature makes this clear: "The pistol, and the dagger, and the peasant coat were ready; Napoleon entered tomorrow."[69] In the second sentence, a tense usage acquired with language exceeds the threshold of automaticization. The resulting fictionalizing effect does not imply (pseudo-)factographic reference (in the sense of an "as if")[70] but causes a spatio-temporal-personal disorientation on the part of the reader. There is not *one origo* in which the reader could put himself but a two-in-one as described above.[71] In narrative fictions, the shift of an *implicit narrative reference*[72] combines with the deictic character of fictions, which makes it possible to perceive meaning *as such*.

At this point it is important to recall that both Roman Jakobson's theory of shifters and Karl Bühler's observations on the way non-symbolic, that is, deictic words function emerged in the context of linguists' efforts to clarify the reference of linguistic signs. This is central for an investigation of fiction insofar as fictions are suspected by literary theories oriented towards or informed by linguistics to abet a hyper-referential understanding of literature (which is why one may not view fiction as a genuinely literary phenomenon). Philosophical theories of fictions, in turn, view them as being without reference. How does such a contradiction come to be? The contradiction is all the more vexing in that the battle lines seem to be completely reversed. Usually it is literary studies that insist on the self-referentiality of literature, while theories informed by an analytical philosophy of language assume that literary language does not in principle differ from non-literary language. On the question of fictionality, however, the reverse is the case. Since philosophical theories, especially in the analytical philosophy of language, understand fiction to be a non-referential practice of language that operates with fictitious claims ("as if"), they believe to have discovered a specific literary phenomenon of the self-referentiality of language. Literary studies, meanwhile, merely regard fiction as an intruder that is of no use for explaining a text's literariness.

Excursus: The genealogy of the concept of the shift

Deixis theory and shift theory have been called on to resolve the contradiction between a-reference and hyper-reference. One of the central tenets of all deixis theories is the assumption that Karl Bühler understands a deictic expression to be an expression "whose referent, whose relation to the object changes from case to case." What is less clear is whether (as Bühler's namesake Axel Bühler assumes) the signified—the "reference (in Frege's sense)"—can also vary.[73] And if referent and signified can switch, does this also imply a variance in the signifier as a third possibility of sign variance in deixis? The fact that the implications of Bühler's deixis theory for semiotics are unclear leads to tensions within deixis theory. Can the referent vary in a *demonstratio ad oculos*, the signified in the *deixis at the level of phantasma* and the signifier in an *anaphora*?

While Bühler may not have cleared up the relationship with semiotics, he has conceptually and systematically articulated the fundamental problem. He distinguishes between the deixis of space, time, and person, which belong together in a triad, and three ways of showing (demonstrative/phantasmatic/anaphoric), which are concerned with the different *semiotic* dimensions of deixis. Yet throughout the history of theories of deixis, the question of how the two sides relate to one another has dropped from view again and again. Without taking the shifting function into account, however, we cannot adequately describe the reading of narrative fictions. Richard Gerrig's *Experiencing Narrative Worlds: On Psychological Activities of Reading* can serve as an example.

In her commentary on Gerrig's book, Marie-Laure Ryan presents what happens in a process of reading as follows: "If I read the word *Texas* in a story, no matter how good or bad the text, I will think about Texas, which means that I will be mentally transported to the place."[74] Ryan herself notes that in this case it is less a matter of deixis than of reference, for "imaginative transportation to Texas is a consequence of the speech act of reference, rather than a consequence of embedding the speech act in a narrative context."[75] Ultimately, no deictic shift at all can be recognized in Gerrig's account. An imaginative transportation that follows the model of projection, in this particular case to Texas, can no longer be distinguished from simple reference. Under these circumstances, it becomes impossible to see any emergence of fiction to be based on deictic shifts. For as soon as the concept of shifting is replaced by that of projection, deixis theory loses all methodological value in answering the question of distinguishing between fictions and facts.

This deficit on the level of the deictica of space/time/person entails a further deficit at the level of the second triad (the kinds of indication). What is problematic here is the implicit thesis that there must first be a place to which one can refer (be it invented or real) in order for the presumed transposition of the reader-*origo* to occur. The objection is that "Texas" (just like "Laputa") is only a linguistic signifier or a name, which has no signified and is not determined by any reference to the world, but only by a self-reference to the linguistic code. Roman Jakobson has elaborated on this point:

The general meaning of a proper name cannot be defined without a reference to the code. In the code of English, "Jerry" means a person named Jerry. The circularity is obvious: the name means anyone to whom this name is assigned ... The general meaning of such words as *pup*, *mongrel*, or *hound*, could be indicated by abstractions like puppihood, mongrelness, or houndness, but the general meaning of *Fido* cannot be qualified in this way. To paraphrase Bertrand Russell, there are many dogs called *Fido*, but they do not share any property of "Fidoness."[76]

What can be said about Fido and Fidoness also applies to Texas and Texasness or Laputa and Laputaness. The question of how fiction comes to be can be resolved neither by the merely self-referential names "Texas" or "Laputa," nor by referring to the actually existing US state or to the "fictive existence" of floating islands in an invented world. What is much more relevant for fiction theory is what lies between pure reference (the real Texas or the invented Laputa) and pure self-referentiality (the relation of the name "Texas" or "Laputa" to the linguistic code). We can systematize our objection by continuing to follow Jakobson's terminology.

In the essay just cited, "Shifters, Verbal Categories, and the Russian Verb" (1957), Jakobson both defines simple linguistic references—alongside "referential" nouns and "circular" names, in which the code refers to the code, or citations, in which the message refers to the message—and distinguishes them from forms of linguistic duplex structures. He calls them *shifters* to designate the overlap of code and message (of language and speech). They are duplex structures because they have both a referential and a non-referential side. The non-referential, self-relational side in turn has two poles, of language (*langue*) and speech (*parole*), that in relation to one another can be differently oriented.[77]

In poetry, the self-relation of language cannot be overlooked because there, the message refers in two different directions: on the one hand to the code (language) and on the other to the world, or to the deictic system of actuality (reference). Reference and self-reference are directed against one another and can be perceived as phenomena of contrast (difference). The fact that there are duplex structures in fictional prose as well, however, is easily overlooked. For here, language refers to the message, and the message at the same time refers to the world or the deictic system of actuality, and since both vectors of reference run parallel, it is as if a *direct* relation of language to the world were created. It can thus seem as if in fictional texts there were a simple reference and as if literary prose were "prosaic."

We now have a better understanding of what Jakobson's "shift" accomplishes. It comes in precisely at this point and makes it possible to experience the parallelism in this form of duplex relation (language/message—message/referent) as a bifurcation. Shifting is that movement by which the fictional usage of language distinguishes itself from the prosaic use of language and dislocates itself into the poetic use of language. Jakobson's insight that the referential relation of shifters is not *suspended* but *deferred* by a relation of the code to the message keeps us from incorrectly assuming that in order to explain fiction one must *either* give up on the possibility of distinguishing between fictional and prosaic language *or* assume a full reference. Such a reference of fictions is then out of the question for those theories of deixis in which the only thing that remains of the shift is the idea of a mobile sign that carries the reader to Texas. They virtually mark the opposite pole of the poetologically uncompromising position of the avant-garde:

Мой жест нелепый усваивают дезертировавшие меридианы.

My helpless gesture is appropriated by absconded meridians.[78]

This sentence from Aleksei Kruchenykh's *Sdvigologija russkogo sticha* [*The Doctrine of Shifts in Russian Verse*] gives us a better idea of the poetic radicality and fictionalizing potential of deictic shifters. Here, the indicative gesture of Bühler's placing-before-the-eyes is not a self-conscious showing of a place by a speaker. The "helpless gesture" is ripped away by a pull of the meridians that are themselves on a flight without destination. Such a deixis is indeed felt as a shift. In its journey around the globe, a lyrical subject without bearing is shifted in a personal deictic shift. Immersion pulls the reader into a movement of flight attempt that is not without its dangers. The original Russian entangles the reader by means of the passive past participle (of the verb *abscond*) in the imperfective aspect (*usvaivayut dezertirovavshie*) because the connection of this participle with the imperfective aspect has a paradoxical effect. The imperfective aspect brings the verbal action into an imperfective perspective; a past, unfinished movement is viewed from within this movement and is thus represented *in actu*.[79] The meridians thus perform a temporal shift from the past tense (*dezertirovavshie*) into the present tense (*usvaivayut*). They capture the present, while this movement of appropriation stands as much in the imperfective aspect as the act of the raid itself.

In his poetological writings, Kruchenykh claims a movement "From Impressionism to the Shifting Image" (*Ot impressionizma k sdvigovomu obrazu*).[80] We follow his insight into the explosive poetological force of the *sdvig* in that we view fiction not as medial illusionism or a deictic impressionism but as a dynamic of shifting differentiated by person, space, and time:

> Сдвиг передает движение и пространство.
>
> Сдвиг дает многозначимость и многообразность.
>
> Сдвиг—стиль современности
>
> Сдвиг—вновь открытая Америка! ...
>
> The shift transmits movement and space.
>
> The shift provides ambiguity and variety.
>
> Shift—the style of the present
>
> Shift—the newly discovered America![81]

How such a shifting proceeds can also be illustrated in a verbal image from Robert Musil's *The Man without Qualities*:

> Der Mann mit gewöhnlichem Wirklichkeitssinn gleicht einem Fisch, der nach der Angel schnappt und die Schnur nicht sieht, während der Mann mit jenem Wirklichkeitssinn, den man auch Möglichkeitssinn nennen kann, eine Schnur durchs Wasser zieht und keine Ahnung hat, ob ein Köder daran sitzt.
>
> The man with an ordinary sense of reality is like a fish that nibbles at the hook but is unaware of the line, while the man with that sense of reality which can also be called a sense of possibility trawls a line through the water and has no idea whether there's any bait on it.[82]

In an "impressionistic" interpretation, limiting itself to the narrativity of the passage, the personal deixis would rest with the narrator, and the reader would vainly identify with a man with "a sense of possibility" trawling "a line through the water." Yet this would mean a failure to realize either the fictionality presented in the text or the shift. The "impressionistic" reader thus unwittingly ends up on the text's fishing line. The irony of the text is that the reader, thanks to an identification with the man "with a sense of possibility," inevitably turns out to be the "man with an ordinary sense of reality" who "nibbles at the hook." In the text's dynamics of shifting, it is only now that the bait is attached to the line, the personal shift is immediately followed by a spatial shift, and it takes place in the very moment the reader falls into the water. The "shift image" of the text comes in even later, namely at the moment one shifts the "sense for reality" beyond the boundary of the text in the direction of one's own sense of possibility and then hears a splash.

This passage is meta-fictional in that deeper sense in which the issue is not to unmask fiction but, as we will explain in more detail in the next chapter, to push ahead to its imaginary ground and imaginary presentness. The sensitivity with which the passage registers the presence of a reader and the attention with which Musil follows the path of the reader's imagination in order to guide it along the unfolding of the text also motivate the deployment of the present tense. This example may serve to illustrate how narrative fictions mediate a primary shift[83] by means of an aesthetic sensation of difference, and also show that narrative fictions are not about any kind of reality effects created by medial subterfuge. The very possibility of perceiving a meaning that narrative fictions open up cannot be actualized if one establishes a referentiality in language only to retrospectively denounce it as illusion. That can only be achieved if one follows the deictic shifts of language.

The deictic shifts to which literary fictions owe their very existence are thus not mere quasi-references or non-referential expressions, never mind variable references that could be filled arbitrarily. Rather, in literary fictions, the code of language enters into dialogue with the message, language into a relationship with speech. For this very reason, the autonomy of language that becomes visible in fiction is not to be equated with an arbitrariness of reference. Without ignoring its knowledge about the autonomy of language, indeed, only *in the knowledge* about this autonomy can fiction make full use of the deictic elements language can provide. It narrates in (and by means of) the effects of a shift between space, time, and person. Our fiction-narratological approach captures this in a formula: *Literary language shifts reference.*

Now we can also understand why the inversion of the battle lines of the various academic disciplines mentioned above arises on the subject of fiction in particular. Literary studies recognize the degree to which the linguistic arsenal of narrative fictions aims at reference. Any understanding of literature devoted to linguistic self-referentiality (an understanding that derives its concept of literariness from the modern paradigm of an autonomous poetry that experiments with language and is sensitive to sound and writing) must find such a transgression of linguistic boundaries to be almost like an obsession with reference. This obsession is judged severely: Fictional narration is said to fall short of the fundamental criteria of literariness, to abandon the pure immanence of lyrical language, and to subordinate itself to the external-referential function of prosaic language. Yet stopping at the boundary of linguistic immanence overlooks that in literary fiction language does not officiously fulfill its referential function; it exercises it with all its power.

Reversely, discourses about language outside literary studies react very sensitively when they see their objects affected by the kinds of primary shifts that come with fiction. Speech act linguistics, historical studies, and the philosophy of language are thus more interested in the (linguistic) reference available in fiction.[84] They are concerned with reflecting on their own discursive practice, with discursively protecting themselves from shifts of reference, and with guaranteeing the existence of their own referents, which is indispensable for any academic discourse. Kendall Walton, for example, a theorist of representation, attempts to restrict the phenomenon of fiction to an area of arbitrary agreement. An illustration is his motto: "Let's say that all stumps are bears."[85] Walton addresses fiction as signing a "make-believe" contract to accept precepts of the imagination.

To a certain degree, we do follow the intuition that fictions operate with speech act situations. But we do not develop this intuition into any kind of pragmatics. We instead discover a structure in the grammar of language that makes it possible to relate any message to place, time, and person. Insofar as grammatical deixis regulates the usage of language in everyday situations, that is, insofar as it grammaticalizes the concrete production of messages, we can determine what a procedure that can be called a poetics of fiction consists in. The procedures of fiction result from a reflexive usage of deixis. While deixis leaves open places in language that a speaker fills with the I–here–now of the message produced by him contemporaneously, within the situation, fiction uses this mechanism to reinterpret readers' self, place, and time.

As we have noted, Karl Bühler[86] already motivates his investigation of the speech situation with the dubious reference of a series of linguistic expressions:

> The logician is inclined by virtue of his profession to see in words nothing more than conceptual signs. If he finds a whole class of words that are not directly conceptual signs, not naming words, then he points out something about them that does make it possible to rank them with names ... Deictic words do not need the symbolic field of language to make their full and complete contribution; but they do need the deictic field and determination from case to case by the deictic field ... by the perceptual factors of a given speech situation.[87]

Speech situations are accessible not only to pragmatic but also to deictic description. What interests us about fiction, then, is neither the fundamental indeterminacy of the referent nor a retreat of language behind meaning. According to our definition, fiction is neither a form of semblance nor a subspecies of metaphor[88] but the language-immanent production of a *perception* of meaning that is based on the devices of reflexive deixis.

In his early formulation of a theory of deixis, Karl Bühler conceptualizes, first, a direct placing-before-the-eyes, second, a phantasmatic deixis, and, third, an anaphoric deixis. These three semiotic (or, in Bühler's terms, sematological) dimensions of deixis can be related to one another in the terms of fiction theory. The analyses of the poetologies of Kruchenykh and Musil given above have made it clear why fiction should not be understood as any simple placing-before-the-eyes. Rather, we should take the "phantasmatic" moment in any deictic shift into account at the same time as we pay attention to how anaphorics perform gestures of showing within language itself. Wherever a fiction effect comes about, the deictic triad (of space, time, and person) stands in connection with all three ways of showing, not only on the level of experience (*demonstratio ad oculos*), but also on the level of the poetics of the work (phantasmatics) and of the medial level (anaphorics).

Equipped with Bühler's theory, let us take another look at the epic past tense that so far we have only thought in Hamburger's terms. We can now describe the epic past tense as an anaphoric deixis, whose effect is a deixis at the level of phantasm: the presentification of a "fictional world." We have already stressed that neither the epic past tense nor presentification are to be understood simply as an arbitrary positing of any temporal deixis whatsoever. Arbitrarily posited deixis is indistinguishable from reference, independently of whether we refer to it afterward as quasi-reference or empty reference. What is decisive in defining fiction is the relationship between phantasmatic and anaphoric deixis. In fiction, the relationship between signifier and signified is such that a shift from code to message (and thus meaning *as such*) can be perceived. Reading fictional language does not mean imagining the existing Texas or a non-existent "Texasness" but following the shift in the present of a text. Actualizing a deictic shift means letting oneself be taken in by the tow of the meridians to discover a new America. Perceiving how the semantic possibilities of a code are achieved in the reality of the utterance implies following Musil's text under the water.

Meaning as such is only perceivable in a dynamic branching of the three ways of showing. For a reader who does not realize the interaction between placing-before-the-eyes, phantasmatic deixis, and anaphoric deixis,[89] the mobility necessary for triggering fiction is lost. This makes it impossible for the text to (re)organize the system of actuality. Without a mediation of real deixis, imaginative deixis, and textual deixis, as we seek to describe them in their semiotic-deictic play of shifts, the difference between fictional and non-fictional texts is reduced to the difference between a real and an imaginary deixis.[90] Ignoring an independent fiction-forming dimension of language, however, means having to resort to an extra-literary criterion for fictionality. Before we could reach a fictional place through reading, we would already have had to gather information about whether this place exists outside the text. It is impossible for such a criterion to explain how the reader might accomplish experiencing the difference between fiction and reality within the very reading that allows for the experience of fiction to arise in the first place. This is why we want to ask how a literary text establishes an imaginative deixis. How are the tenses used? How is focalization deployed to enjoin the reader to perform an imaginative deixis? What strategies do literary texts develop to ensure that a reader does not posit a deixis to the real? How can we describe the semiotic-deictic interplay of shifts that opens up a perception of meaning and makes it possible to experience a shift between language and utterance? What does a textual deixis consist in that lets us dive into the water? How do fictional texts again and again manage to get the bait on their fishing line?

Combining narratology, fiction theory, and deixis theory

We are now at the stage in our readings in methodology at which we will critique these various methods in relation to one another and attempt to combine some of their productive moments. It has become clear what connection there is between a theory of deixis and Hamburger's fiction theory, but also that the poetics of shifting is absent from her theory. The fact that her critics pay even less attention to shifts than Hamburger did herself can be illustrated by a systematic argument often used against her. According to this argument, the epic past tense is a special case of "free indirect discourse,"[91] which does not allow for conclusions about the shift of spatio-temporal and personal deixis to be drawn that are as sweeping as Hamburger's are. This objection is based on doubts concerning the combination and the dynamic of shifting of epic past tense, space, and person. For narratologists, an epic past tense does mean presentification, but they do not accept its connection with the transposition of the *origo*, that is, with the displacement of the reader into another "here and now" and into another subjectivity (a possible person and, with it, a plunge into the water).

With regard to the (verbal) grammar of literature, there is a preference, based on the analysis of language, of tense over spatial categories (until perhaps one day there will be a language of literature in which topos is a morphological category). But from the point of view of fiction-narratology, that is, in view of narrated fictions of linguistic provenance, we must insist on the equal valence of the three deictic levels that are space, person, and time.[92] This is directed both against Genette's understanding of literature as a pure time-art (for which tense seems to play no role) and against Hamburger's exclusive concentration on tense structures (which assumes the timelessness of literary fiction).

In the context of our integration of theories of narration, fiction, and deixis, we can turn our initially critical reading of Margolin's essay into a positive reading. From a narratological perspective, Margolin had to be criticized for viewing the temporal shifts beyond their relation to the narrative levels and their appearance in fictions. From a fiction-theoretical perspective, Margolin saw temporal shifts only as a deviation of tense from the times stated, that is, as a mere semantic paradox of temporality that cannot explain how fiction comes about. From the viewpoint of deixis theory, however, space, time, and person must be viewed in combination, such that Margolin's mono-perspectival view of temporal shifts can be supplemented with the two other parameters provided by deictic shift theories.

The processes by which deictic shift theories receive and adapt historical concepts is marked by a preponderance of fiction-theoretical moments over narratological ones. This is true in particular of Bühler's conception of an I-*origo*, which makes its way into deictic shift theories via Hamburger's fiction theory and which they adapt by interpreting it as a deictic center. This center is to be understood as a mental or cognitive construct. The adaptation of narratological concepts in terms of fiction demonstrates the dominance of fiction-theoretical questions. On the one hand, the deictic concept of *sujet* (narration as movement through the narrative) is a fictionalized one. And on the other, a fictionalization can equally be seen in the concept of the *fabula*: "Most events occur in a deictic center ... The events tend to occur within the mental model at the active space-time location."[93] While on the level of the *sujet* the question comes up whether the story was narrated or invented, on the level of the *fabula* the decision to be made is whether one is dealing with courses of events in a world or with a world that changes in (and is changed by) such courses of events. This question is of some significance for the history novel, and thus also for the altermodern novel of the past, which tends to underscore the historicity of the world and the part that fictions play in it.

In its cognitivist version, the concept of a deictic center additionally helps to explain those processes of reading in which, for example, the order of events in the *fabula* is produced (against any disorder in the *sujet*). In this model of deixis, the question of how a chronological *fabula* sequence comes about is answered by saying that the events are arranged around the deictic center. Only when fictionality is given priority over narrativity does it make sense to conceive of narration as a movement through the narrative. Such a reversal remains utterly unthinkable as long as narration is imagined as a process of storytelling. It becomes immediately graspable, however, when we think of a camera traveling, moving through the very world that it gives us to see. This leads Erwin Segal to refuse the idea of a fictional narrator: "There is no existing fictional narrator."[94] Altermodern narration is *in* the fictional world.

At the beginning of this chapter, we announced that we not only wanted to acknowledge narratology and fiction theory in their conceptual efforts, but also to acknowledge the methodological objects or phenomena that they observe in their (and our) material. In this way, the epic past tense and focalization as forms of temporal and spatial deixis can be translated into a deictic shift theory. Yet we have not yet come across separate reflections on personal deixis. Accordingly, a syncretism of personal and temporal shifting, which stands in relation to this blank space, has often been raised as a criticism of Hamburger. For our attempt at systematizing deictic fiction theory, it is important to distinguish misunderstandings and legitimate points of criticism in the relevant debates. This is especially true for the criticism that the epic present tense effects no presentification at all[95] and that the contradiction between the past tense and the future temporal adverb is merely due to the fact that two personal deixes exist within a single temporal deixis.

We share the criticism that Hamburger does not recognize the personal difference at the basis of the temporal shift in her model sentence "Tomorrow was Christmas." But this does not mean that there is no such shift. The genuinely narratological insight that one must distinguish between a deixis of the narrator and a deixis of the character is something that we consider a beneficial result of this misguided criticism. While tense, in this case the past tense, refers to the deixis of the narrator, the deixis of the adverb "tomorrow" clings to the character. Temporal deixis and personal deixis split. A doubled, or even contradictory temporal deixis thus becomes recognizable.

Alongside the double temporal deixis, we can also already name a double spatial phenomenon: focus. The very same overlapping of the perspectives of narrator and character that Gisa Rauh describes for time are depicted by Dorrit Cohn for focalization. In what follows, we will therefore speak of *focus* wherever we turn our attention to the doubled spatial perspective of a two-in-one. When we look at tense and focus in combination, in order to complete the descriptions of a double tense and a double perspective, we must detect a two-in-one in all three deixes and make it the foundation of fictional shifting, in personal as well as in temporal and spatial deixis.

Spelling out the spatial-temporal-personal dynamic of shifting in a fiction-narratology

Now that we have brought various methods together, we can turn to elaborating the conceptual tools of fiction-narratology. The integration of deixis theory, fiction theory, and narratology allows us to compile a set of analytical categories. The *narratological* persons of reader, narrator, and character always shift within the *deictic* triad (space/time/person), i.e., in combination with time and space, because a two-in-one structure underlies each of them. This structure exists between the poles of a *fictional* dynamic of shifting (a/syntopy, a/synchrony, doubling). In terms of deixis, we can for the time being summarize this fiction-narratological arrangement as follows:

– Temporally, the following narrative deixis is possible:

time of the character, time of the narrator, and time of the reader, each related to the possibilities of contemporaneous/non-contemporaneous (past)/synchronous

– Spatially, the following narrative deixis is possible:

space of the character, space of narration, and space of the reader, each related to the possibilities of here/there (absent)/simultaneous

– Personally, the following narrative deixis is possible:

she or he of character, I of the narrator, and you of the reader, each related to the possibilities of self (internal)/other (external)/double (*Doppelgänger*).

The set of analytical categories can also be represented in a *schedule of literary shifts*, namely along the lines of the characters and modalities we use to describe the functions of the present tense. Fictional shifting can then be traced as a movement through the rows and columns of table 2.1.

This table shows the nine possible deictic moves that result from the three deictic categories of space, time, and person, which are bound to each other but each operate independently from one another. Our schedule demonstrates that from the perspective of a fiction-narratological deixis theory, the *I–here–now-origo* must not be thought of as a point, as a purely linguistic theory of deixis presumes. In our schedule, the *origo* is recognizable as a diagonal line from the upper left to the lower right; we have marked it in italics. Since within the framework of a linguistic theory of deixis the dissociation of the I-*origo* effected by fiction cannot be recognized, such a theory can also not explain the transition from everyday speech to literary fictions. From a fiction-narratological perspective, however, the dissociation of the temporal meaning of tense has to be the occasion for inquiring into the dissociation of all parameters of deixis. Instead of an undifferentiated shift of all three categories, we then see a deictic triad whose categories allow for nine possible moves.

This, then, is the way of systematically describing the linguistic markers of fiction, namely the deictic markers, in their coordinated collaboration in narrative texts that we have been looking for. At the same time, showing the difference between the everyday usage of a deictic *origo* and genuinely poetic deixis once more leads to the assumption that there are only pragmatic or paratextual markers of fiction. Narrative techniques such as the

Table 2.1 Schedule of literary shifts

	Space-person (S1)	**Time-person (S2)**	**Space-time (S3)**
TIME (R1)	*now* (contemporaneous)	non-contemporaneous (past)	synchronous
SPACE (R2)	there (absent)	*here*	simultaneous
PERSON (R3)	double	other (external)	*I* (internal)

epic past tense, the asynchronous present tense, focus, or interior monologue trigger a deictic dissociation and a dynamic of shifting that can be read off the distorted or paradoxical shape of every deictic parameter.

(1) *Temporal deixis*: By means of narratologically diversifying and deictically extending Hamburger's fiction theorem with various dimensions of shifting, we have been able to gain new and further nuances and insights into her classical example "Tomorrow was Christmas."[96] When the reader of the sentence follows the fictional shift of reference, i.e., presentifies the past tense, she does so because of an overlapping of the time of the character and the time of the narrator, an overlapping of the past tense (which can be explained by the perspective of the narrator) and the *tomorrow* (which can be explained by the perspective of the character). Fiction comes into effect through the differentiating relation to the third term of personal deixis. The two-in-one of a presentification of what is past comes into effect in the contemporaneity of the time of reading. A fiction effect requires, however, that the medium at hand allow for a temporal-deictic shift in the first place. A fiction induced by a temporal deixis can only come into effect by means of an elementary tense structure that makes it possible to move away from the contemporaneity of reception and to negate the *now* (in this case through a *was* and a *tomorrow*). In contrast to the impressionistic Texas, which we grant no fictional quality, Hildesheimer's Tynset, fictionalized according to the motto *not here, not now*, can serve as an example of how a temporal *now* is negated in moving away from a spatial *here* and thus indicates an elementary fictionalization.

(2) *Spatial deixis*: For the spatial figurations of deixis (space of the character, space of narration, space of reading), this can be explained by an analogy with focalization, which we have characterized as an overlapping of the spatial perspectives of narrator and character.[97] The two-in-one of the perspectives of narrator and character claimed by Cohn for focalization needs to be augmented by a reader's perspective. In order to take the necessary extension of the narratological perspectives by fictional deixis into account, we speak of *focus* rather than of focalization. In Russian, for instance, the grammar of the verb contains a temporal focus, namely its aspect, which allows for a choice between a transcendent perspective on events and a perspective immanent to them. The use of the imperfective aspect in the past tense (much like the use of the past progressive in English) has a specific temporal effect that, as we have mentioned, has a fictionalizing effect that is similar to that of the epic past tense:

> Я открыл глаза: утро зачиналось.
>
> I opened my eyes: the morning was beginning.[98]

An analogous effect can be observed in Franz Kafka's story "The Burrow." There, events are portrayed at one and the same time from a temporal perspective that is immanent to them and another that transcends them, such that a temporal focus emerges in this story as well. Although German grammar knows of no distinction between an immanent and a transcendent aspect of the verb, we can here get a sense of aspect in German, too (and in the English translation). The story leads to the elaboration of a sublime narrative perspective that has been conceived of as an "eternal present":[99]

> Ich weiß nicht, ob es eine Gewohnheit aus alten Zeiten ist oder ob doch die Gefahren auch dieses Hauses stark genug sind, mich zu wecken: regelmäßig von Zeit zu Zeit schrecke ich auf aus tiefem Schlaf und lausche, lausche in die Stille, die hier unverändert herrscht bei Tag und Nacht, lächle beruhigt und sinke mit gelösten Gliedern in noch tieferen Schlaf. Arme Wanderer ohne Haus, auf Landstraßen, in Wäldern, bestenfalls verkrochen in einen Blätterhaufen oder in einem Rudel der Genossen,

> ausgeliefert allem Verderben des Himmels und der Erde! Ich liege hier auf einem allseits gesicherten Platz—mehr als fünfzig solcher Art gibt es in meinem Bau—und zwischen Hindämmern und bewußtlosem Schlaf vergehen mir die Stunden, die ich nach meinem Belieben dafür wähle.
>
> I do not know whether it is a habit that still persists from former days, or whether the perils even of this house of mine are great enough to awaken me; but invariably every now and then I start up out of profound sleep and listen, listen into the stillness which reigns here unchanged day and night, smile contentedly, and then sink with loosened limbs into still profounder sleep. Poor homeless wanderers in the roads and woods, creeping for warmth into a heap of leaves or a herd of their comrades, delivered to all the perils of heaven an earth! I lie here in a room secured on every side—there are more than fifty such rooms in my burrow—and pass as much of my time as I choose between dozing and unconscious sleep.[100]

The grammar actualizes the connection between focus and tense in the aspect. The aspect is thus to be understood as both tense and focus, and consequently as time-focus. A transcendental aspect corresponds to an external focus, and an immanent aspect to an internal focus.

In the following chapter we will see the extent to which the highly elaborate shaping of focus in the great novels of the late nineteenth century (whose possibilities were particularly and masterfully exhausted by Flaubert) can be conceived of as a perspectivism of simultaneity. At the end of the twentieth century, we can see a temporal equivalent of this simultaneous perspectivism of focus in the *simultaneous narration* of novels that are projected on an equally grand scale, from Thomas Pynchon's *Gravity's Rainbow* to David Foster Wallace's *Infinite Jest*. The fundamental reinvention of the genre and its linguistic texture in altermodernism, after the "end of the novel"[101] proclaimed by avant-garde modernists (and not just by Mandelstam), is neither a "return of narration" nor a neo- or retrofictionality. Instead, like focus, it is a simultanistic technique of the novel.[102] No technique is to be regarded as what is left over of another.

(3) *Personal deixis*: The following remarks already provide an outlook for the following chapter. For in regard to the personal

two-in-one, we find that at this point in our study we are still lacking the terms for a complete development and concrete discussion of personal deixis. For the time being, we can only list various partial moments, for instance the relation of personal deixis to focus, to the various forms of two persons in a dual voice,[103] or to the narratological thesis that the past tense is not presentified in first-person narratives.[104]

For the third-person perspective of this two-in-one, let us recall that it is only in third-person narration that focus, as a simultaneous perspective of narrator and character, liberates that dizzying measure of fictionality whose uniqueness is manifest in the experience of the "subjectivity of a third party as a third party." Unlike what is the case in first-person narration, focus here unfolds the fiction-generating paradoxes that come about in the use of verbs of interior processes in combination with the third person singular, a use that suggests access to the consciousness of a third party. From a systematic perspective, the two-in-one of a doubled personal deixis that arises in the narrated monologue thanks to introspection (which introduces the new literary technique of focus to third-person narration) is evidence that person, too, is differentiated by the space-time. There is a distinction between *he* and *I* that is induced spatio-temporally (as an ego-time loop or self-distantiation). At this point in our argument, we may already surmise that as a consequence, metamorphoses of space and time appear in first-person narratives, as they do, for instance, in Kafka's "The Burrow."

This question cannot yet be sufficiently explained for the first-person perspective of the two-in-one. We will first have to look back into the history leading up to the interior monologue, which is the first present-tense genre. In the pathographies of fiction of the nineteenth century, we already encounter an *imaginary present tense*, which promises to elucidate how we can conceive of a personal deixis that is exposed to unstoppable shifting and rips open a space for an imaginary other.

3
The imaginary present tense

Until quite recently, narratology insisted that all fictional narration is retrospective in its very principle. Accordingly, the past tense was the paradigmatic tense of any narrating genre. In our discussion so far, we have presented the arguments literary theory makes against generalizing a past present into the temporal horizon of all narrative fiction. Our objections, which also move the present tense into the foreground, draw on the two perspectives developed so far, the literary-historical perspective of the first chapter and the methodological perspective of the second.

Looking back from the apex of a successive development—the conquest of the present tense by the novel in the twentieth century—from the moment when novels are being written throughout in the present tense, we can detect a series of forerunners in Romanticism, in the avant-garde, etc. These literary forms of the present tense have barely received any attention and—as long as every narrative present was explained (away) as a historical present—could not even be seen. When we described the modern present-tense forms in the opening chapter we touched briefly on the emergence of the interior monologue. In the present chapter we follow the intuition that one of the necessary conditions for the present tense taking the relay from past tense is the novel's increasingly dominant ability to highlight the imaginary stimulus for fiction[1] to the detriment of the narrative formation of fiction. In the history of literature, the development of the present-tense novel marks a shift of dominants from narration to fiction. This means that under the dominance of fiction, a *textual imaginary* takes shape and appears in the present tense. The regency of the epic past tense and its gesture of historical retrospection fall victim to the tensions that arise because historical narration tried, in the interest of a more profound access to history, to integrate "fiction" into the historical novel. In the pathographies of fiction, which emerge from an imaginary that (as we will show) failed to take form, we see an instability of classical narrated fiction that present-tense novels will recuperate. In the altermodern novel of the past, narration obtains its formal principle from out of fiction.

This is the point at which we can also apply a perspective from the history of concepts. This perspective suggests that we will have to revise the narratological dogma of the unavoidable retrospectivity of all narration in light of developments in fiction theory. We started with Käte Hamburger's classical analysis of fiction as a form of time of literary language. According to Hamburger, the use of tense in literary texts reflects not only their narrativity, but is decisive for constructing their fiction and for provoking immersive effects. We have generalized this approach and narratologically extended it. Beyond the evidence that the manifold descriptions of this effect can claim for themselves, we have described it systematically as the result of a *deictic shifting*. In this chapter we will trace the dimensions of the concept of fiction itself.

In Wolfgang Iser's conception, which is seminal to our own fiction-narratological approach, fictionality is no longer determined by its counterfactual character, in mere difference from some kind of reality. It is defined by the procedures it uses to medialize an imaginary. According to his thesis, our silent knowledge of the difference between reality and fiction can only become explicit by bringing in a third: the imaginary. Seen in this way, fiction is not only distinct from reality, but furthermore, the distantiation of fiction from reality occurs by putting itself in relation with an imaginary. Taking a triadic relation as a basis resolves an ambiguity characteristic of fiction theory that we find, for instance, in Odo Marquard and Aleida Assmann. Both authors describe fiction in terms of its differential quality, but also recognize its tendency constantly to switch places. Thus Marquard, for instance, retraces the path from reality to "ficture" in order to task aesthetic thinking with an antifictional mission.[2] Assmann thinks the collapse of the opposition between fiction and the real even further and links it to the question whether the difference (between fiction and the real) is itself to be regarded as fictive.[3] When in the twentieth century a certain constructivism in the understanding of the real becomes dominant, this implies the involvement of structures that can, at bottom, not be distinguished from fictional structures. In the face of a well-founded panfictionalism of constructivist and system-theoretical (and in the end also nominalist) thinking, we nonetheless do not wish to retreat to a position of normative pragmatism. That would make any particular practice merely the place where arbitrary boundaries between fiction and the real would be negotiated.[4] Its qualities, devices, and effects can thus not be specified, which usually leads the proponents of a pragmatic fiction theory to argue that such boundaries do not exist. Our attempt at defining fiction in this chapter consists in specifying the forms of an always precarious difference from an imaginary. *Unnoticeability* of difference, *undecidability* of difference, and *indistinguishability* are for us the three essential forms of an imaginary that becomes manifest in fictional narration.

In the twentieth century, an as-if-theory of the real comes with an as-theory of fiction. This gives a positive sense to the concept of fiction, which liberates fiction theory from its traditional identification with philosophical criticism of fiction. This turning point allows us to notice that revising the notion of fiction involves a reinterpretation of the manifestations of the imaginary in delusions.[5] Delusion in turn no longer appears as a phenomenon of excessive positivity that creates inexistent worlds and hallucinates perceptible worlds. It appears in its subtractive character, that is, as an effect of feigning that continues as the real retreats. Only a new concept of fiction no longer identified with a criticism of fiction makes it such that phenomena such as Gertrude Stein's infinite speaking[6] or the voices that speak in Beckett's protagonists no longer need to be explained by a pathogenesis of fiction but instead conquer the literary space of an imaginary.

In the first chapter we examined the assumption that narration and fiction fundamentally refer to one another. In the second chapter, to advance the fiction-narratological approach necessary for a poetics of the narrative present tense, we engaged in a methodological reflection on narratological conceptual tools. In the present chapter, which treats the interference of narration and fiction in the present tense (texts) of the nineteenth century, a parallel attempt will try to elucidate this relation from the side of fiction theory. Our basic assumption throughout, that narration and fiction belong together, will now be motivated by their common relation to an imaginary. We will trace the development of a textual imaginary in its three functions. First, the imaginary grounds fiction, thus contributing to the shift of dominants in the novel from narration to fiction. Second, its temporal mode, non-contemporaneity, gives rise to the present tense in its first (not yet narrative) form in the interior monologue. Third, altermodernism's present tense of the past develops a non-contemporaneous past, that is, a past that never was a present. While in the fourth chapter we will define asynchrony in the terms of the philosophy of time, here we are interested in how this figuration of time arises from impulses of the imaginary. In altermodernism, the imaginary becomes narrative and thus rests on the temporal mode of non-contemporaneity.

To these findings we can add the historical observation that the fictionality of modern and altermodern present-tense novels makes its imaginary basis visible in a different way, and refers to it in a different way, than classical fiction does. In what follows we will primarily discuss two present-tense phenomena that already appear in narrated fiction. Interior monologue and the *stream of consciousness* assigned to it at the beginning of the twentieth century are joined by literary hallucinations in nineteenth-century stories of delusion. Inspired by Iser's dictum according to which "it is only in madness that the imaginary takes on a comparatively pure presence,"[7] we explicitly understand such phenomena, encountered under the regime of narrated fiction, to be "pathographies of fiction."

We have already encountered the interior monologue in the context of establishing the present tense as a concept to explain the anti-narrative structures in Virginia Woolf's *The Waves*. The stream of consciousness, too, belongs to the immediate forerunners of the narrative present tense. We read the use of the present tense in nineteenth-century pathographic fictions as an indicator and precursor of a fully accomplished imaginary present tense. This raises the question of the relation of the imaginary to both interior monologue (and the technique of the stream of consciousness) and to literary hallucinations. We will have to clarify whether there is a necessary connection between the present tense and the imaginary, which would be the basis for the affinity—often claimed but never proven—of modern present-tense forms to the interior monologue.

(Obviously the present tense achieves a mimesis of the purely contemporaneous character of processes of ideation, perception, imagination, hallucinations, and dreams.) The historical significance of the imaginary present tense can be determined as a liminal phenomenon at the edge of the system of narrated fiction. Instead of understanding the interior monologue as a phenomenon of pure decadence, for instance, we emphasize the productive meaning of present-tense forms, which initially failed but begin to emerge in the depths of literary inventiveness.

In the interior monologue we see the imaginary present tense as a historical formation. Independently of this specific formation, its temporal mode of non-contemporaneity embodies a layer of the present tense as such that is also to be found in later fictional narratives written in the present tense. Only by defining how the imaginary present tense functions in the matrix of narrated fiction does it become clear how the imaginary present tense works as the substrate of narrative and fictional forms in the twentieth century. As a precursor to these forms and in order to collect material for a systematization, we will consider examples of the imaginary in fictional prose that feature literary processes gone haywire as well as failed or overdone medializations of the imaginary.

Once again, we derive our arguments from primary documents of literary thought. In the four literary pathographies of fiction we will work with, the present tense flares up at significant points and draws attention to itself in symptomatic ways. First, we will observe how fiction is set into motion in all its ambivalence by an imaginary in E. T. A. Hoffman's *The Golden Pot*. We see a deterritorializing and reterritorializing imaginary: on the one hand going off the rails in hallucinations and dreams (significantly written in the present tense); on the other hand restrained by fictionality. What is most significant for us here is the medialization of the imaginary in a single text, from which the fantasia of the library noted by Foucault springs and into which it is absorbed again.[8] In Gogol's *Diary of a Madman*, also written partially in the present tense by a first-person narrator, we examine a slow descent into madness within a story. At its end, the event that crosses the boundaries can no longer be reconstructed. Instead, a fantastic chronology (The of 34 ҒердиятА th, yrea 349) has charted new paths. One of Dostoevsky's early texts, *The Double*, allows for a twofold schizophrenic division to become visible at the textual level. Delusion is always simultaneously present with the fiction and the character in two Golyadkins (the older and the younger). And even if the textual schizophrenia long remains unexposed, the end of the novel makes its point thanks to a retroactive re-adjustment of the reader-*origo* from the fictional world into the world of delusion.

While in the first three texts to be discussed the *sujet* retrospectively recovers the surprising course of events—we will discuss this as the motif of the *loop*—the reconstruction of events in Strindberg's *Inferno* is driven by a persecution complex that as it were recovers itself in a metafictional maneuver (of a *sujet*-fake) in order to exhibit itself as literary delusion. These notes, written almost entirely in the present tense, succeed in making their fictional character disappear right before the reader's eyes.

The present tense of interior monologues

Narratology usually classifies interior monologues as a genre of the present tense that, on the one hand, is not narrative, and whose fictional character, on the other, is not easily determined. As a result, one is compelled to focus on its documentary or quasi-documentary character. From that point of view, there is in interior monologues a documentary present tense, a *mental present tense* that designates the present of a stream of consciousness. But we would like to take the interpretation of the present tense in interior monologues further. In a first step, we follow Dorrit Cohn, who defines the interior monologue as a "fictional mimesis of mental life."[9] Cohn acknowledges that the present tense of the interior monologue is fictional, yet she also attributes a further, a mimetic, function to it. This suggests reading and interpreting the interior monologue according to the pattern of a realistic novel, a pattern thus transposed from outer onto inner life. Such a switch in perspective, however, threatens to make the world of the protagonists disappear. The novelistic mimesis of the world is based on the focal device of looking outward. When, however, in the claustrophobia of the interior monologue both the outer and the inner can no longer be brought to cohere in a focus, the result is an implosion of the fiction (or looking outward) or a collapse into the interior. We will come back to this point in the context of a becoming-self-reflexive of focalization.

The second step goes beyond any interpretation of the interior monologue that reads the present tense "as if" it were documentary. In the first chapter we have shown that *simultaneous narration* is only achieved in the fully developed fictional present tense of the altermodern novel, which is able to interlock interior and exterior in such a way that they continually merge. This shows *simultaneous narration* in fictional present-tense novels to be a functional equivalent of the technique of focus from two perspectives in realistic narrated fiction, which is given a temporal interpretation. In a third and last step we would then like to develop a notion of fiction that no longer argues with any idea of mimesis. Instead, it starts with the relation Wolfgang Iser established between the fictional and the imaginary. It will turn out that the intention of the present tense in the interior monologue is to bring out, to validate, and to shape an imaginary in its temporal mode of non-contemporaneity. We would like to conceptualize this present tense in the interior monologue as a *non-contemporaneous present tense*.

The present tense of the interior monologue thus has three meanings. It is a documentary, mimetic, and imaginary tense, and all three are relevant aspects. Arguing both with and against Weinrich, we have shown how the narrative and fictional forms of the present tense slowly move away from their origin in extra-fictional (factographic) description. It cannot be a question here of setting off the documentary aspect of the present tense in the interior monologue as a clinical stenography against the descriptive present tense. Neither can the present-tense (contemporaneous) aspect of the present tense be made congruent with the "transparent minds" (Cohn) of realistic novels' mimetic fiction, and it should not be reconciled either with the non-contemporaneous events of a narrativity that pursues itself. Nonetheless, what is at stake here is nothing less than the exposition of an innovation in the history of literature, a systematic discovery by means of which the novel once more reinvents itself after it has come to an end in the avant-gardes.[10]

The imaginary present tense of the interior monologue marks a point of transformation in literary history from traditional narrated fiction to modern and then altermodern fictional narrations insofar as it does not appear only as a mimetic present tense of the present but, as a fictional and narrative tense, it draws on the non-contemporaneity of the imaginary.

Pathographies of fiction

Our reflections on the linguistic deixis of spatial and temporal parameters left open the question of how to think the deixis dependent on person that is included in the dynamic of shifts. Now, we would like to show how the dynamic of the category *person*, understood as the two-in-one constellation *I–Other*, is linguistically actualized in time and in space.[11] Only in this way can we explain how immersion can be located within a deictic system of reality or which temporal arrangement readers are being entangled in when they are included in an immersive loop. With Hamburger and purely linguistically oriented theories of deixis, one would have to understand the character-*origo* as a "time-space of an (other) I" (which would then be "prepared" to amalgamate with the reader-*origo*). Instead, we will speak of a "time-space of an other (I)." Understood this way, there can never be anything like what literary studies used to conceptualize as "identification." It is more likely that a reader put himself in relation with a linguistic *time-space of the other*.

Obtaining the self-image (Lacan)

Theorems about the imaginary often have an affinity to theoretical reflections about language and time. With regard to Lacan, Alain Juranville recognizes the different temporalities of three layers immanent to language, immanent for "the triad of the real, the symbolic, and the imaginary ... is contained in language itself."[12] The real is defined as "the time proper to the chain of signifiers;" "it is the suffering (*souffrance*) of pure time, appearance and disappearance ... that which cannot be anticipated."[13] Inversely, "the lack that is situated in the imaginary" clings "to anticipation,"[14] in which suffering comes with a return to the self. The temporality of the symbolic, finally, is contingent on an "articulation in which the possibilities, if not the event that comes up suddenly, can be anticipated. The pure transition of time with which a new possibility is opened up is maintained."[15] Juranville thus asserts an "essential synchrony of all symbolic elements in the presentness of the system."[16] In the *synchronous temporality of the symbolic* thus understood, a relation between I and other articulates itself. In symbolic temporality, there is no imaginarily anticipated return to the self and no sudden appearance of an unpredictable real, but an other is synchronously present as other. In this Lacanian understanding of the symbolic and its synchronous non-present, the other is *present only as one who is absent*. The temporalities of the real, imaginary, and symbolic dimensions of language (its instantaneousness, its relations of anticipation, and finally its relations of non-/contemporaneity) allow for a different description of the dynamic that literary studies call "presentification."

Having extended a tense-structural deixis theory of fiction theory to include the aspect *person*, we can now differentiate presentification. It is a complex course of events that does not simply presentify uni-directionally but relates to all three temporalities of language. These linguistic events involve instantaneous and anticipatory temporalities as well as temporalities that move into the non-present of a symbolic present tense. They thus refer to a folded *origo* of the reader and narrative other (character or narrator) on whose configuration the character of narration and fiction depend. Typical of nineteenth-century narrated fiction in the past tense is a kind of *loop* into which the three ecstasies of time are tied. (Toward the end of the fourth chapter we will introduce the asynchronous counter-model of a time that *bifurcates* in the present.) For a subject, the three ecstasies of time can be brought into a succession by means of the imaginary:

> The act of anticipation ... posits the three ecstasies of time that are joined together in it and projects them in the direction of the coming of the futural that is to come. It is itself the opening of time—as a future that retrieves the past and lets it arrive. The past does not pass by itself, it has to be pulled. The present is the site of the knot. The future (*futur*) produces as an act of anticipation the future (*avenir*) in which the past is what comes back.[17]

The succession described here already produces the structure of a narration in which a series of events is projected toward an unknown future,[18] in order to be called up, in the very process of completion, as past by a *sujet*. Here two possibilities diverge: either the medialization into a fiction succeeds, that is, the integration of the times in a present forms a knot, or it merely reactualizes itself in its failure, in a delusion.

According to our hypothesis that the imaginary present tense is a symptomatic phenomenon on the edge of the system of narrated fiction, we will first work out how the image of such an image of a loop that successfully ties together the three times[19] applies in E. T. A. Hoffmann. In this story, however, as in two more by Gogol and Dostoevsky, we will only indicate those moments at which these loops begin to come undone. Hoffmann's *The Golden Pot* is a first limit case insofar as the text succeeds in tying a loop, i.e., in bringing together the times, despite the obvious transgression of its hallucinating protagonist. The imaginary set in motion by two scribes is recuperated at the end of the text and is manifest in the conclusion in the present, that is, in the symbolic present tense of its language.

E. T. A. Hoffmann's fictional breakthrough to the imaginary present tense

Three different meanings can be found for the use of the present tense in the fourth vigil of E. T. A. Hoffmann's tale. The text begins with a direct address to the reader by the narrator, written in the present tense. This might seem like a breaking of fiction, but it in no way endangers the regime of narrated fiction. Alongside it, we find, second, the reinforcement of fiction that is characteristic of the historical present tense, and, third, an attempt at fictionalizing the reader. The narrator attempts to draw the reader into the fiction and even goes so far as to try to make him a co-protagonist:

> Wohl darf ich geradezu dich selbst, günstiger Leser! fragen, ob du in deinem Leben nicht Stunden, ja Tage und Wochen hattest, in denen dir all' Dein gewöhnliches Tun und Treiben ein recht quälendes Mißbehagen erregte ... Du schlichst mit trübem Blick umher wie ein hoffnungslos Liebender, und alles, was du die

Menschen auf allerlei Weise im bunten Gewühl durcheinander treiben sahst, erregte dir keinen Schmerz und keine Freude, als gehörtest du nicht mehr dieser Welt an. Ist dir, günstiger Leser! jemals so zumute gewesen, so kennst du selbst aus eigener Erfahrung den Zustand, in dem sich der Student Anselmus befand. Überhaupt wünschte ich, es wäre mir schon jetzt gelungen, dir, geneigter Leser! den Studenten Anselmus recht lebhaft vor Augen zu bringen. Denn in der Tat, ich habe in den Nachtwachen, die ich dazu verwende, seine höchst sonderbare Geschichte aufzuschreiben, noch so viel Wunderliches, das wie eine spukhafte Erscheinung das alltägliche Leben ganz gewöhnlicher Menschen ins Blaue hinausrückte, zu erzählen, daß mir bange ist, du werdest am Ende weder an den Studenten Anselmus noch an den Archivarius Lindhorst glauben, ja wohl gar einige ungerechte Zweifel gegen den Konrektor Paulmann und den Registrator Heerbrand hegen, unerachtet wenigstens die letztgenannten achtbaren Männer noch jetzt in Dresden umherwandeln. Versuche es, geneigter Leser! in dem feenhaften Reiche voll herrlicher Wunder, die die höchste Wonne sowie das tiefste Entsetzen in gewaltigen Schlägen hervorrufen, ja, wo die ernste Göttin ihren Schleier lüftet, daß wir ihr Antlitz zu schauen wähnen—aber ein Lächeln schimmert oft aus dem ernsten Blick, und das ist der neckhafte Scherz, der in allerlei verwirrendem Zauber mit uns spielt, so wie die Mutter oft mit ihren liebsten Kindern tändelt—ja! in diesem Reiche, das uns der Geist so oft, wenigstens im Traume aufschließt, versuche es, geneigter Leser! die bekannten Gestalten, wie sie täglich, wie man zu sagen pflegt, im gemeinen Leben, um dich herwandeln, wiederzuerkennen. Du wirst dann glauben, daß dir jenes herrliche Reich viel näher liege, als du sonst wohl meintest, welches ich nun eben recht herzlich wünsche, und dir in der seltsamen Geschichte des Studenten Anselmus anzudeuten strebe.

Let me ask you outright, gentle reader, if there have not been hours, indeed whole days and weeks of your life, during which all your usual activities were painfully repugnant ... You crept to and fro with downcast gaze like a rejected lover, and none of humanity's many and varied activities gave you either joy or pain, as though you had ceased to belong to this world. If you have ever felt such a mood, gentle reader, then you know from your own experience the state in which Anselmus found himself. And indeed, kind reader, I should like to think that I have managed by now to bring the student Anselmus vividly before your eyes. For in the night watches in which I am recording his extraordinary story, I have still to recount many peculiar events, which, like a ghostly apparition, turned the everyday lives of ordinary people topsy-turvy, and I fear that you may end up believing neither in Anselmus nor in Archivist Lindhorst; you may even have some unjustified doubts about Sub-Rector Paulmann and Registrary Heerbrand, although the latter two worthy gentlemen, at least, are still walking the streets of Dresden. You are now, kind reader, in the fairy realm of glorious wonders, whose mighty strokes summon up both supreme bliss and extreme horror, and where the grave goddess raises her veil so that we may fancy we see her face—but her grave expression often breaks into a smile, and that is the impish humour that teases us with the bewilderments of magic, which our spirit so often reveals to us, at least in our dreams. Try, kind reader, to recognize the well-known shapes that, as the saying goes, cross your path every day. You will then believe that this magnificent realm is much nearer at hand than you had previously thought; and that is what I heartily wish you to believe, and what the strange story of Anselmus is supposed to convey.[20]

What becomes legible is the Romantic writer's strategy to no longer turn to his reader merely in order to break with the narrative. Wishing to vivify the events and fearing for the reader's faith in the fiction, he cannot rely on a rhetoric of the historical present tense. His metafictional commentary accordingly follows up with a reference to an imaginary, to the play of daydreams, which quickly takes on the promising traits of desire. Not least of all, this provokes the danger of being carried off by the deafening force of the imagination into uninhibited hallucinations.

A mild form of daydreaming is shown in a scene in which the Counsellor's daughter Veronica, enthusiastically involved with the student Anselmus, imagines her future and the text performs a dual switch of tenses. At the moment in which the daydream completely fills the present, the text, too, jumps into the present tense, and Veronica really "hears":

Veronika überließ sich ganz, wie junge Mädchen wohl pflegen, den süßen Träumen von einer heitern Zukunft. Sie war Frau Hofrätin, bewohnte ein schönes Logis in der Schloßgasse oder auf dem Neumarkt, oder auf der Moritzstraße—der moderne Hut, der neue türkische Schawl stand ihr vortrefflich—sie frühstückte im eleganten Negligé im Erker, der Köchin die nötigen Befehle für den Tag erteilend. "Aber daß Sie mir die Schüssel nicht verdirbt, es ist des Herrn Hofrats Leibessen!"—Vorübergehende Elegants schielten herauf, sie hört deutlich: "Es ist doch eine göttliche Frau, die Hofrätin, wie ihr das Spitzenhäubchen so allerliebst steht!"—Die Geheime Rätin Ypsilon schickt den Bedienten und läßt fragen, ob es der Frau Hofrätin gefällig wäre, heute ins Linkische Bad zu fahren.—"Viel Empfehlungen, es täte mir unendlich leid, ich sei schon engagiert zum Tee bei der Präsidentin Tz."—Da kommt der Hofrat Anselmus, der schon früh in Geschäften ausgegangen, zurück; er ist nach der letzten Mode gekleidet; "wahrhaftig schon zehn," ruft er, indem er die goldne Uhr repetieren läßt und der jungen Frau einen Kuß gibt. "Wie geht's, liebes Weibchen, weißt du auch, was ich für dich habe?" fährt er schäkernd fort und zieht ein Paar herrliche, nach der neuesten Mode gefaßte Ohrringe aus der Westentasche, die er ihr statt der sonst getragenen gewöhnlichen einhängt. "Ach, die schönen, niedlichen Ohrringe" ruft Veronika ganz laut und springt, die Arbeit wegwerfend, vom Stuhl auf, um in dem Spiegel die Ohrringe wirklich zu beschauen. "Nun, was soll denn das sein", sagte der Konrektor Paulmann, der, eben in *Cicero de Officiis* vertieft, beinahe das Buch fallen lassen, "man hat ja Anfälle wie der Anselmus."

Veronica abandoned herself, as young girls will, to delicious dreams of a happy future. She was a Counsellor's lady, living in a handsome residence in Castle Lane, or on the New Market, or in Moritz Street; her fashionable hat, her new Turkish shawl, suited her perfectly; she took her breakfast in the window alcove, wearing an elegant morning gown and giving the cook instructions for the day. "But don't spoil the meat course, for it's the Counsellor's favourite dish!" Passing dandies cast upward glances at her, and she overhears them saying: "What a charming woman the Counsellor's lady is, and how beautiful she looks in that lace cap!" The lady of Privy Counsellor Y.

sends a domestic to ask whether the Counsellor's lady would care to visit Linke's Restaurant today. "Give your mistress my very best compliments and say that I am very sorry, but I have promised to have tea with the lady of President Z." Then Counsellor Anselmus returns, having gone out early to attend to his duties. He is dressed in the latest fashion. "It's ten o'clock already, I declare," he cries, making his gold watch strike the hour, and giving his young wife a kiss. "How are you, my pet, can you guess what I've brought you?" he goes on teasingly, and from his waistcoat he produces a pair of magnificent ear-rings in the latest style, which he puts in her ears to replace those she was wearing before. "Oh, what lovely dainty ear-rings," cries Veronica out loud throwing away her work and jumping up out of her chair to look at the ear-rings in the mirror. "What on earth is the matter?" said Sub-Rector Paulmann, who had been so engrossed in Cicero's *De Officiis* that he now nearly dropped the book; "you're getting as bad as Anselmus with your crazy fits."[21]

Veronica is so caught up in her daydream that it "jumps" into the present of the narration and "calls" to her in the present tense. While she is already back in the *fabula*, her father, Sub-Rector Paulmann, speaks in the past tense of narrated fiction and promptly denounces the *lapsus temporae* of his Romantic avant-gardist daughter as a fit. In fact, a spatial and temporal ambiguity emerges. The sentence in the present tense could still have come from the daydream and Lady Counsellor Veronica could jump in her daydream. Or we could already have returned from the future, returned to Sub-Rector Paulmann's office. We find ourselves here and there, in the future and in the present, to the extent that the temporal organization of the text distances itself from the image of the time loop into which present, past, and future are tied in the matrix of narrated fiction.

This drift of the present tense culminates in the finale of the tale, written entirely in the present. After the narrator has addressed the reader one last time and after another breaking of the fiction provides a glimpse of the imaginary, there is a peculiar role reversal. The Romantic narrator, who is having trouble with finding an ending, receives a letter from one of his characters that reveals him to be the author of *Tomcat Murr*. The *fabula*-character of the archivist[22] (who had also once employed the adolescent dreamer Anselmus as a writer) commends alcohol and, during the *sujet*-narrator's drunken stupor, takes over writing the story. The result: three pages of pure, hallucinatory present-tense prose. A hundred years before the modernist procedures of an imaginary novel, such a medialization of the imaginary is of course bought at the price of hallucination and delusion or alcohol abuse. Only in the last paragraph does the hung-over author wake up. At the very last moment, he manages to close the loop of narrated fiction. He now remembers his exhilaration in the past tense and finds himself back among the living. The final passage, which invokes the life of poetry, reads:

> Die Vision, in der ich nun den Anselmus leibhaftig auf seinem Rittergute in Atlantis gesehen, verdanke ich wohl den Künsten des Salamanders, und herrlich war es, daß ich sie, als alles wie im Nebel verloschen, auf dem Papier, das auf dem violetten Tische lag, recht sauber und augenscheinlich von mir selbst aufgeschrieben fand.—Aber nun fühlte ich mich von jähem Schmerz durchbohrt und zerrissen ... Da klopfte mir der Archivarius Lindhorst leise auf die Achsel und sprach: "Still, still, Verehrter, klagen Sie nicht so!—Waren Sie nicht soeben selbst in Atlantis, und haben Sie denn nicht auch dort wenigstens einen artigen Meierhof als poetisches Besitztum Ihres innern Sinns—Ist denn überhaupt des Anselmus Seligkeit etwas anderes als das Leben in der Poesie, der sich der heilige Einklang aller Wesen als tiefstes Geheimnis der Natur offenbaret?"

> For the vision in which I had seen Anselmus in bodily form on his estate in Atlantis I was indebted to the arts of the salamander. It was splendid, too, that when the scene had dissolved into mist, I found it clearly and legibly described in my own handwriting on the paper that was lying on the purple table. Now, however, I felt pierced and lacerated by sudden anguish ... At that moment Archivist Lindhorst tapped me gently on the shoulder and said: "Hush, my worthy friend! Don't complain like that! Weren't you in Atlantis yourself a moment ago, and haven't you at least got a pretty farm there, as the poetic property of your mind? Indeed, is Anselmus's happiness anything other than life in poetry, where the holy harmony of all things is revealed as the deepest secret of nature?"[23]

Gogol's imaginary time-fuse or "date none"

In reading the following mad narrated fiction, written some two decades after *The Golden Pot*, too, we would first like to examine the role of the present tense in narrated fiction generally. Only then will we, in a second step, examine Gogol's *Diary of a Madman* to discern an *indistinguishability* of the imaginary. Not least of all, this indistinguishability can be seen, third, in a complete de-ranging of space and time that unfolds in step with the progression of the diary keeper's insanity and leads to chaos in the dating of his entries.

In Gogol's first-person tale, present tense and past tense alternate regularly. The past tense is assigned to the events at the level of the *fabula* (which concern the fictional character). The passages in the present tense belong to the *sujet* and concern the first person as narrator. On October 4, near the beginning of the text, we read: "Today is Wednesday, and so I was in my superior's study."[24] While the "is" refers to the writing of the diary entry and its dating on the Wednesday that is today, the "was" refers to the events that are noted in the diary and are fictionally presentified by the reader. As the notes progress, however, larger and larger zones of indeterminacy spread in the first-person commentary. One example is a soliloquy from November 11, a few diary pages later, that continually drifts off into short hallucinations:

> Хотелось бы мне заглянуть в гостиную, куда видишь только иногда отворенную дверь, за гостиною еще в одну комнату. Эх, какое богатое убранство! Какие зеркала и фарфоры! Хотелось бы заглянуть туда, на ту половину, где ее превосходительство,—вот куда хотелось бы мне! В будуар: как там стоят все эти баночки, скляночки, цветы такие, что и дохнуть на них страшно; как лежит там разбросанное ее платье, больше похожее на воздух, чем на платье. Хотелось бы заглянуть в спальню … там-то, я думаю, чудеса, там-то, я думаю, рай, какого и на небесах нет. Посмотреть бы ту скамеечку, на которую она становит, вставая с постели, свою ножку, как надевается на эту ножку белый, как снег, чулочек … ай! ай! ай! ничего, ничего … молчание.

> I'd like to peek into the drawing room, where you sometimes see only an open door into yet another room beyond the drawing

room. Ah, such rich furnishings! Such mirrors and china! I'd like to peek in there, into that half, Her Excellency's—that's what I'd like! Into the boudoir, with all those little jars and vials standing there, such flowers that you're afraid to breathe on them; with her dress thrown down there, more like air than a dress. I'd like to peek into her bedroom ... there, I think, there are wonders; there, I think, there is paradise, such as is not even to be found in heaven. To look at the little stool she puts her little foot on when she gets out of bed, at how a snow-white stocking is being put on that foot ... aie! aie! aie! nothing, nothing ... silence.[25]

In the English translation, the reader has the impression of repetition. Aksenty wishes to see through the open door into the drawing room, whereupon the drawing room manifests itself in his imagination; he wishes to see into the boudoir, whereupon the thrown dress materializes in the air and as air. In the original Russian, however, a narrative succession emerges, in which one space brings forth the next and sets a successive spatial (deictic) shift in motion. Second, at the end of the quote there is a significant grammatical difference. There is a reflexive verb with which the stocking pulls itself up the leg. It also remains unclear to whom or what the snow-whiteness belongs, which reveals that the sentence has no clear subject. The stocking thus turns out to be a metonymy for the narrating character, who pulls himself up the soft little foot.

When in the last stammered words, the present tense and verbs generally drop out, they lose their relevance. After the imagination of the narrator has settled into the young woman's stocking, cries are heard ("aie! aie! aie!"), followed by a linguistic fainting fit ("nothing, nothing ... silence"). In this passage, then, the imaginary has an even stronger effect than it does in Hoffmann. It no longer takes the harmless form of a drunken stupor, which could still be captured in a magical text. It follows a drift that infects the text itself to end up in silence and the extinction of the narrator.

Now on to the present-tense entry of December 3, which is less an expression of aphasia and a de-ranging of language than of an increasing confusion about how to contain the marginalized present tense by means of the paradigmatic or auctorial past tense:

Не может быть. Враки! Свадьбе не бывать! Что ж из того, что он камер-юнкер ... Может быть, я какой-нибудь граф или генерал, а только так кажусь титулярным советником? Может быть, я сам не знаю, кто я таков. Ведь сколько примеров по истории: какой-нибудь простой, не то уже чтобы дворянин, а просто какой-нибудь мещанин или даже крестьянин,—и вдруг открывается, что он какой-нибудь вельможа, а иногда даже и государь ... что скажет и сам папа, директор наш?

It can't be. Lies! The wedding won't take place! So what if he's a *kammerjunker* ... Maybe I'm some sort of count or general and only seem to be a titular councillor? Maybe I myself don't know who I am. There are so many examples in history: some simple fellow, not only not a nobleman, but simply some tradesman or even peasant—and it's suddenly revealed that he's some sort of dignitary, or sometimes even an emperor ... What is Papa himself, our director, going to say?[26]

Once again, the already mentioned hallucination of what is hoped for or imagined is manifest as reality in the present tense, in the literary procedure of realization. The hero has become his boss's son-in-law, and he will soon turn out to be an imaginary emperor as well. As the madness keeps spreading in the narrator's soliloquies, the fantastic becomes increasingly legible on the level of the story as the hallucination of the hero going mad. At the end we will know that the protagonist is not the emperor that he believes himself to be. We also know without a doubt that in the fiction he is by no means a simple farmer. Yet between hallucination and fiction it remains indistinct whether he is a member of the bourgeoisie or the nobility.

What initially accompanies the diary entries as a commentary in the gnomic present—"The Englishman is a great politician. He fusses about everywhere"[27]—is a soliloquy of the hero, then starts to transition indiscernibly into the speech of madness. The *sujet* is haunted by the very de-rangement that fantastically spreads in the *fabula*. We will see, in the context of the complete de-rangement of dating, how the moment at which the de-rangement becomes manifest and the two levels of *fabula* and *sujet* and the first-person narrator can no longer keep the events and his mad interpretations apart, the tenses bolt and alternate in wild haste.

What so far we have shown for the use of the present tense in relation to the narrative levels and the narrative personnel we can equally trace in the temporal de-rangements, which are joined by spatial ones. Before we analyze this deictic movement, we might point to the character and various modes of de-rangement. In Gogol's *Diary*, an imaginary in fiction comes to express itself through a slow, imperceptible process of de-rangement that cannot be located in any distinct event. Not the least of reasons for this may be that there are shifts from the very beginning of the text that initially look as if they were identical with the establishing of fiction. As the protagonist notes the scolding of his boss, the date is already written in the English style, with the day after the month:

> Он уже давно мне говорит: "Что это у тебя, братец, в голове всегда ералаш такой? Ты иной раз метаешься как угорелый, дело подчас так спутаешь, что сам сатана не разберет, в титуле поставишь маленькую букву, не выставишь ни числа, ни номера". Проклятая цапля!

> For a long time already he says to me: "Why is it that you have such a hotchpotch in your head, brother? You rush about frantically, you sometimes confuse a case so much the devil himself couldn't sort it out, you start the title in lowercase, forget the date [in Russian, *chislo* means both date and number] or number." Cursed stork![28]

In this opening passage, the de-ranging, the forgetting of dates and numbers, could thus already have been legible. But it does not come to the fore because the foreground is taken up by fantastic events: two dogs, Maggy and Fidèle, start to speak and soon thereafter to write letters to one another. In the dogs' letters as well, the dates are missing, without us noticing at first reading. Instead, our attention is absorbed by the fantastic quality of the events. Todorov's definition, according to which fantastic narrative events are characterized by the undecidability of their natural or supernatural origin, applies here. In the dogs' letters we observe an inversion of the fantastic and the fictional. It is no longer the dogs writing letters to one another that seems fantastic but the circumstance that the protagonist gains information about himself and the other (acting) protagonists in the story from their letters, information that has been kept secret at the level of the story. Both the (fantastic) dog letters and the (fictional) information gained from them turn out to be hallucinatory. This means for the imaginary in question that the real and the unreal remain indistinguishable. We can generalize this form of narrative: Gogol's story narrates an unnoticed (by the reader) going mad of the protagonist as the indistinguishability of fiction (of the text) and hallucination (of the character).

We have taken Iser's remark that the imaginary attains to a comparatively pure present in delusion as the starting point for a hypothesis according to which there ought to be a tendency toward the present even before the "properly-so-called" present-tense texts of the twentieth century. Our interest in such a delusional present tense in the nineteenth century consists first and foremost in clarifying its relation to the narrative and fictional organization of texts. That is why we are less interested in the thematization of delusion, in texts, that is, in which delusion is only raised to the level of motif, without narration and fiction being affected by attempt on the part of the imaginary to break out. Of greater instrumental value for our problem are those stories of madness in which we can observe how delusions or hallucinations enter into the narrative and fictional levels of the text and thus affect the system of narrated fiction itself. Stories of delusion in the nineteenth century thus confirm the hypothesis with which we set out to look for a present tense before the present tense. When the matrix of narrated fiction affects itself with an imaginary, a present tense appears that twentieth-century prose will go to great lengths to integrate into narrative and to form into fiction.

Narrated fiction, in contrast, does not yet leave any room for the imagination and drives it to the madhouse, something that Hume might already have surmised when he wrote that the imagination "is liable to become a cannibal and turn on itself."[29] The matrix of narrated fiction digests itself.

The two sets of questions we have discussed so far, Gogol's use of tense on the one hand and the destabilization of the narrated fiction on the other, can be followed up with what we would like to call Gogol's "date futurism." For what cannot be read in the narrative, the onset of delusion, becomes visible in the symptomatic use of the present tense, to be sure, but above all in the impossible dates. The first thing one notices in reading the diaries is an ascending series of dates, which initially still seeks to dissimulate numerically what is already nonsense in the calendar (5th, 8th, 43rd, 86th play with the homonomy mentioned above of *chislo* as both *number* and *date*). Parallel to this, times of intervals emerge—"The 86th of Martober. Between day and night," "Date none"—and with the entrance of delusion, time disappears altogether—"The day had to date,"[30] "Don't remember the date. There was no month, either. / Devil knows what there was." In what ensues, a new way of figuring time begins in a rather imaginary Spain—"I discovered that China and Spain are absolutely one and the same land ... I advise everyone purposely to write Spain on a piece of paper, and it will come out China"—and the narrator opens up entirely new dimensions thereafter in the Russian (imperfective) past tense as well:[31]

> Но меня, однако же, чрезвычайно огорчало событие, имеющее быть завтра. Завтра в семь часов совершится странное явление: земля сядет на луну. Об этом и знаменитый английский химик Веллингтон пишет ... Луна ведь обыкновенно делается в Гамбурге; и прескверно делается. Я удивляюсь, как не обратит на это внимание Англия.

> But, nevertheless, I was extremely upset by an event that is going to take place tomorrow. Tomorrow at seven o'clock a strange phenomenon will occur: the earth is going to sit on the moon. This has also been written about by the noted English chemist Wellington ... For the moon is usually made in Hamburg, and made quite poorly. I'm surprised England doesn't pay attention to this.[32]

Several times, the narrator runs up vehemently against the epic quality of the past tense, with which the sentence begins in Russian. We read "tomorrow ... will occur" and "is going to take place tomorrow." He fictionally catapults himself to Spain, making an imaginary detour via the moon: "And for the same reason, we can't see our own noses, for they're all in the moon." Personal disintegration is tied up with temporal confusions and spatial jumps—"And so I'm in Spain, and it happened so quickly that I've barely come to my senses"—that lead the narrator to Spain, China, and the moon, a journey through space and time that the matrix of narrated fiction makes take place in a madhouse. Stage by stage, entry by entry, Gogol's text spells out this drifting off in always funny, comical, and grotesque steps.³³

The third to last entry—"The Englishman is a great politician. He fusses about everywhere"—bears the date "January of the same year, which came after February."³⁴ The dating of the previous entry—"Madrid. Thirtieth Februarius"—corresponds to how narrated fiction intrigue functions, even overdoes it in terms of semblance. There is, of course, no thirtieth of February, but the Englishmen fussing about everywhere seem to have colonized even the month and to speak through the calendar itself. In place of the Russian *fevral*, "what reigns here is a Russified *fevruary*. The *February* that shines through lets us guess that the English secret service must have had a hand in this and that we are dealing with a spy story that leads its protagonist into a padded cell. The temporal leap within this eternal thirtieth of February leads all the way to avant-garde and beyond to 'The Year 2000, 43rd of April'."³⁵

The text unfolds the inversions, reversal, and de-rangement of time on the level of its language and thereby exposes itself to a process of linguistic destruction. Once again we can refer to Roman Jakobson, who states that deictic shifters belong to later developments in language acquisition and thus are among the first to get lost in aphasias.³⁶ Applied to Gogol's story, this means: While the story is imprisoned in the madhouse of narrated fiction, Gogol's absurd language succeeds in a futuristic departure. His text initiates a time travel through literary history, in which the renunciation of sentence structures, verbs, and grammar in futuristic and absurd poetry marks the literary extreme that dates the last entry: "The of 34 ἑϱµηνιλ th, yrea 349."³⁷

Gogol's story lets us read an unbridled imaginary that manifests itself in a delusion of language, an imaginary whose fundamental nihilism we may, with Sartre, call "nihilation."³⁸ This form of the imaginary, which we see embodied in Gogol's story of madness, makes it clear why no successful narrated fiction emerges. A terrorist imaginary, like a time-fuse, lies unformed in this fictional *Diary of a Madman* whose nihilating potential destroys the structures of fiction and the levels of narration. These latter are corroded to the extent that they do not manage to banish the imaginary in a chronotopically coherent fictional world, to the extent, that is, that they fail to tie the narrative thread into a tight loop.

We view the poetologies of Gogol, E. T. A. Hoffman, and, in

what follows, Dostoevsky, as poetologies in which the delusion of an imaginary affects narration and fiction. The imaginary leads to undecidabilities and to an indistinguishability of narration and fiction. What happens in regard to these second and third forms of fiction-narratological in/difference to the imaginary—when no medical Grand Inquisitor appears on the scene to call the hero by name and see to it that he is committed—will be shown at the end of this chapter in our discussion of Strindberg.

Doubles

"It was a little before eight o'clock in the morning when Yakov Petrovitch Golyadkin, a titular councillor, woke up from a long sleep."[39] This presentifying scene, conforming to the ideal type of narrated fiction, opens Dostoevsky's novel *The Double*. Only paratextual or intertextual previous knowledge[40] would let readers suspect that the protagonist will soon declare: "I am not myself, but somebody else strikingly like me."[41] The schizophrenic motif of the double that lends the novel its name is actualized by Dostoevsky's text at several levels. Before analyzing this in detail, we would like, in an excursus, to present focalization itself as a procedure of doubling. Only then will the thematic doubling of character become apparent, and we will finally come to understand to what extent the narrator is a double of the character. Against this backdrop we will also be able to understand the connection of the two-in-one phenomena of binocular focus and dual voice.

In our schedule of deictic shifts at the end of the preceding chapter, we alluded to the fact that spatial, temporal, and personal two-in-one phenomena are of central significance for the dynamics of shifting in narrated fiction. Fyodor Dostoevsky's *The Double* will allow us to develop the overlay of a double personal deixis with a binocular "focus" and to clarify the differences between *focus* and the narratological concept *focalization*.

Excursus: Focus as a double in narrative technique

What we know from narratology as focalization goes back to a literary move in which the procedure of looking inside characters' interior transitions to a form of personal narration, such as we can read in Dostoevsky. Only through this crossing of introspection and third-person narrative does *psychonarration* emerge. This form of narrative is distinct from the practice of previous third-person and first-person narratives. In first-person narrative, since as early as the eighteenth century, the perspective or outlook of the first person was toward itself. Only with the realist novel of the nineteenth century does the difference between perspective and focalization, which narratology deems to be fundamental, become relevant.[42] Once we use the concept in the sense of our fiction-narratological system, we would like to speak of *focus* rather than *focalization*, since this is consistent with taking into account a third perspective, that of the reader, and therefore with integrating the two-in-one of focalization into a deictic dynamic of shifting.

We would now like to trace how internal focus turns up in the history of literature at the moment that the practice of introspection, at first exclusively associated with first-person narrative, is adopted by personal narration. Assuming that perspective and focus form a couple proves to be fruitful not only because in a consistent focus there is presumably always a consistent perspective, but also because the prior and subsequent development of narration in literary history is more clearly visible when we assume such a systematic correlation. This is especially the case when the aim is to avoid the danger of narratological overdifferentiation, i.e., the formation of synchronous double terms for individual narrative categories.

The distinction between perspective and focus is not a transhistorically valid narratological nuance. Not every perspective differs from a focalization, and not every type of focalization can be meaningfully recognized to be different from a perspective. Yet the distinction is of particular value for classical narrated fiction. Let us look, therefore, at the two categorizations of (a) zero-focalization and (b) external focalization in terms of their perspectival dimension or perspectivity: (a) omniscient auctoriality implies a perspective of overview, but there is no focalization, whereas (b) the neutral view of characters, which knows nothing of characters' interior life, is not a neutral perspective, only focalization.

From the viewpoint of a fiction-narratological method, which is aware of the various dominants, we can see that every narration restricts the number of realizable categories. No text can actualize all categories. When we define focus as a phenomenon of doubling, we do so to restrict a universal horizon of narrative distinctions to the ones that are historically possible in each case. Literary history is not a progressive history, and it is not at all the case that texts become more and more complex over the course of that history and incorporate more and more categorial distinctions. Instead, older forms are translated into new ones, and procedures that in a new paradigm are only insufficiently motivated die off.[43]

In retracing the historical trajectory, we notice that "focalization," theoretically differentiated by narratology for narrated fictions, must be understood as a metamorphosis of "perspective." Only by decontextualizing, by looking only at the time when narrative perspectivization transforms into focalization, can we see them both as comparable categories. Not the least of our aims in the typological reduction or de-differentiation of "perspective" and its double, "focalization," is to open up a historical dimension. The path toward a historical narratology cannot lead us to tie the categories of narratology into a diachronic succession. Fiction-narratology is to describe a categorial dynamics of transformation. In the course of this transformation, focus emerges as the fictional dimension of perspective. This is a third justification for our speaking of focus.

Our first criterion for differentiating focalization and focus was the inclusion of a third person alongside narrator and character—that of the reader. Our second criterion was the integration of focus into a deixis of time as well (temporal focus). Our third criterion now is situating focus in spatial deixis as a transformation of perspective. Viewed from within the system of narrated fiction, we see no narratively sustainable or useful focus in the history that comes before the system, and we see no perspective, in the strict sense, in the history that comes after. This leads to a distinction between the following three historical formations by means of different variants of "perspectivism": (1) a total, only metaphorical perspective; (2) a perspective from narrated fiction, that is, focus; (3) a multiple perspective, which, in the end, means a dissolved perspective.

(1) The "total perspective"

The distinction between perspective and focus has little or at least restricted heuristic value for the literary epoch preceding the system of narrated fiction. Like Dorrit Cohn, we see the reason for this in the fact that in this narrative regime the expression of protagonists' interior life is usually encountered only in first-person narratives. To this extent, the often-mobilized easy parallel between the invention of novelistic narration and perspectival painting in the Renaissance is only metaphoric. The geometric perspectivism of Renaissance painting has no equivalent in literature.[44] In a "total perspective," the omniscient narrator is precisely not a narrator with a perspective, for he does not restrict his view to what would be visible from his perspective. He always sees more than is possible. The "overview" often brought up in narrative theory is more of a non-perspectival map and precisely not a (geometrically constructed) bird's-eye view.[45] In the case of pre-perspectival view we are thus dealing with total or absolute visibility: everything can always be seen from all sides at the same time. But here, there is no looking inside characters from the outside.

(2) The doubling of perspective in narrated fiction qua focus

How does focus arise in narrated fiction? Renouncing the comprehensiveness of representations in favor of the restricted view of a particular perspective initially seems so unappealing that focus has to be a substantial enrichment of narrative technique and narrated fiction. This brightest of stars in the heavens of procedures of narrated fiction is the focalizing person. The story can be told from out of this person, and at the same time, a narrative or a narrator is able to look inside it. At the danger of taking the wordplay too far: the invention of focus amounts to a concentration of the narrator's gaze, an intensification that succeeds in penetrating *into* its protagonists and narrating *from out of* their perspective. Focus is a filter or magnifying glass because in focus, a perspective is synchronously at work. On the one hand, this is due to the angle with which focus restricts the knowledge about the world of the fiction, limiting the view to what a single person can see. On the other hand, this self-restriction to a single view, to a single starting point of the gaze, is the condition for looking into the protagonists. It is not by chance that Genette's only characteristic of fiction is this most important *insight* (in the fullest sense of the word) of narrated fiction.

This much for the dimension of the changes in narrative technique that come with focus and can be verified narratologically. In terms of fiction theory, we may note that this new, one-eyed focal perspective makes fictional space plausible *in toto*. This distinguishes it from the doctrine of total perspective, which tries to make individual fictional objects plausible by representing many sides (as many as possible). Focus posits a gaze *within space*, whereas perspective only gives a view *of space*. In perspective, the space represented solely unfolds from out of the position of the viewer. Later, with Kharms, this limiting of perspective takes on the form of a literary motif we already cited: an absolute nothing behind the character's back.[46]

Only with the gaze *from out of* the character can something like surroundings form. Only with focus is the viewer placed into the center of a (potentially universal) space that can be conceptualized as a "fictional world." Put differently: While focus arises in the transfer of the interior view from the first-person narrative to the third-person world of the novel, it is this subjectification that connects focus to an intensification and extension of the meaning of fictionality that is typical of narrated fiction, indeed even constitutes its horizon.[47] The point at which focus participates in the construction of the dynamic of narrated fiction comes with narrators' insight into their characters, a development of their interior life, a shaping of their view of the world, indeed, a participation in their subjectivity, their passions, and, finally, their imaginary.

(3) Manifold perspective

The multiplication of perspective amounts to its dissolution and leaves behind the shambles of in-spections that can also be conceived of as post-perspectival narration. Here we can pick up on a phenomenon already discussed in the first chapter, rethink it poetologically, and refine it. Simultaneous narration, which is described in literary history (by Monika Fludernik, Suzanne Fleischman, and many others) as deviation, appears to us to be a late (altermodern) development of focus. We consider this to be the real reason for the present tense's change in status, first postulated by Fiona Björling, from a mere deviation to a basic tense.[48] Focus turns back toward first-person narrative, from which it is originally imported as "simple insight," only at the end of a long development. In Marcel Beyer's *The Karnau Tapes*, for instance, we can see how a dual focalization resolves the inconsistency of the retrospective autobiography in relation to the (temporal) focus. In every autobiography there is the perspective of two egos, separate from each other in time, whose identity with one another across the temporal boundary of memory is not recognizable in retrospective narration.[49] Only in simultaneous narration does a temporal focus appear that develops the procedure "focus" under the conditions of an asynchrony of the present. In altermodernism, focus achieves the simultaneization of temporal asynchrony with spatial asyntopy. In so doing, focus succeeds on the personal level in involving memories in the narration in a new way. These memories are no longer presentifications of former presents that turn up from out of the past; they are steps back into the past.

We have arrived at a neuralgic point within the historical typology described above. What is important for the imaginary present tense in the nineteenth century is less altermodern multi-focalization than the pharmacological effect of focus within the matrix of narrated fiction. Focus is its doping, it enables narration's *illegal* peak performances—illegal in the assessment of the literary avant-gardes that follow, for instance in Carl Einstein's infamous *Fabrication of Fiction*. It is thus no wonder that integrating the imaginary in such high doses quickly accelerates the collapse of the system (which allows for the comparison with Derrida's *pharmakon*).[50] This is the main relation of focus to the imaginary, whose conspicuity in delusion is a side effect of the nineteenth-century's self-confident realism. As a liminal phenomenon of the system of narrated fiction, focus for the first time uncovers something that will, in the subsequent modernist development of internalizing the world of the novel, find its (only restrictedly narrative) form in the interior monologue. Focus exposes the internal life of its protagonists as it is expressed in soliloquies, internal speech, and streams of association. Slightly exaggerated, focus in narrated fiction overexerts itself in the attempt to integrate an ever-increasing overdose of the imaginary, that is, in the attempt to make it accessible to literary symbolizing.

This process is, on the one hand, celebrated as subjectification. There is also, on the other, a de-actualization of the fictional world, that is, a noticeable shift toward the imaginary. Furthermore, the narrator, who grants us insight into an interior world, does not necessarily retreat or even disappear in focus, but settles into the consciousness of his character. This "third eye"[51] that Gogol's madman Poprishchin talks about potentially leads to a split in the character. In Dostoevsky, this is legible in the protagonist Golyadkin's creation of a younger double who cannot be seen by anyone but the madman—only the narrator somehow mysteriously seems to be with the double. In complete serenity, Dostoevsky's narrator brings his work to an end, in which the character, desperately trying to protect himself from the superior power of the double, can no longer separate delusion from reality.

We have shown how focus, from a narratological point of view, is to be understood as a double of the narrative technique of perspectivizing. It is, however, a double in yet another sense. Focus is an instrument of a literary delusion. Flaubert's long-held dream—"I have long pondered a novel about madness, or rather about the *way* one goes mad"[52]—has only seemingly not been fulfilled. Instead of materializing in a single work, it is present in all his works as focus, and perhaps nowhere more emphatically than in the hubris of his programmatic statement, "*Madame Bovary, c'est moi.*"

Let us—after we have seen the two-in-one at a personal level in which the character and the narrator are involved in the formation of an Other—return to the literary object of this chapter. There is little distance between the essential deludedness of personal narration and the delusional figures to whom Dostoevsky gives focus in *The Double*:

> "Гораздо было бы лучше, если б всё это было лишь так только,—беспрерывно думал он про себя.—Действительно, подобное темное дело было даже невероятно совсем …"
>
> Только что господин Голядкин решил, что это совсем невозможное дело, как вдруг в комнату влетел господин Голядкин-младший с бумагами в обеих руках и под мышкой.
>
> "It would have been a great deal better if it had all been just nothing," he kept incessantly thinking to himself. "Indeed, such a mysterious business was utterly improbable … in short it's an utterly impossible thing."
>
> My Golyadkin had no sooner made up his mind that it was an utterly impossible thing than Mr. Golyadkin junior flew into the room with papers in both hands as well as under his arm.[53]

The scene begins with a glimpse into the character of the older Golyadkin, absorbed in pondering a story that he clearly wants to deny, and it ends with the appearance on the scene of an (imagined) Golyadkin junior. At first glance the passage has the effect of a psychonarration, in which a narrator depicts a scene in the office through the focalization person of Golyadkin senior. At second glance, however, the two Golyadkins are also to be read as the synchronization of an internal and an external perspective. Understood in this way, however, they are not two characters. They have to be combined in a single one. The fact that the narrator depicts Golyadkin senior only from an internal perspective and Golyadkin junior only from an external one is something that readers only notice the moment when they realize that Golyadkin junior originates in the delusion of Golyadkin senior. But how can such a split be narrated? How can the narrator describe a character flying into the room when the character only exists in the mind of another character? The position of the narrator becomes dubious and allows for a textual schizophrenia to come to light.

Three forms of literary delusion, or the loss of distinction

To better describe the effects of textual schizophrenia, let us examine the conditions under which delusion joins narration and fiction. Before we continue the analysis of Dostoevsky's novel, we would like briefly to systematize these conditions.

There are three forms of literary delusion. They can be divided according to the deictic differentiation of persons. We observe (1) an *unnoticeability* of delusion at the fictional level of the character (of the protagonist); (2) an *undecideability*, this time for the reader, whether it is a delusion or a fiction that appears between the narrative levels within a work; (3) an *indistinguishability* of the imaginary and fiction, which implies a deterioration of the ability to distinguish on the part of the author as well. While our concern in what follows will primarily be with the last two forms, let us briefly address the first to provide a contrast.

(1) Unnoticeability of delusion within fiction

The first form of delusion is a *being-unnoticed*. It only affects characters in a narrating fiction. They are the only ones not to notice their delusion. Such is the case in Cervantes's *Don Quixote*, where it is the protagonist alone who is infected by the delusion. Both the narrative and the fictional organization of the novel remain immune. The character remains the sole instance of personal deixis to be unable to differentiate fiction from delusion. Narrator, author, and reader are not affected. There is a further argument to be developed from this. All that is affected by the deictic shifts is the world of the character. The fiction itself remains largely untouched. In the course of this shift, the world of the characters successively separates from the fictional world, a separation noticed by everyone but the protagonist.

(2) Undecideability between delusion and narrative (fiction)

The second form of madness is the fabrication of an *undecideability* by narrative means. The delusion of a character is not sufficient. In addition, the delusion is integrated into the (fictional) construction of the text.

One of Kafka's miniatures with the programmatic title *The Truth about Sancho Panza* thinks Don Quixote's madness further and assigns it an *undecideable* form:

> Sancho Pansa, der sich übrigens dessen nie gerühmt hat, gelang es im Laufe der Jahre, durch Beistellung einer Menge Ritter- und Räuberromane in den Abend- und Nachtstunden seinen Teufel, dem er später den Namen Don Quixote gab, derart von sich abzulenken, daß dieser dann haltlos die verrücktesten Taten aufführte, die aber mangels eines vorbestimmten Gegenstandes, der eben Sancho Pansa hätte sein sollen, niemandem schadeten. Sancho Pansa, ein freier Mann, folgte gleichmütig, vielleicht aus einem gewissen Verantwortlichkeitsgefühl, dem Don Quixote auf seinen Zügen und hatte davon eine große und nützliche Unterhaltung bis an sein Ende.

> Without ever making any boast of it, Sancho Panza succeeded in the course of years, by feeding him a great number of romances of chivalry and adventure in the evening and night hours, in so diverting from himself his demon, whom he later called Don Quixote, that his demon thereupon set out, uninhibited, on the maddest exploits, which, however, for the lack of a preordained object, which should have been Sancho Panza himself, harmed nobody. A free man, Sancho Panza philosophically followed Don Quixote on his crusades, perhaps out of a sense of responsibility, and had of them a great and edifying entertainment to the end of his days.[54]

The notion of "undecideability" is borrowed from Todorov, who uses it to describe a characteristic ambiguity of the fantastic.[55] In general, it is the construction of fantastic narrations that makes it impossible to decide whether an event should be interpreted as natural or supernatural. What is fantastic is not the fantastic things that are going on. In analogy, we do not understand the delusion expressed by an imaginary present tense to be an excess of imagination. In E. T. A. Hoffmann, for example, we saw that the fantastic can accommodate delusion. And even in Gogol, the delusional quality of the events is for a long time wrapped in the cloak of the fantastic. There is undecideability, for example, when narration forms doubles of characters. Another possibility becomes apparent when a narrative focus is exaggerated in a schizophrenic split character.

Yet in order for a narrative undecideability to come about at all, there must be a collaboration of the fictional level as well. Otherwise, the world of delusion does not appear as different from the fiction. Fiction provides deictic motivations for suspicious inversions of space and time to such an extent that the decision about whether or not these are delusional can only be made in narrative retrospect. In Gogol's story, the separation of the two worlds becomes possible only very slowly and through a retroactive judgment. Spatial and temporal de-rangements—the Martober in a Spain that is like China—are made distinguishable at the narrative level by a dynamic of fictional shifting, which means that the reader can judge the character's delusion only retrospectively. Reading the narrative is determined by a slow separation of fictional shift and delusional de-rangement, whose decisive moment, however, cannot be determined narratively. Rather, what the *Diary* demands is a judgment or a decision about which of the two levels, the delusional or the fictional, forms the literary or imaginary basis of the narrative. Whether it is possible to reintegrate this undecideability into a narrative loop depends on whether or not we can still consider it to be fantastic.

(3) Indistinguishability of delusion and fiction

The third form, an indistinguishability of hallucination and fiction, only exists when indistinguishability has arrived on the third personal level, the level of the author. Accordingly, if the attempt to recuperate the imaginary is to succeed, the awakening that saves the day can be made possible only by the author.

Don Quixote may once again serve as an example, even if only in the form of an allegory. This time, Don Quixote is represented by Borges' motif of the delusional Pierre Menard, another author of *Don Quixote*. Menard has created a text that cannot be distinguished from that of Cervantes. Borges' story is an allegory of the third form of indistinguishability, in which an insane author entirely blurs the boundary of fiction and delusion.[56]

With regard to the affinities between the particular forms of delusion and tense, we can note: At least the last two forms, which we analyze as *undecideable* and *indistinguishable* onset and continuation of delusion, have an affinity to the present tense. In terms of its function, the *imaginary present tense* can, for the time being, be defined via the effort to make the functioning delusion literally *experienceable* for the reader. This is attempted by means of narrative undecideability (the event is unidentifiable and therefore rendered inactual) and fictional indistinguishability. This is also what we see in present tense use, at the latest in the second form, the undecideability of delusion and fiction. In this second figure, which we observe with increasing frequency starting in Romanticism, the imaginary is medialized in the narrative and provokes an undecideability of narrative levels. The mad soliloquies in the present tense we encounter over and over in this chapter are an early demotivation of the use of the past tense. Only in the third form, however, does an imaginary become completely *of* the present tense, that is, it no longer stands in need of any estrangement of the past tense. The consistent accomplishment of the *imaginary present tense* creates a hallucinogenic reader perception, in which fiction and the imaginary are indistinguishable and collapse into one another.

Dostoevsky's other doubles

The three shapes of delusion are three ways in which the two-in-one can appear, three ways that indicate—unnoticed, undecidably, or indistinguishably—a co-presence of the imaginary in the text. These three ambiguities relate to the person, narration, and fiction of the texts. This means that it remains ambiguous who is who, what happens, or what is narrated, and finally what the facts are or what was invented:

> Это не Крестьян Иванович! Кто это? Или это он? Он! Это Крестьян Иванович, но только не прежний, это другой Крестьян Иванович! Это ужасный Крестьян Иванович! ...
>
> Крестьян Иванович, я ... я, кажется, ничего, Крестьян Иванович ...

"That's not Krestyan Ivanovitch! Who is it? Or is it he? It is. It is Krestyan Ivanovitch, but not the old Krestyan Ivanovitch, it's another Krestyan Ivanovitch! It's a terrible Krestyan Ivanovitch!"

"Krestyan Ivanovitch, I ... I believe ... I'm all right, Krestyan Ivanovitch."[57]

An imaginary present tense appears wherever there is undecideability and indistinguishability. In the passage quoted, this takes place on the personal level. It slowly crystallizes in the hero's soliloquies, which transition to an inner speech. Aage A. Hansen-Löve has convincingly demonstrated how a literary technique of exchanged speech, which originates in the epistolary novel, transforms into a relationship between narrator and character—with ludicrous results for Golyadkin. While in Dostoevsky's early epistolary novel *Poor Folk*:

> the narrative style of the entire work is divided into two positions, Dostoevsky dislocates this split from now on into the interior of his hero, who, exposed to a certain schizophrenia, can no longer preserve the boundary between delusion and reality. This technique of *"inner speech,"* masterfully developed by Dostoevsky, the thrilling juxtaposition of various styles and judgments in one and the same statement, set a new direction for the future.[58]

The *inner speech* of the text, which in narrated fiction remains hidden as his own speech in the character, in Dostoevsky acquires linguistic materiality. In the story "A Gentle Creature," this materiality is recorded in a "fantastic stenography."[59]

What in narrated fiction indicates or triggers fiction, namely the narrative technique of focus, in Dostoevsky is characterized in its imaginary figure and portrayed as the present of delusion. The trigger of fiction becomes a motif of delusion. This can occur as an exalted inner narrative, such as in "A Gentle Creature," where the narrator turns to the reader in the traditional present tense of the *sujet*. Or it can lead to hallucinatory dialogues with one's own double and soliloquies that are also written in the present tense. In Dostoevsky, however, the voice, which becomes manifest as a dual voice, is associated with the motif of delusion and fixes it as an "inner voice." Only in a present tense that calls for a pure imaginary does the voice turn into an audible resonating body, as in Beckett's *Company*:

> A voice comes to one in the dark. Imagine ... To one on his back in the dark a voice tells of a past. With occasional allusion to a present and more rarely to a future as for example, You will end as you now are ... Apart from the voice and the faint sound of his breath there is no sound.[60]

Let us now look at how Dostoevsky in his *Double* works on or manipulates the deictic space-time shifts of his figure:

> Но согласия господина Голядкина, кажется, никто и не спрашивал. Герой наш почувствовал, что вдруг чья-то рука упала на его руку, что другая рука немного оперлась на спину его, что его с какою-то особенною заботливостью направляют в какую-то сторону. Наконец, он заметил, что идет прямо к дверям. Господин Голядкин хотел было что-то сказать, что-то сделать ... Но нет, он уже ничего не хотел. Он только машинально отсмеивался. Наконец, он почувствовал, что на него надевают шинель, что ему нахлобучили на глаза шляпу; что, наконец, он почувствовал себя в сенях, в темноте и на холоде, наконец и на лестнице. Наконец, он споткнулся, ему казалось, что он падает в бездну; он хотел было вскрикнуть—и вдруг очутился на дворе. Свежий воздух пахнул на него, он на минутку приостановился; в самое это мгновение до него долетели звуки вновь грянувшего оркестра. Господин Голядкин вдруг вспомнил всё; казалось, все опавшие силы его возвратились к нему опять.

> But Mr. Golyadkin's consent no one apparently thought of asking. Our hero was suddenly aware that someone's hand was laid on his arm, that another hand was pressed against this back, that he is guided in a certain direction with peculiar solicitude. At last he notices that he is going straight to the door. Mr. Golyadkin wanted to say something, to do something ... But no, he no longer wanted to do anything. He only mechanically kept laughing in answer. At last he was aware that they were putting on his greatcoat, that his hat was thrust over his eyes; finally he

felt that he was in the entry on the stairs in the dark and cold. At last he stumbled, he felt that he is falling down a precipice; he tried to cry out—and suddenly he found himself in the courtyard. The air blew fresh on him, he stood still for a minute; at that very instant, the strains reached him of the orchestra striking up again. Mr. Golyadkin suddenly recalled it all; it seemed to him that all his flagging energies came back to him again.[61]

But it is not only Golyadkin's flagging energies that are revived, those of the narrator who follows him everywhere are, too. Mixed in, there are a few jumps in time and space (indicated, for instance, by a deictic "suddenly"), into which the narrator has no insight. He turns out to be exposed to the chronotopical blackouts of his protagonist. What we see in these snapshots—the coat, the door, the stairs, the street—is less cinematic prose than a kind of fudging on the part of a narrator who has failed to motivate the elliptic quality of his narrative.[62] The (unachieved) *fabula* is thus defictionalized and claimed to exist independently of the narrative. In the second chapter we presented such tricks in narrated fiction by way of an analysis of the narrative figure of the ellipsis. Understood this way, Dostoevsky's narrator begins to disguise himself. While usually, the instruments of focus place him in his character so firmly that he is the only one who perceives his character's schizophrenic double, in the ellipsis of the passage above he denies his insight and his participation in the destiny of the character he makes up. At the end, the positions of narrator and character are switched. In delusion we can see what Stanzel claims to be true of every narrator: the narrator is a fictive character in his own text. In Dostoevsky the reverse side of this narrated fiction presents itself as a partial aspect of the latent insanity of focus. The narrator cannot invent himself, neither outside nor inside his text: in his text he can only make (himself as) the character disappear.

What up to that point presented itself as internal perspective and external focus, as portrayals of our hero's world of thought by his narrator, now turns out to be internal focus. The fictive world of Dostoevsky's double is that of a madman. This recalibration leads to a renewed shift of the reader-*origo*. In this moment we step out of the character. What thematically concerns the plot level in Cervantes' *Don Quixote* (and thus stabilizes the matrix of narrated fiction), the texts of delusion in the narrated fiction from

E. T. A. Hoffmann to Dostoevsky extend to narration itself. Since they began to apply the technique of focus, the texts have started to obscure the shift character of deixis. In order to situate the reader-*origo* in the protagonist, the deictic shift is presented as an identificatory amalgamation. The narrator seems to retreat in order to open up the fictional world for the amalgamation of the reader-*origo* with the I-*origo* of the character. At the end of the story, however, it often turns out that what was waiting for us in the characters were only the narrator's doubles. The reader is made to experience the squinting latent in any textual focus. Delusion affects the mechanisms of fiction itself, and puts the reader into the unpleasant position of not being able to *decide* about the status of what he has read. The reader thus shares the latently delusional experience of someone hallucinating, namely *not to notice* the hallucination because it *is not distinct* from his perception.

At the end of the stories discussed here, delusion often takes the form of a supremacist nihilism that once again sends the fiction back into the darkness from which it had come. In Dostoevsky's story, this is a black carriage, which the hero gets into at the beginning of the story and in which the story ends. What happens in between becomes a matter of doubt once the madman is exposed and his world has collapsed. Did anything happen at all? The whole cosmos of the novel unfolds from inside a black carriage cube, which will provide the occasion for hallucinogenic metamorphoses of space right through to Peter Weiss's *The Shadow of the Body of the Coachman*.[63] Hallucinogenic texts create metafictional black boxes, blame the entire fiction on the imagination of the reader, and *indistinguishably* always begin where they end.

Tense confusion—Strindberg's indistinguishable present tense of delusion

Only with Strindberg's *Inferno*, written 1894–1897 and published before the turn of the century, do we finally see the first case of a fictional pathography almost entirely written in the present tense. The remaining rudiments of the past tense merely pertain to the narrative arrangement of certain events by the protagonist, who sporadically rears up as a narrative authority. In the attempt to obtain a contrasting order of present and past, he at one point turns to the perfect tense:

> Absolutely alone, I take my mid-day meal in my room, and I eat so little that the waiter pities me. For eight days I have not heard the sound of my own voice, which begins to grow feeble for want of exercise.[64]

Only intermittently a ghastly thin classical narrative framework can be surmised. Even when we encounter a past tense, it is hardly an epic past tense. More likely it is an intermittently narrative past tense that engages in retrospection only in rare moments. It is joined (in rare exceptions) by narrating interventions that expand, subdivide, and explain, albeit not only in taking recourse to the past tense but also to the discussing tenses, the present, the perfect, and even the future tenses:

> I discover in him intelligence above the average, a melancholy temperament, and unbridled sensuality. But behind this mask of a cosmopolitan I begin to divine another character which disquiets me, and the full discovery of which I postpone to a favourable opportunity.[65]

Strindberg ties references forward and references backward into a paranoid narrative that hints at an intrigue or a threat beyond the present of the instant. Before we turn to the structural connection of present tense and fictional pathography, here is another passage that is incisive in its mixing of tenses:

> It is no mere accident, for on certain days the cushion takes the shape of terrible monsters, such as Gothic dragons and serpents; and one night after I have spent a hilarious evening, I am greeted on my return by a mediaeval demon, a devil with a horned head and other appurtenances. I was not at all frightened; it looked so natural, but it also made on my mind the impression of something abnormal and unearthly.[66]

While E. T. A. Hoffmann's fictional author finally awakes after a heavy intoxication—even if he was hung over and holding a fantastic manuscript—Strindberg's absinthe abuse produces a delirium in the style of an autobiography. In terms of tense, we encounter a rarity, a gnomic past tense ("I was not at all frightened") that engages in autobiographical retrospection while at the same time an uncanny present tense remains in charge.

Being exposed to unsettling events implies a narrative double bind. To the extent, one might say, that there is *no* narration, a diabolical plot emerges from the intrigue typical of the *fabula*. The narrator cannot narrate the conspiracy as (hi)story, he does not choose, assess, or judge. Instead, simply everything is significant. The *sujet* does not narrate the *fabula*, it is incessantly haunted by it:

> I am condemned to death! That is my firm conviction. By whom? By the Russians, the Pietists, Catholics, Jesuits, Theosophists? ... At the moment that I write this, I do not know what was the real nature of the events of that July night when death threatened me, but I will not forget that lesson as long as I live.
>
> If the initiated believe that I was then exposed to a plot woven by human hands, let me tell them that I feel anger against no one, for I know now that another stronger hand, unknown to them, guided those hands against their will.
>
> On the other hand, if there was no plot, I must suppose that my own imagination conjured up these chastising spirits for my own punishment. We shall see in the sequel how far this supposition is probable.[67]

This passage recalls the Englishmen and Spaniards from the *Diary of a Madman*. The first-person narrator of the *Inferno*, however, is more adept an autobiographer than Gogol's diary-keeping protagonist, much more skilled in metafictional deceptive maneuvers. The alternative interpretations offered up to the reader in the short term cannot really be considered but are only introduced for them to turn out to be undecideable in the finale of the *Inferno*—"I part from my friend—my executioner—without bitterness. He has only been the scourge in the hand of Providence,"[68] as the last paragraph has it. It is an intrigue that, at the same time, is not an intrigue.

Such a literary device, operating with all permissible and impermissible deceptive maneuvers, shows us how one can pay homage to the power of delusion without being committed to a clinic. In a counter attack, Strindberg's alter ego manages to denounce his doctor, who judges his fiction to be delusion, as a murderer:

> When my friend enters after a minute, it is I who am seized with compassion. He, the surgeon, who is accustomed to witness suffering without emotion, he, the advocate of deliberate murder, is an object of pity indeed. He is pale as death, trembles, stammers, and at the sight of the doctor standing behind me seems on the point of collapse, so that I feel more panic-struck than ever.[69]

All of a sudden, "Strindberg" has a second doctor, whose diagnosis counters that of the cold-blooded murderer. Although the way that the doctor looks over his shoulder might lead us to suspect that he originates in the imagination of someone writing, it is only the mention of the doctor's library and of "Strindberg's" scientific writings that makes it clear that he is an invention. The fact that "Strindberg" again and again swaps the address between his friend the "physician" and his friend the "doctor" shows the two medical professionals to be doubles. Shortly before the entry of August 12, which marks the beginning of a recovery, we read:

> If I take a book at haphazard out of the doctor's library, it always gives the explanation I was looking for. Thus I find in an old chemical treatise the secret of my process for making gold ... An essay on matter which I have written and sent to a French review is immediately published. I show the article to the doctor, who betrays his annoyance, since he cannot deny the fact. Then I say to myself, "How can that man be my friend, who is vexed at my success?"[70]

In terms of spitefulness, "Strindberg's" attack leaves nothing to be desired. He leaves the disavowed, broken-down physician, condemned to remain powerless against the literary fame of his patient, as a healthy man. As this competition between the (literary and medical) readings continues, he even manages to ensnare phenomenological psychoanalysis, namely in the person of Karl Jaspers. Strindberg's delusional maneuvering deceives Jaspers by distracting him from the fictionality of the *Inferno*. In his manifesto of phenomenological psychoanalysis entitled *Strindberg and Van Gogh*, Jaspers unfolds the (narrative) procedurality of madness by showing how disturbances that successively settle in the world of perception fulfill the essential function of making it possible to recognize the processes of madness as such.[71] He pays special attention to a scene in Strindberg's *Inferno* in which the first-person narrator complains to the landlady of his hotel about three pianos that can be heard in the surrounding rooms.

To suspect a disturbance in perception here, as Jaspers does, is certainly not entirely wrong. The overhasty assumption of an autobiographical reference, however, overlooks Strindberg's or, rather, "Strindberg's" fictional calculus. It may be that Jaspers, against the background of classical narrated fiction, took the present tense to be a symptom of a madman and as a factographic present. We, however, understand it as a fictional present tense, in which the protagonist invents the story of the three pianos for his landlady in order to prevent her from delivering a letter he suspects to contain a hotel bill. Destitute, the hero seeks to dodge the economic realities of his existence. Delusion at this point lies less in the disturbance of perception than in the hubris of the calculus of reality[72] with which the first-person narrator computes the probability of the fiction: How many pianos do I have to set up so that no one will read the bill?

What we have here is a metafictional textual play in Iser's sense, that is, the formation of the imaginary in a literary fiction, not the documentary present tense of an autobiography.[73] If what we found when we analyzed E. T. A. Hoffmann's romantic metafiction was a *breaking of the fiction in the present tense*, then in Strindberg it is rather a matter of a *present-tense breaking of the fiction*. In the history of literature, his text comes only slightly before the first interior monologues and *stream of consciousness* prose, which absolve their authors—and the present tense of their texts—from the testimonial function of a medical report. Furthermore, in *Inferno* it is difficult to decide whether the *sujet* is less fictional than are the incredible perceptions that it (allegedly only) records. The maneuvers with which Strindberg tasks his readers integrate him and expose him to the (hidden) hallucinations of the text. Hallucinations are originary images of the power of imagination, and they become fictions as soon as it is possible to share them with others in linguistic communication.

The forms of time of fiction and the imaginary

At this point we would like once again to summarize our procedure in this chapter. Starting from the phenomenon of the interior monologue, we looked for the possibility of a present tense in the history leading up to the inner monologue. In doing so, we came across a "delusional" present tense within past tense narration. The delusional present tense of the nineteenth century is an imaginary (present tense) that is not or only insufficiently integrated into narrated fiction. Once the imaginary is entirely integrated into fiction, this leads to a switch of perspective in how fiction itself is understood, a switch we can trace in Aleida Assmann, Wolfgang Iser, and Dorrit Cohn.

According to Assmann, fiction is no longer to be understood *in* difference to something, for instance to truth or reality, but *as* a difference that always comes into play the moment *something*, truth or reality, becomes contested. In an argument about reality, for instance, fiction is denounced as unreal, in an argument about truth as lie, and finally in an argument about legality as deception.

The critique of fiction maintained all the way up to modernism always unearthed new aspects of fiction. In the end, however, it only ever understood fiction negatively, as deviant. Only in a conception that sees fiction positively as the formation of an imaginary is fiction no longer to be attached along an axis of deviant estrangement. It necessarily includes an analysis of the imaginary. In our view, Dorrit Cohn, too, subscribes to this intuition of Wolfgang Iser's. Cohn does not seek out the difference just mentioned at the boundaries of reality and fiction, but at those of consciousness and unconscious. Correspondingly, her book *The Distinction of Fiction* does not begin with the question of how the difference between reality and fiction can be analyzed at all, but with analyses based on Freud.

The intuition to understand fictions as products of language so similar to those produced by the unconscious that they might be mistaken for them has guided our analysis of unnoticeable, undecideable, and indistinguishable delusion in fiction. Indistinguishable fictions insist on the circularity of the endeavor to task consciousness with making judgments about the status of its byproducts and with judging the difference of delusion and fiction as the difference between reality and fiction. Such byproducts, if we can believe Foucault's *Madness and Civilization*,[74] accumulate only in the process of the constitution of a rational consciousness. In introducing the interior monologue at the beginning of this chapter, we raised the question of the historical meaning of the imaginary present tense.

At that point we could not yet decide whether the imaginary present tense should be viewed as a closed literary form or as a historical phenomenon of decadence at the end of the system of narrated fiction, which might be replaced by the narrative and fictional present tenses that follow (at the latest in altermodernism). The imaginary present tense in the nineteenth century might, however, have paved the way for discovering a much deeper structure (of temporal bipolarity) that is a condition for the success of the altermodern present tense. The latter is able to refute the accusation of embodying a merely tautological emphasis on the present only because it does not refer to the *present* of fiction. In its temporal mode of *non-contemporaneity*, the imaginary becomes a structural moment of the connection of the temporalities of narration and fiction in the twentieth century.

Asynchrony, in which the contemporaneity of fiction and the retrospectivity of narration are embodied, is held together internally by a non-contemporaneous present tense. Viewed in terms of literary history, the asynchronous present tense becomes a moment of historical transition in the shift of the dominant from narration to fiction. Against this non-contemporaneous present tense, in which narrative fiction gives new expression to the character of literature as time-art, the critique of fiction by the avant-gardes ultimately falls short. We observe a negative parallelism: the imaginary present tense—starting from the interior monologue—finds its way to stable narrative and fictional forms, and the metafictional exposures[75] of fictional procedures increasingly turn out to be ineffective. Their effectiveness relied on an implicit agreement with their opponents that only becomes explicit in the evaluation of the interior monologue as a bourgeois phenomenon of decadence or as the destruction of realistic narration.

We already encountered this hidden agreement in the avant-garde's evaluation of the present tense as a factographic tense. A fictional preparation of facts achieved by the epic past tense could only be dismantled through the use of the present tense or through metafiction. This fiction regime loses its effectiveness to the degree that a fictional narration appears, dominated by the imaginary, a narration that does not at all reject the metafictional insights of the avant-garde but instead continues to pursue them ever further. The literary work of the metafictional present tense does not (as narrated fiction and factography imagined) lead back to the realm of facts, but advances into the substratum of the imaginary by narrating fictionally. John M. Coetzee, for instance, who has been very successful in making the present-tense novel a matter of course, projects a metafictional *fabula* in his *Slow Man*. There, an author-character does appear, but by no means to make fiction disappear with a sovereign gesture sending the reader back to the ground of linguistic facts. Instead, the story actualizes the doubling to which an imagining author and a focalized character are subject.

Going through the pathographies of fiction makes an alliance between the classical and the altermodern novel visible. Altermodern simultaneous narration is based on a development and generalization of the simultaneous perspective of focus familiar from narrated fiction, in which simultaneity is interpreted temporally. Conceiving of the imaginary as a temporal mode of non-contemporaneity allows us to recognize in the imaginary present tense a catalyst for the past meaning of the *fictional present tense* in altermodernism.

Starting from the thesis that the question of the imaginary at the same time implies the question of the substance of fiction, we have worked with literary texts that set up their fictions very near the border to the imaginary, again and again risking the collapse of the fictional world in order to follow the impulses of the imaginary. The de-actualizing power of the imaginary cannot be grasped in any understanding of fiction that views fiction in terms of counterfacticity. No ontological border can be drawn between the fictional and the imaginary; both are inactual. By looking at the tenses, however, we can grasp a difference in the status of temporality—the difference between non-contemporaneity (the temporal mode of the imaginary) and contemporaneity (the form of time of fiction). These definitions enable us to answer a question concerning the temporal modality of fiction that has so far remained open. This modality can neither be understood as the "presentification of the past" nor as the "timelessness" described by Hamburger. The analyses of the imaginary present tense in the nineteenth century allow us to specify the time-figuration of presentification as the collaboration of a fiction oriented toward synchrony and a narration oriented toward anteriority under the dominance of narration. The non-contemporaneity of the imaginary is compatible with both and serves as a "catalyst." The non-contemporaneous temporal mode of the imaginary is a precursor of fictional contemporaneity, in which the tendency of fiction to synchronize takes shape.

In the next chapter we will also look at the fundamental function of the imaginary in relation to the altermodern time-figuration of asynchrony. In fictional narration the efforts of fiction to synchronize transform much like the drive to anteriority does in narrated fiction. We will discover an anterior present tense that makes non-contemporaneity the foundation of understanding the past. Narration, which traditionally has made its claim to the past in the gesture of retrospection, in altermodernism finds a pure past with the help of the non-contemporaneity of the imaginary. The expression of such an anterior past, which has never been present and can never be fictionally presentified, is a non-contemporaneous present tense that distances itself from itself.

4
Tense philosophy

An "absolute present tense" has been used to argue in the name of aesthetic theory against any philosophy of art that sees itself exclusively as historical. We agree with Karl Heinz Bohrer in so far as he separates out the present tense from the evocative flow of history. But we also think that, in the translation of history into time, one cannot stop at an idea of the present tense divested of all ties whatsoever. From the standpoint of a poetics of time and to the extent that "time" itself is understood from out of literary language, the present tense can be seen as asynchronous. It is not aesthetic (absolute) or even, to follow Alain Badiou, *unaesthetic* (eternal).[1] For us, Bohrer's polemical demand to examine categories of time "in their semantic-grammatical form" rather than as "a psychic-moralistic ... experience of limits"[2] can only mean to begin with the phenomenon of tense, which constitutes time grammatically, and to examine it both linguistically and philosophically.

In tracing the process of a post-historical translation of "history" into "time" we are also tracing a change in the understanding of history itself. Yet the elimination of the future from theorizations of history in no way amounts to declaring history *in toto* to be literarily obsolete. Quite to the contrary, in the altermodern present tense we see precisely a reinvention of the history novel as time novel. A quick look at historical studies may help to clarify this. After the separation of the philosophy of history from historical studies, historians themselves are less and less able to do anything with the "future," since there are simply no documents from the future. This is also the reason why historical studies have increasingly taken "presents" as the basis of their analyses, which they, of course, understand above all to be synchronous (cf. Ingold's study on the year 1913, Gumbrecht's on the year 1926, and Schlögel's on the year 1937).[3] A rare approach of an asynchronous understanding of history can be found in Jacques Rancière. Yet we do not share his understanding of time, for in assuming a future he tends to fall back into a model of time based on successive movement. In the narrative innovations of the *Annales* historians, for instance, Rancière sees a modification of the conception of history. Historical narration is transformed into scientific historiography by staging the transition from an epic past tense to a descriptive present.[4] Fernand Braudel, in his history of the Mediterranean, makes use of an allegorical (that is, a lyrical) present tense.[5] In doing so, he appeals to a poetics of knowledge in which it could never be decided which word is being used in its actual meaning and which in its figurative meaning. The historian invents his presence at historical events, for instance at the death of a king, in order to distill an allegory of the end of the history of events (*histoire événementielle*). Braudel thereby conveys a knowledge about the illusionary succession of all *fabula*-events, which he deprives of the power to symbolize a historical process. History in the sense of layerings [*Ge-Schichte*], that is, of a sedimentation of presents, belongs to a past future. As a political promise, Rancière locates this insight decades earlier, in Flaubert's involuntarily democratic narrator.[6]

The distinction between the writing of history and literature, too, runs along the limit to the future. Literature's role in this is, not least of all, to produce (historical and political) truth. Looking at Tolstoy's *War and Peace*, Rancière goes beyond the thesis that literature "anticipates, in its fictions, the scientific truth to come." In Tolstoy's novel:

> it is a real battle, along staggered fronts, that its polemics presents us with. Literature, as such, passes itself off as truth talk, and sets its history, woven from the host of obscure gestures made by anonymous people, against the fictions of the powers that be and their translation into historiography.[7]

The critical potential that the literary reflection of history draws from literature as (an art of) time must thus not be lost in overly hasty political pathos but, as an objective possibility of literature, demands a philosophical grounding.

Philosophy of time

Obviously, a chapter on the philosophy of tense provokes the question whether truth, sense, and language are themselves temporal. And reversely, to what degree is our understanding of time marked by language or, more precisely, by the grammar of tense? A meaningful discussion of this question can only take place on a linguistic level. And for us, it ties in with a question of narrative technique that is also the starting point of this chapter: the direction of time. What we will need to conceptualize in the following pages is the novel's poetic knowledge of temporality. What readers of novels know implicitly because they permanently and synchronously create this knowledge in the process of reading is this: retrospective narration creates a prospective course, and reading the retrospective *sujet* creates a prospective *fabula*. When we seek to theoretically catch up with this narratological insight into the functioning of fictional text, our procedure is diametrically opposed to the usual philosophical way of doing things. The classical relation between philosophy and literature, in which the former makes utterances about literature and the latter is only used to provide examples, minimizes opportunities for making literature and philosophy mutually productive. In contrast, we will refer ourselves to the (merely apparent) paradox that the philosophy of time *tells* us something about literary writing and reading and the novel *knows* something about time.

In order to bring both philosophy and literature into a constructive conversation with one another, we need to use a theoretical language that is equally close to both of them. Such language, incomprehensively, seems almost entirely to have disappeared from literary theory in recent years. The centrality of reflections from the field of linguistics for our poetics of the present tense is also apparent in the way we set up this final chapter. We discuss Sebastian Rödl's linguistically informed analytical-philosophical thesis, according to which temporal statements are made possible in the first place by a bipolar predicative unity of tense. Then, we mobilize Gustave Guillaume, who, not by chance, has been associated with the "claims of an avant-garde understanding of linguistics."[8] In Guillaume's multidimensional model of language, in which the individual temporal functions of language are incorporated into a dynamic process, the categories of tense can be projected onto the categories of mode and aspect. This will allow us to return to the question of the direction of time, raised but not settled by philosophers such as McTaggart or Russell. According to Guillaume, language is not only situated in time or internally structured by time. Rather, language forms an image of time in the first place in the sense that a linguistic chronogenesis produces the chronological progression of time naturalized by all of us. Guillaume's work also makes the projection of different times onto one another internally plausible—for instance, that the *present will* be a *past present*. We will also find this inner interweaving, especially of past and present, in Gilles Deleuze, whose theory of language is built in large measure on Guillaume's dynamic linguistics.[9]

In order to answer the question of a poetics of the literary knowledge about time, then, we mobilize philosophies of time inspired by linguistics rather than theories that are inspired by phenomenology or favor a future (Heidegger), present (Husserl), or past (Bergson) experience of time. We are not primarily concerned with the aesthetic-literary experience of time but with the role language plays in constituting the experience of time as such. We would thereby like to avoid the circle described by Paul Ricœur in *Time and Narrative*. Ricœur makes narration the basic condition of our temporal experience; inversely, we have access to the idea of a chronological course of time only through training in reading literary *fabulas*. The very fact that it is possible to create a progressive course of the *fabula* or plot in and while reading, however, cannot in our view only be traced back to a cognitive schema formed by the conditioning of reading that would allow for following the course of a *fabula* (for this would indeed give rise to a circle). First and foremost, what is deployed in reading is a product of the two-dimensional tense system of language itself. The tenses let us know that time advances (in the *fabula*), while we only perceive its passing (in narration). This literariness is carried out in exemplary fashion in the reader's brain, which processes an epic past tense and thereby produces a chronological time-image. A non-chronological image of time can only arise at this same level. It makes use of a different tense and accordingly works on the cognitive schemata in order to establish new (present tense) *fabulas*. The development of an asynchronous present tense requires learning a new way of reading.

The philosophical theories we draw on share some basic traits. For instance, they do not presume any concept of time. Instead of articulating a particular theory of time, they first assume that it is not known what time is, whether it is, and how we get to the ideas we have of it. The philosophies of time discussed here are more devoted to the question of a "language of time." John McTaggart, for instance, starts with the question what we can learn about time from the words language has available for it. Bertrand Russell's considerations of anteriority facilitate an entirely new understanding of continuity. And Sebastian Rödl begins his reflections on the properties of temporal utterances with the category of tense. The analytical philosophies of time we use refrain from assuming a pre-linguistic essence of time. This makes it possible to link them up with our hypothesis that tenses are not to be understood as merely referential. They belong to the grammatical categories of shifters and thus generate a mobile (and in the case of narrative fictions a shifting of) reference. We follow up our discussion of analytical time philosophies (McTaggart, Russell, Rödl) with a linguistic explanation (Guillaume's) of the emergence of chronology to comprehend what these philosophies tell us about literary language. They refer us to a poietic moment, that is, a pro-ductive (in every sense of the word) moment. In conclusion, we will see how three of the paradoxes of the past delineated by Deleuze lend themselves to a systematization of various literary ways of dealing with the knowledge about time that is proper to language.

Time as the apparent impossibility of simultaneity (McTaggart's series of time)

McTaggart's succinct formula for a first understanding of time, which he calls the A series, reads: "an event, which is now present, was future and will be past."[10] He defines as the B series what literary theory will later call "untensed time,"[11] a concept of time in the form of a twofold relation of *earlier—later*. While the A series is always liable to the suspicion that it is a mere illusion,[12] the B series, according to McTaggart, seems to be "more objective, and to be more essential to the nature of time." Yet McTaggart wants to show that it is only in reference to the A series that the B series has a temporal sense at all. Without engaging with the various implications of McTaggart's conception of time, we would like to point out the incompatibility he emphasizes between the three characteristics of time that are "future," "present," and "past." All three can be attributed adjectivally to any event without being able to be attributed to it *simultaneously*. In other words, McTaggart stresses the impossibility of simultaneity:

> Our language has verb-forms for the past, present, and future, but no form that is common to all three. It is never true, the answer will run, that M is present, past and future. It is present, will be past, and has been future. Or it is past, and has been future and present, or again is future and will be present and past. The characteristics are only incompatible when they are simultaneous, and there is no contradiction to this in the fact that each term has all of them successively.[13]

For our purposes here, it is important to point out that neither in the A series nor in the B series is there a clear direction (or two possible directions) to be discerned. Even the relation of *earlier* and *later*, which seems to have an unambiguous chronological order, loses this order as soon as it is referred to the A series. And a third series, the C series, manages merely to create succession without setting a direction. Numerically arranged, the C series is merely an ordered series [*Reihen-Folge*], and "a series which is not temporal has no direction of its own, though it has an order."[14]

From illusionary consecutiveness to factual preceding (Russell)

What directions, then, can time take, or which option is supported by the better argument? Does time arrive from the future? Or does it spring from the past? In discussing this question, it might help to remember an example of Bertrand Russell's with which he seeks to illustrate that temporal succession is incompatible with the assumption that time is continuous: "A cinematograph in which there are an infinite number of pictures, and in which there is never a *next* picture because an infinite number come between any two, will perfectly represent a continuous motion."[15]

There is no fundamental (numerical) order, which (as in McTaggart's discontinuous C series) could be interpreted as temporal consecutiveness—however illusionary, that is, anchored only in subjective consciousness, it may be—and thus acquire a direction. A relation of precedence, in turn, can in fact be articulated. On our reading of Russell, two temporal moments can never be *consecutive* because an infinite number of moments can be inserted between them. A continuous *preceding*, in turn, is possible for exactly the same reason: "[T]he continuity of the motion is shown in the fact that, however near together we take the two positions and the two instants, there are an infinite number of positions still nearer together."[16] A theory of time thus has to think time according to Russell's Law of the Series in a model of time without future. In this model, there is no time that advances from the past to the future. Temporality arises from a continuous passing, that is, as anteriority.

We can now connect the question of time series' direction and their reality-content to the enduring narratological debate about the character, direction, and status of the courses of both *fabula* and *sujet* and then pose the question of their asynchrony. Russell's concept also helps us to elucidate an important theoretical nuance in the transformation, already mentioned several times, of conceptions of narrativity. The comparison with other discursive fields (physics, linguistics, literary theory) sheds new light on the fact that the *sujet*, with its retrospective orientation, can claim a factual status for itself, while the prospective *fabula* appears to be fictional. We therefore read Russell's well-founded doubt concerning the actuality of "consecutiveness as a continuous chronology" in homology with the insights into the fictionality of the course of the *fabula* pioneered in the first decades of the twentieth century.[17] Russell's proof of the factuality of anteriority is a theoretical insight into time that makes parallel theses in literary studies (theses advocated since Russian formalism) more plausible. By means of Guillaume's tense-linguistic theorems (also first formulated in the 1920s and 1930s), we will describe a third level and put it to poetological use. This further step concerns the linguistically manifest arrival of the text, of the *sujet*, from the future of reading as well as its transformation into a chronological, fictional course of the *fabula* that springs from the past. This process is to be understood as essentially carried by the tense system of language.

But first, back to Russell's logic of succession, which makes it possible to understand "events" as processes of supersession. What is superseded in each case becomes something that precedes, and from this process, anteriority continuously arises. This leads us to derive the following alternative minimal formula for narrativity: one thing supersedes another. Such a principle of change differs from a model in which narrative sequence is understood only as successive, as consecutive, and thus only as a movement oriented toward the future. In contrast to such a model of fictional-narrating supersession, a disadvantage of traditional explanations by way of the habitual consecutiveness of narrated fiction stands out: They cannot explain how the progression of narrative structures can ever come to an end without the narrative elements accumulating.[18]

Russell's reflections on succession also provide an important poetological impulse for understanding present-tense asynchrony, which they make a central question. "In all cases where there is a change within what is present in one experience, there will be succession, and therefore absence of simultaneity, between two objects which are both present."[19] What becomes visible here is the possibility of discerning in the present an absence of simultaneity, even if Russell only considers it in terms of its relation to succession.[20] For a long time, it seems difficult to interpret the absence of simultaneity or synchronicity as non-synchronicity. One of his examples nonetheless shows that elaborating a non-synchronicity in the present also makes the differentiation of the present conceivable. From this difference in turn springs a successive order: "Suppose that I see a given object A while I am hearing two successive sounds B and C. Then B is simultaneous with A and A with C, but B is not simultaneous with C."[21] What comes to the fore in this *oxymoron of successive synchrony*, we identified in the first chapter as a neuralgic point of modernist present-tense novels. These have long spent their efforts on redeeming or resolving the aporia of synchrony, the aporia posited in narrative technique or in narratology that it is impossible to experience and narrate at the same time. We can now distinguish between two literary attempts to get this paradox to disappear—a synchronous succession and a successive synchronicity.

We have already presented the first solution, the attempt of the modernist present tense to evade the dialectic of the stop and go, with the help of Peter Weiss' *The Shadow of the Body of the Coachman*. Weiss' narrator attempts to short-circuit synchronicity and succession in order to synchronously narrate the flow of experience. This is considered to be altogether impossible, although from the perspective of Russell's example, separating the senses of sight and hearing makes the synchronous participation in experience (e.g., by listening) and its narration by way of the organs necessary for writing (in the case of writing on paper, the eyes and one hand) possible. Sitting on the toilet, the first-person narrator reports how he hears (but does not see) the servant working and synchronously takes notes. In Russell's description something is heard in succession but seen simultaneously and the oxymoron is defused, as it were, into a tension between two kinds of sense data: the material given to the senses and its temporal index (experience) on the one hand and the material provided by the senses to be recorded (narration) on the other. In this way, the aporia of synchrony temporarily dissipates, only to return[22] in the history of perception as the overtaxing of the senses by synchronous media (of sound and image).[23]

The second possibility can be demonstrated by way of the thought experiment with which Russell makes the oxymoron of *successive synchrony* disappear, namely "by denying that any numerically identical particular ever exists at two different instants: thus instead of the one A, we shall have a series of A's ... one for each instant during which we had thought that A endures."[24]

We may read the ominous black car in *Mrs. Dalloway* as a poetological analogy to this; the car is "handed on" from one passerby to another and has no "autonomous" existence. Similarly, in Woolf's literary experiment *To the Lighthouse*, two novellas are connected by an interval to achieve a chain of "moments of being."

The two different solutions also indicate where to find the line that separates the past-tense time novels of classical modernity (with temporal figures such as Proust's involuntary "time regained" or Musil's "great midday") and the modernist present-tense novel (Beckett's "waiting for time," Hildesheimer's "not here, not now') and why they cannot both be subsumed under the shared category of an "absolute present tense." For only the modernist present-tense novel confronts the paradox of *successive synchrony*, which nonetheless remains unresolved for a long time once the narrative present tense has posed the question. In the context of the modernist aesthetics of time, we thus encounter poetologies of the novel in which one category, either succession or synchrony, takes the foreground to conceal the other element of the contradiction; the paradox is obscured. Either the novel pays homage to a radical devotion to the moment and neglects its own procedural character, or it multiplies successions on the textual level and relegates synchronous moments to the background (as in Proust's excessive use of analepsis and prolepsis). But what is still lacking is the temporal understanding of asynchrony that we are looking for, of a present that detaches and splits from itself, of an asynchrony that can be made out in the present itself and that sets itself apart from numerical or cinematic succession.

In what follows, we would like to continue to think in the direction that begins to show in Russell. It leads us to the altermodern present-tense novel because it starts from the relationship between asynchrony and the present. In order to get there, we need to explain a figure of thought of Russell's, that of an "absence of simultaneity between two objects which are both present."[25]

In his *ABC of Relativity*, Russell spells out why synchronicity can, at most, be described as simultaneity:[26] "There is no difficulty about the simultaneity of two events in the *same* place, such, for example, as seeing a light and hearing a noise."[27] Things are different (to continue with this example) when we ask whether two events taken each by itself, i.e., not judged from the standpoint of a viewer, are synchronous with one another: "How should we naturally decide whether two events in different places were simultaneous?" Russell justifies his negation of what we may call "objective synchronicity" in the terms of the theory of relativity. The invariability of the speed of light means that space and time can be translated one into the other:

> If, for one body, the two events are simultaneous according to the definition, there will be other bodies for which the first precedes the second, and still others for which the second precedes the first. We cannot therefore say unambiguously that two events in distant places are simultaneous.[28]

Two spatially separated events can be present and yet non-synchronous without—and this is the crucial point—necessarily conceiving of the "absence of synchronicity" as succession. We can now apply this thought to Russell's reflections on the continuity of time and the non-reality of temporal succession.

Russell's elegant presentation shows that time—despite two centuries of pathos-laden assaults on the part of an aesthetic regime against a one-dimensional, continuous, and linear-chronological time—can indeed be conceived of as continuous in a highly original way. Time is indeed continual, indeed linear, and has only one direction. Nonetheless, what remains unthematized by Russell is the *process* in which that which precedes supersedes some other precedent. It can now be described as the differentiation of the present into synchronicity and non-synchronicity. It is the intrusion of change into the present, where continuity emerges on the one side and discontinuity on the other. This process is also responsible for the asymmetry that gives time a direction.

"In order for a part of the past to be touched by the present instant," Walter Benjamin writes, "there must be no continuity between them."[29] Past, or more precisely precedence or anteriority, arises only if there is a differentiation of the present, and it arises only thanks to such differentiation. Whenever a further moment enters in between two other moments, a relation of precedence arises. Only when a Y enters in between X and Z does X precede Y. While on the one side a discontinuity between X and Z arises thanks to the intrusion, a continuity between X and Y arises on the other. At the end of this chapter, turning to Edward Branigan and Gilles Deleuze, we will further discuss this idea of a passing of time tied to the differentiation of the present, both in narratological and in philosophical terms.

Bipolarity of temporal utterances (Rödl)

After these philosophical reflections on temporal series, courses, and successions, we now need to reflect on a present that constitutes these sequences by differentiating or superseding itself. To reach the understanding of asynchrony we seek, we need to bring out the details of the present's lack of unity, uniformity, and synchronicity. Over against a monologism of the present or a pointillism of succession, an understanding of the tenses emerges that is able to specify their inner polarity. In recent years, Sebastian

Rödl has presented such a theory of temporal bipolarity, especially in his book *Categories of the Temporal*.

Rödl explains one of the fundamental specificities of temporal statements by means of the difference between the temporal copula on the one hand and the atemporal (= logical) copula, which designates an object falling under a concept, on the other: "[A]n object is what falls under concepts; a concept is under what objects fall."[30] Substance and state, in turn, are connected to each other by a temporal copula, which is not determined by any "falling under." For time neither determines the thing nor the determination under which it falls. It determines the unity of thing and determination as a unity of *S was A* and *S is A*. "What falls under determinations in the present or in the past is a substance, and what determines substances in the present or in the past is a state."[31] In contrast to the "atemporal copula ∈" and its "timeless unity of object and concept," the "predicative unity of the tense is the form of consciousness of temporal position."[32]

In this bipolarity, we can see the essence of a tense structure. Temporal determinations of past and present are incomplete or impossible as long as they do not appeal to their other. This theorem will help us to account for why one must not conclude any *untensed time* (B) from the paradoxical tense usage in literature and also, conversely, for why one cannot assume any *tensed time* (A) even in present-tense novels, which emphatically insist on their unmediated present-character. Rather, all the fictional narrative literature examined here traverses a *double un/tensed time* (prospection and retrospection). Literature thus works on a fundamental tense-theoretical division into two. The unity of all temporal statements is determined "by this contrast: present—past. It is a *bipolar* unity, present and past being its poles."[33] This does not designate a temporality that would belong to each of the elements, it denotes the necessary contrast in the form of temporal utterances. "The form of a temporal thought is in the first instance *S was/is A*, and only someone who thinks such thoughts can refer to times [*Zeitpunkte*]."[34]

This explanation of the temporal polarity of utterances about reality can be placed in a direct relationship to Hamburger's thoughts on the time-form of fictional statements. The meaning *it is*, claimed by Hamburger by means of presentification for the epic past tense of an *it was*, can thus be put into a tense-philosophical context. We are now in a position to better understand what the system of narrated fiction knows. In the novel of narrated fiction, S *was* refers to S *is* (and thus, simply stated, to the presentifying present of the *fabula*). The relation of language to the utterance (*was~is*) highlights the double relation presented above, that is, the reference of language to itself and the shifting that occurs in the process.[35] Furthermore, it brings out that the connection between the two consists in the presentification that takes place in the present of each reading. Insofar as our final object, an asynchronous present tense of the past, is concerned, we can distinguish three different time-poetological forms of knowledge.

(1) *was~is*: As the tense-logic of narrated fiction continues, there are two problems, above all, that come up, an indistinguishability and a breaking point: the latter is the breaking point within the matrix of narrated fiction we analyzed in the first chapter, which is approached in a genuinely new way only by the altermodern *it is*. The inaccessibility of the form of the past—wherever one finds *it was* written down there is no possibility of communicating *it was*—can be explained by way of the characterization given above of the double relation (which is proper to fictional prose). Insofar as language refers to the utterance and the utterance refers at the same time to the world or to the deictic system of reality, it seems as if there were a direct reference of language to the world since the two vectors of reference run parallel. Fiction, then, would fall back into being a simple reference: the reading of a *was=was* that appears would detemporalize the tense such that no temporal utterance would be possible any longer.

The indistinguishability at issue also concerns the pathographies of fiction we analyzed in the previous chapter. In the few cases where the tense-logic of narrated fiction writes *it is*, the *it is* cannot be defined as a temporal copula and generates an undecideable propositional logic: *is* it delusion or fiction? This is exactly what the (not at all marginal) stories of delusion from the nineteenth century draw attention to with their marginalized present tense. The reader is confronted with the fact that, in a kind of short-circuiting, the atemporal and the temporal copula are surreptitiously identified with one other, that their relationship with one another is undecided in the imaginary narration, or even that a (meta-)fiction can push a difference between them to the point of indistinguishability.[36] In those canonical cases, however, in which the narrated fiction, enjoying its "quality of semblance," deliberately overlooks the fictional quality of its present tense, the present tense can serve the epic past tense as a (hyper) fictional, "historical" present tense: its formula reads *(is~was)~is*. This present tense thus also makes its pre-temporal capacity for temporal locating[37] accessible to the epic past tense (as a rhetorically vivified *it was*).

(2) *is~is:* Rödl's definition of temporal utterances allows for a precise formulation of the basic problem of the early present-tense novel. Temporal utterances must be structured such that "what is at a time must be distinct from the time at which it is ... A thought that is articulated into substance and state makes this distinction."[38] The modernist present-tense novel levels this contrast, and it expends all its efforts on precisely this problem. In the switch of tenses to the present tense, the present tense also runs the danger of losing its capacity for temporal location, which it possessed as "historical present tense." It runs the danger of being understood no longer as a temporal copula, but only as a logical one. This is apparent in certain historical positions, for instance in the factographies or, throughout various epochs, in stylizations such as the gnomic present tense. This does not, however, justify the conclusion that the present tense is fundamentally oriented toward *discussing* (as Weinrich has it). What in the first chapter we analyzed as a problem of non-fictionalizing and not-getting-to-narration can also be discussed as a dilemma that arises in the theory of time thanks to the consistent use of the present tense. Released from an implicit *was*, the copula *is* runs the danger of petrifying into an atemporal copula. It may well be that the possibility of such an implosion of temporal bipolarity (and thus of a loss of temporal meaning altogether) was the reason for the centuries-long skepticism about using the present tense as a narrative tense.

In the first chapter, we saw in the fact that the *is~is* of literary prose is difficult to distinguish from a prosaic *is=is* is the reason for the factographic avant-garde's conviction that it was immune to fictionality. Yet the proximity to the atemporal copula is also responsible for the problems the modernist present-tense novel comes up against when it nonetheless attempts to narrate (a present-tense *fabula*). *Is=is*, however, is an unambiguous, non-fictional relation of reference to objects that atemporally fall under concepts. The case of the hypothetical *was~was* is similar, and can barely be distinguished from a *was=was* (a historical-factographic utterance): there is an unambiguous relation of reference. Neither in *is=is* nor in *was=was* does the grammar of time, and thus of tense, become visible. Instead, a mere reference of language to time is asserted.

The cases of the two temporal contrasts of *was~is* and *is~was* are different. They are not to be understood as merely referential but to be counted among the tensed times of grammatical categories, that is, among the shifters. In their double un/tensed time, the figurations of time that are presentification and asynchrony make it possible to experience the grammar of tense (and shift reference).

(3) *is~was*: In this third temporal polarity, we encounter Russell's sense data oxymoron discussed above, which functions as the catalyst for a new understanding of time. The oxymoron of synchronous succession can be explicitly reformulated as a temporal bipolarity and paves the way for a philosophical understanding of the asynchronous concept of the present with which the present-tense novel familiarized us. Running counter to Hamburger's thesis of de-temporalization, the literary usage of the present tense triggers a reflection on the temporal meaning of the present-tense *it is*. It does not limit the tense to uttering or discussing, but creates narrative and fictional structures that are asynchronous-present to uttering or discussing.[39] For the question of a bipolar unity of temporal propositions with which we are concerned, a reformulation by analogy reads: the atemporal copula *is* acquires its temporal sense *is/was*. In relation to Sebastian Rödl's other polarity of *was/is*, one could also think that when the altermodern novel writes *is*, it simply means *was*.

Yet let us go beyond this point at which the temporal copula *was/is* is neither used to address the time of things nor a time of specification, and follow Rödl to the point at which *was/is* designates the (bipolar) unity of things and determination. We then see that an asynchronous *is*, that is, a split *now*, does not lend itself to the production of any unity of state and substance. According to Rödl, the temporal copula designates "a *bipolar* unity, present and past being its poles." Against this philosophical backdrop, it becomes clear that the altermodern present-tense novel actualizes more than one pole (more than its own pole) of the temporal copula. The asynchronous present-tense novel, with its present that splits and detaches from itself, not only "pastifies," as it were, but calls the unity of both poles as such into question. The asynchronous present tense is about a non-organic time, a time that does not come together in any unity with itself.

The formation of time through language: Gustave Guillaume

The philosophical theorems on tense just discussed can now be examined as to how they unfold into a theory of language. What seems particularly helpful to us in this endeavor are Gustave Guillaume's linguistic reflections, first published in the 1920s, which find application in practically all literary languages we work with here.[40] According to Guillaume, grammatical structures (that is, the cooperation of aspect, tense, and mode) do not depict temporal experience. Rather, in practice, every language[41] catalyzes a reformulation, which is itself experienced as a temporal process, of an unspecific perception of time as an understanding of time that is accessible only through language. A time that is somehow experienced as arriving and as abandoning the present in the direction of the past is reformulated by language as a time that springs from the past in order to open or extend itself through the present and into the future. Much like in Russell, who noted that only anteriority is granted factuality and that the everyday chronological understanding of time is illusory, we find in Guillaume the basic assumption that the experience of prospective time is formed by language usage in the first place.[42] The *operative time* of language (of the verb) transforms an original *universal time* into an image of time, and this transformation actualizes a process of chronogenesis.[43]

The language system has developed a cooperation of tense and mode, that is, it has set up a second temporal dimension for the triad of forms of time (future, present, past), understood as a triad of modes (*in posse, in fieri, in esse*). In this two-dimensional time model, mode and tense can be projected onto one another in such a way as to actualize the process of reversal or reformulation just mentioned. In order to make the reflections that follow more accessible, Table 4.1 assembles the superpositions that according to Guillaume establish the experience of time.

Table 4.1

	Past	**Present**	**Future**
in posse	incomplete past	opening	hypothesis
in fieri	frame	opposition	tension
in esse	succession	reversal	prediction

In posse: Guillaume develops this first mode of time mainly from the future tense and ascribes hypotheticalness and openness, that is, incompleteness, to it. Like the other two-dimensional times, *in posse* also exercises its function on all the others. Time, as future alone, cannot yet be experienced in its amorphous quality.

In fieri: Guillaume's explanation of the *présent* shows it to include a countering (a quality obvious in the German *Gegen*wart). This means that the present is the central operator of the linguistic reversal of the course of time. The amorphous time that arrives from the future reverses course in the present. The opposition of this encounter of two courses of time acquires its conclusive shape, as we will see, only in a cut in the *in esse* mode.

According to Guillaume, the present acquires its shape when both other times are introduced into it. The introduction of the incomplete and hypothetical moment of the future puts tension on, extends the present, or opens it up. And as long as *in posse* and *in fieri* cooperate, the present remains an open tension [*Spannung*]. Only the introduction of the past completes the present as extension [*Spanne*]. This provides us with a linguistic explanation of how the present acquires its final outline only thanks to the introduction of a past moment into it. The present only becomes itself by extending toward its other. This must by necessity be formulated as a paradox: the first step of the present always already consists in the fact that the past turns against itself in order to become present. The present becomes a segment of time only thanks to two cuts made by the passing of the past and by the passing of the future. In that they relate to one another as a "completed epoch," both cuts delimit the present. At the same time, the passing of the two other times (future and past) through the present lets the present pass in an open completion.

In esse: The *in esse* is what introduces cuts into time, and the extension of the present results from the passing of a future on the one hand and the completion of a past on the other. The future becomes present the moment it passes as future and "completes" the transition from subjunctive to indicative.

The past is understood as pure distantiation or as the cut of a completion—an action (walk), for example, is completed in the verbal participle (walked), in which the verbal activity comes to its final[44] *esse*. In relation to itself, the (passing of the) past unfolds as pure differentiation or as contrasting from a preceding moment.[45] In this first re-introduction of the past into the past, the past completes its cut as a cross-section of time (*vision sécante de l'image verbale*), which it then presents as a pure withdrawal of the past from itself. Such a past raised to the power of itself, as it were, produces the image of a pure series of cuts. In this sense, it is as if the past is introduced into the two other times twice. First it completes the future and establishes the interface with the present. And then it completes the present as extension, an *époque*. In the unfolding of an incomplete future moment in the past, we thus obtain the verb-image of an incomplete past, that is, of a past that has never been a present,[46] but was infinitely postponed and never became actual.

The temporal paradox of the epic past tense's presentification, too, occupies a symptomatic place in Guillaume's system, namely at the point at which Guillaume has some trouble with the introduction of the present into the past. This difficulty results from his understanding of the present as a pure countering [*Gegeneinander*]. The introduction of this pure *counter* into the past must result in something like the model of a counter-past, that is, of a past that turns against itself. Guillaume cannot avoid this *counter*-conception insofar as it is responsible for the chronological turning point in time with which the tense system is tasked. To avoid such a paradoxical *de-temporalizing* presenting (de-pastification, de-futurizing) [*Gegenwärtigung (Ent-Vergangenheitlichung, Ent-Zukünftigung)*], Guillaume attempts to describe a temporal countering or opposition of two correspondences: (1) a relaxation or de-tension, *in posse*/of the possible, that corresponds to the transition into completion (present into past); and (2) an ex-tension of the possible (*in posse*) that corresponds to the (opening) exit from being (*in esse*). The distinction of these two correspondences must, according to Guillaume, be maintained in all their applications outside the present—or else detemporalization occurs.

Such a de-pastification of the past[47] is nothing more than the principle of presentification we find in fictional texts in the form of the epic past tense. This is therefore also where the tenses of narrated fiction (besides the epic past tense, the historical present) are to be located. The historical present tense, according to Guillaume, opens up the extension into the past: it is a means for creating a more vivid and direct impression of past events.[48]

Narrative chronogenesis and mirror stages of narrated fiction

Following this brief summary of Guillaume's speculations in the linguistics of tense, we would like to exploit their potential for the theory and history of literature as well. According to Guillaume, language forms a complete understanding of time by virtue of its grammatical structures alone. This is not to say that it depicts an experience of time. It is the simple *usage* of language that accomplishes the transformation of an amorphous perception of time into a chronological image of time. Language begins this process of reformulating with a (hypostasized) originary sense-certainty of time that necessarily sees time as arising in the present and flowing into the past. The production of a successive chrono-logic, which structures all of our everyday understandings of time, is only the result of language acquisition and the chrono-genesis linked to it. As announced above, this can be illustrated by the figure we have elaborated with Russell, which combines a factual retrospective course with an illusionary prospective or chronological *fabula*.

The counter-flow of *fabula* and *sujet* is interpreted as a grammatical achievement of language. It situates us on the level of a linguistic ontology for which literary theorists (like Genette and Bohrer) have occasionally aimed but have hardly ever secured with arguments. On this level, the narrative devices of analepsis and prolepsis, which since Lev Vygotsky have often been analyzed as deviations, come to be seen in a new light: as the forms in which the tenses create an image of time. The narratological thesis of the contrary orientations of *fabula* and *sujet* is an interpretation of the grammatical achievements of language. Reading a *fabula* chronologically thus does not mean to impute referentiality but to follow the change in direction of time achieved by the tense system of language. The linguistically induced contrary courses of *fabula* and *sujet* also offer—beyond the traditional argument against the present tense that one cannot simultaneously experience and narrate—a reason for the retrospectivity of narration.

A related narratological question is whether and how literary language further develops this understanding of time. What is decisive here is that the present shows itself to be the site where the chronology of the *fabula* and the retrospection of the *sujet* run counter to one another. In this sense of countering, the present becomes conceivable as critical, as the site of decision. In every narrative moment, two vectors of time extend in the directions of the past (*sujet*) and of the future (*fabula*). However discontinuous a *sujet* may appear to be in a narratological analysis, it cannot be experienced as anything other than continuous or, rather: the *sujet* is either experienced as continuous or it has no *fabula*. There is always a moment inserted into the present of the process of reading. Even if these insertions occur discontinuously, they still produce a continuous preceding in Russell's sense. Or, to formulate it from the perspective of Guillaume's speculative linguistics rather than that of analytical philosophy: it suffices to read the language (of the *sujet*) for the temporal succession to revert, in each moment, into illusionary succession (of the *fabula*). All it takes is alphabetization; no instruction in narrated fiction is necessary.[49] Narrated fiction knows of this genuinely linguistic moment of illusion. Every narrated fiction thus actualizes an event to be found in the grammar of language, and in that it causes the factual anteriority of the *sujet* to revert into the fictional succession of the *fabula*, it makes the event of language as such the possible object of an experience (in the present of reading).

Literary knowledge

The traits that all genuinely literary narrative texts share can also serve as the basis for a distinction between their various kinds of literariness.[50] The following variants of such an implicit knowledge of language can be found in the three forms of the novel that we have examined, narration in the past tense, present-tense narration in modernism, and present-tense narration in altermodernism. Thus the central question becomes: What is the novel's philosophical knowledge of time?

(1) What the epic past tense knows

Narration in the past tense produces a fictional arrangement of *fabula* and *sujet* running counter to one another, which repeats and retrieves the process of appropriating time in the acquisition of language. Something of this phantasm or desire is expressed in Walter Benjamin's memory, cited earlier, of grasping something in early childhood, by means of which his

> hand slid the letters into the groove, where they would be arranged to form words. My hand can still dream of this movement, but it can no longer awaken so as actually to perform it. By the same token, I can dream of the way I once learned to walk. But that doesn't help. I now know how to walk. There is no more learning to walk.[51]

We take the liberty to contradict these beautiful thoughts. For the epic past tense presentifies the act of learning to read each time anew and thus always hits the bull's eye, as it were. The greatness of its fiction has its measure in the celebratory identification of the one reading with the promise of a fictional wholeness in language. In the epic past tense, narrated fiction encounters language, and in this mirror it receives an imaginary unity that constantly restores itself. Narration in the past tense acquires its permanent self-confirmation from this complete fulfillment of a perpetual linguistic function, and it is rewarded by an addiction to reading that has already lasted for centuries. This is the ontological reason for the enduring success of narration in the past tense, which will not come to an end. Narrated fiction in the past tense was and is an autopoietic *perpetuum mobile*.

(2) What the modernist present-tense novel knows

Narration in the present tense sees through the illusionary character of a successive chronology (instituted by the *fabula*), which seems to unfold in a countering present. The early present-tense novel aims at the present's moment of reversal with which every illusionary succession begins. Its modernist phantasm of blasting literariness from out of the production of fiction and illusion always aims for literal language. This literal language introduces a void into the bourgeois illusion of plenary speech and hopes to achieve, with the "end of the novel," a destitution of the ego in the interest of a new, reified, or at least different human being.[52] By means of ever more and new antagonistic counter-languages, the avant-garde's purist concepts for cleaning up language seek to remain in possession of the present.[53] The excitement of avant-garde language is captured in the motto "Language is a revolution." No (hi)story reverses by itself, language alone can cause time to reverse. In the years of the revolutionary avant-garde, the oxymoron of a successive synchrony concurrently articulated by Russell becomes a reality.

Like the avant-garde, the modernist present-tense novel focuses on the decisive moment that overwhelms its protagonists. Just as their authors are stuck in language, in the countering of Guillaume's present, modern protagonists like to hesitate in an eternally vacillating present tense as well. Of the numerous variations of the massive problems modernist protagonists have with making decisions, those of Kafka's "heroes" are particularly telling, not least because they have given rise to a symptomatic theoretical discussion. Already for modernism, the category of "decision," which we want to reclaim in what follows for (altermodern) asynchronous present-tense narration, is central, albeit in a particular interpretation. For Dorrit Cohn, we mentioned, Kafka's modernist present-tense text (*is~is*) is a case of an *eternal present*. The altermodern present-tense author J. M. Coetzee objects to such a reading: "To say ... that 'the crucial events of life happen not once, but everlastingly,' therefore misses the point. There are no 'crucial events' as opposed to other events: there is only what is happening now, and this is always crucial."[54] In the modernist emphasis on the presence, each and every moment is the most important. Modernism's fidelity to the instant involves denying it the possibility of transforming into the prospective *fabula*. In abandoning the chronology of the *fabula*, modern present-tense texts eternalize the moment of decision that Coetzee analyzes in Kafka without making use of the dimension of a reversal (inherent to this moment) for elaborating a new model of fictional narration.

(3) What the altermodern novel knows

The altermodern present tense of anteriority contests the all-importance of the question of whether or not there is a course (of the *sujet*) because it knows how fundamental the *counter*-dimension of the present is for the emergence of the (fabular) past. Time does not come and go; it is always present in language. We cannot acquire language the bourgeois way, nor appropriate it the revolutionary way, nor can we lose it, as conservatives fear. This can be clarified by a look at the time novel of classical modernism. If language cannot be lost, as the epigones (Thomas Mann) of the past tense believe, then it does not have to be regained, as the melancholics (Proust) think, or be secured mythologically (Joyce). What the altermodern novel raises to the status of being the decisive moment of language, in opposition to the modernist present-tense novel (and also to the classical modernist time novel in the past tense), is what we, along with Guillaume, call the *past's cutting into the present*. This present tense of the past is determined by its decisive anteriority.

Poetologically speaking, altermodernism is not so much bothered by modernity's revolutionary (*is/is*) attempts to reverse time. Its implicit narratological objection is that it is not only the chronological succession of the *fabula* that is illusory, which is the reproach directed by the avant-garde at classical narrated fiction. Instead, the point of reversal (*was~is*) is itself illusory because no present effects a turn. The present only ever causes something preceding to (factually) emerge. The altermodern present tense of the past thus has a correlate in a narrative-asynchronous decisionism. Accordingly, the most appropriate counter-image to the loop of narrated fiction, which binds the three times into a knot, is that of forking, introduced by Edward Branigan:

> I believe that one of the valuable tasks of interpretation is the uncovering of these hidden "narrative morphs," of these *nearly true* versions (or drafts) of the plot, which may lead toward—or be the result of—an experience of *déjà vu* or the *uncanny* in watching a fiction. A forking-path plot makes explicit the causal hypothetical, "What if?" In other cases this sort of hypothetical is merely implicit or else suppressed in a text under a more general, "as if."[55]

The making-congruent of *what happened* and *as if* is synonymous with the coming together of narration and fiction in the new figure of the *what if*. Such a *what if* expresses the interlocking of fiction and fact, which we already saw in altermodernism in the first chapter. The stable separation of reality and fictional utterance, for which Hamburger's *as* (brought into play to counter a mimetic *as-if* concept of fiction) seemed to be a sufficient criterion, is invalid in the altermodern present-tense novel.

The altermodern present tense is not a garden of forking paths at the ends of which the present tense tragically encounters its past. He is fifty. He wears a tunic with a collar and gilt embroidered breastplate. He is thirty. And no one ever hears the screaming of the rocket. Nothing about the events is certain, and we narrate them in the present tense. In the "disnarrated narrations"[56] of altermodernism, the present forks and detaches from itself. An interruption is introduced into time but the time frame does not change. It is in this way that a past has an interrupting effect in the present and can nonetheless be narrated in it, along with it, in the present tense. In the present tense of linguistic events, the literalness of the text separates from fiction. In altermodernism, we read what reading always was: we read how *fabula* and *sujet* emerge from the present tense at the same time.

As modernists, we still tried to smash the mirror of language—and language looks back at us in manifold ways. Even shattered glass is reflective. Here we hear a voice turn up in another voice. Only now does the adult world speak to us. There we see the documents and do not understand them. Only when we read them again do we learn to understand them. It is not the phantasm of writing the last of all novels that drives altermodern writing, but learning to read again with every sentence. Always anew. Always now.

Cut.

Asynchronous synthesis (Deleuze)

The present is the only dimension of time that exists. Differentiating itself, it creates past and future, but it is not the reason for the succession of time. "The synthesis of time constitutes the present in time."[57] Although the present creates past and future as dimensions of the present, it falls into time. A present conceived of not in the terms of a metaphysics of presence[58] but arises as asynchronous present when a difference emerges in the repetitions of habit. The habit that is the basis of an (atemporal) present merely repeats; past and present only emerge as a difference. It is this time-instituting synthesis that lets the present pass.

At this point we can see a first paradox of the past (P1): the past is synchronous with the present it has been; it is to be understood as the reason for the passing present. "Time does not escape the present, but the present does not stop moving," Gilles Deleuze writes, for the present "constitute[s] time while passing in the time constituted."[59] This entails the necessity of another synthesis to serve as the basis for time. Hence the shift to the second synthesis, to "memory" as pure past. Memory does not simply reproduce the past in the present but also reflects it. "The active synthesis of memory constitutes it as the *embedding* of presents themselves."[60] We have already encountered this embedding or staggering several times as a possibility of altermodern literature—as a response to the necessity of connecting the past and the asynchronous present.

To understand why the present can pass at all, it is not sufficient to think the past as synchronous with the present. It must also be understood as the synthesis of time as a whole. Deleuze defines this coexistence with all other times or dimensions of time as a second paradox (P2):

> The past does not cause one present to pass without calling forth another, but itself neither passes nor comes forth. For this reason the past, far from being a dimension of time, is the synthesis of all time of which the present and the future are only dimensions.[61]

As we saw in the altermodern present-tense novel, it is not sufficient for a philosophy of time "to say that it was. It no longer exists ... but it insists ... with the former present."[62]

What we discussed in Guillaume's linguistic terms can now be spelled out philosophically. The cuts of the past do not only let the present pass, they also let the future enter into the present. It takes the cut of the past in relation to the future, that is, the passing of the future for a merely extended present to form an *époque*. The third paradox of the past (P3) is thus the *pre-existence of the past*—the first two concern its synchronicity with the present and its coexistence with time as a whole. When the novels of Pynchon or Simon spend their efforts on impossible relations of time, this is not only due to certain motifs (the supersonic rocket, war trauma); it finds its deeper cause in the virtuality of such a pure past. This general past has never been present and could never have been present. As non-present and non-manifest, it is inaccessible to non-fictional narration as well. That is why fiction is not a dimension of narration that could be dispensed with (which would correspond to the theoretical fiction of a non-fictional narration) but its necessary complement. This is the basic thesis we have methodically followed in our fiction-narratological approach. Narration without fiction could not match up to its own intention (of retrospectivity). Narration can live up to its claim to comprehensively develop all the dimensions of the past only with the help of the *form of time that is fiction*. By means of fictionalizing, narration has access to those dimensions of the past that constitute the paradoxes of the past as well.

The poetological aporia of the epic past tense we have so often evoked—that the past closes itself off to the past tense because and in that the past tense presentifies the past—can now be articulated with more precision. On the one hand, classical narrated fiction turns the synchronicity of the past with the present it once was into its poetological agenda, and in precisely this move, on the other hand, it closes the past off to its past tense. This is a paradox concerning the past in itself, its "pre-existence," in Deleuze's terms, as "a substantial temporal element (the Past which was never present) playing the role of ground."[63]

The altermodern novel knows of language's own possibility to grasp a time understood as pure past. A pure past cannot be recognized in a simple past, as we have pointed out in relation to Guillaume, but only in its reflective form of the past's being-past. This is the fundamental *non-presentness of the pure past*. In view of such a non-presentness of the past, the epic past tense (and along with it, the presentification of narrated fiction) reaches the limit of its productivity. The fact that it helps express the paradox of the synchronicity of the past with the present makes no difference. The figuration of time that is presentification thus ultimately disavows the non-presentness of the past instead of highlighting it. A past that has never been present naturally

Table 4.2 Overview of the paradoxes of time in narrated fiction and fictional narration

	Authors	Narrativity	Fictionality	Time aimed for	Paradoxes of the past
narrated fiction	Dickens, Raabe, Goncharov, Zola	present *sujet* narrates past *fabula*	presentification	past present	synchronicity with the present (P1)
classic modernist time novel	Proust, Musil, Joyce, Thomas Mann, Woolf	*sujet* takes time for the past (of the *fabula*)	temporalization	(past) time	co-existence with all time (P2)
modernist present-tense novel	Updike, Hildesheimer, Weiss	present *sujet* narrates present *fabula*	presenting	(present-tense) present	paradox of the passing present[64]
altermodernism	Simon, Pynchon, Vennemann	(present) *sujet* distinguishes itself from present *fabula*	asynchrony/non-contemporaneity	(non-present) past	pre-existence (P3)

eludes the presentifying epic past tense of narrated fiction. Only through the tense innovation of the altermodern present tense (and the time-figuration of asynchrony that emerges with it) can such a past, which it is impossible to presentify, become the object of fictional narration *in its non-presentness*. The altermodern present tense recognizes that (only) language has the power to define the boundaries of the present. It exercises this power by establishing different boundaries and by making it possible to experience the shifting establishment of boundaries as an event immanent to language. The means to accomplish this is a present tense that deviates from itself.

Thanks to the three paradoxes of the past, we are now able to see in the course of literary history we traced in the first chapter two distinct phases of a critical engagement with the poetology of classical narrated fiction. Wherever modernity makes use of the present tense, it breaks away from the attempts (that are bound to fail) of classical narrated fiction to confront the first paradox (P1) and to capture the past as such. In contrast, altermodernism, by spending its efforts on the third paradox (P3), seeks to keep open the demand that narrated fiction wrongly imagined it had already responded to. And thanks to the efforts of narration to live up to its own intention fully to unfold all the dimensions of the past, altermodernism recognizes the systematic necessity for narration to distance itself from the past tense. The development of a narrative present tense of the past is motivated by the possibility that a (hypothetically assumed) non-fictional narration may not live up to its own intentions (of retrospectivity). Only such an altermodern present tense can give expression to the third paradox of a pre-existence of the past (P3). The development toward the altermodern present tense, which in the first chapter we called the "present tense of the past," can therefore also be conceptualized as the emergence of a *present tense of pre-existence*. A present that distances itself from itself gives form to the non-presentness or non-present of such a past.

Before turning to the first phase of engaging with the poetology of classical narrated fiction, we have to reformulate one last premise of the opening chapter. The developments in literary history, the possibility of distinguishing phases and forms that supersede one another, do not, for all that, imply a linear history. After the reconstruction of the paradoxes of the past and of the temporal paradoxes of narration that go along with them, such a continuity has lost its self-evidence. Nonetheless, in terms of a poetics of time, there is a parallel between the figurations of time that are presentification and asynchrony and the forms of time that are narration and fiction we use to describe the way literary developments relate to one another. Our methodological focus has been on how previous points of reference were established and problems of fiction were further developed, what new solutions were offered for narration, and why previous attempts at finding a solution were dismissed. We started from the idea of an asynchrony of positions and developments and from the question of how the various tense-poetologies relate to one another.

Modernism, as the first phase of a delimitation from classical narrated fiction, relates critically to the past tense, while altermodernism, as the second phase of the engagement with the question of how to deal with the past, is characterized by an alternative to the paradox of presentification. Viewed superficially, it might seem as if modernism and altermodernism were taking turns in expending their efforts on demolishing a central pillar of narrated fiction—the past tense in the first case, presentification in the second. Assuming a progress in literary history, it might seem as if both of them were dedicated to a common refutation of the old paradigm. But when we look at how they relate to the possibility of narrating the past, we see a contradiction in their poetological opposition. Both phases are lined up against the past tense of narrated fiction. Yet they move away from the hubris of the system of narrated fiction, and especially from its inherent claim to narrating the past, in opposite directions. Although modernity and altermodernism thus seem to form a common front against the epic past tense (a front marked by the use of the present tense), they contradict one another with regard to the question of whether the past can be narrated or not. Altermodernism claims this to be possible, modernism denies it.

The special position of the modernist present tense apparent in the table above—it does not spend its effort on any paradox of the past—thus has an additional systematic justification. Confronting the second paradox (to mention this only briefly for reasons of completeness since it does not concern the genesis of the present) is the chosen task of the modernist time novel, which emerged, not coincidentally, alongside the first present-tense novels. The reason why it is so difficult to distinguish the time novels of classical modernity from the great novelistic tradition of the nineteenth century is that, logically, the second paradox of the past (P2: the coexistence of the past with time as a whole) can be seen as a generalization of the first paradox (P1: synchronicity of the past with the present).

We are thus dealing with four different poetics of time and, accordingly, with diverging claims: a claim to the past in narrated fiction; an absolute desire for time in classical modernism (still written in the past tense); a longing for the present in the modernist present-tense novel; and an asynchronous present tense of the past in altermodernism. These four poetics of time make it clear that the developments of literary history we analyzed in the first chapter are in no way to be understood in terms of a dialectical sublation. The thesis "the past can be narrated" and the antithesis "the past cannot be narrated" are not simply resolved in a synthesis by the altermodern present tense of the past, in which the historical positions of the past tense of narrated fiction and the present tense of modernist would be "sublated." We are dealing with an antinomy that is proper to fictional narration per se that persists in altermodern narration. The tenses of fictional narration are antinomic because they a priori aim to achieve a unification with their bipolar temporal counterpoints and attempt to make them unequivocal to themselves.

Even if we do not understand antinomy in the strict Kantian sense,[65] we can use Kant's non-dialectical table of judgments, and especially of judgments of quality, to illustrate the irresolvable tension that conditions the possibility of *both* narrated fiction *and* fictional narration. More or less explicitly, the affirmative judgment of the paradigm of the past tense always says (a) "the past can be narrated"; the negative judgment of the modernist avant-garde says (b) "the past cannot be narrated." If "infinite judgments must, in transcendental logic," unlike in traditional logic, "be distinguished from affirmative ones,"[66] this has poetological relevance for the altermodern history novel, for the infinite judgment of the altermodern present-tense novel says (c) "the past is a non-narratable one." The non-presentness of a pure past cannot simply be narrated in a different way but only as *non-narratability*. This should in no way be misunderstood as an empty gesture of repetitive deconstructions. An infinite judgment is defined by an affirmative form, but an affirmative form that contains a negative predicate. As Kant specified in his *Logic*:

> the infinite judgment indicates not merely that a subject is not contained under the sphere of the predicate, but that it lies somewhere in the infinite sphere outside its sphere; consequently this judgment represents the sphere of the predicate as restricted ... In negative judgments the negation always affects the copula; in infinite ones it is not the copula but rather the predicate that is affected.[67]

In the case at hand, this predicate is the understanding of the past itself. Accordingly, the present-tense novel brings to light a concealed temporality of the copula. The utterances *the past was not* or *the past is not present* take on the following new forms: *the past is (and was not)* or *the past is/was non-present*. The judgment about the past in the altermodern novel is infinite because it transfers the bipolarity of temporal utterances discussed above into one another. The fact that in the sentence, *the past is and can be not-narrated*, both the subject and the copula can be temporalized by a paradoxical narration is based on altermodernism's poetological knowledge. The past itself affects and cuts through the present *is*:

Am Abend legte

Ich mich hin und

denke, am Morgen

stehe ich auf und sinne.

In the evening

I laid down and

think, in the morning

I wake up and ponder.[68]

The three judgments of narrated fiction correspond to the actualizations of the fundamental polarity of tense in narrated fiction already touched on: (a) a "naïve" fictional presentification in the case of *was/is*; (b) the modern present tense *is/is* as tautological and skeptical of fiction; (c) the asynchronous present-tense novel with the peculiar fictional form of time of an *is/was*.

Even if it is only in and with altermodernism that Deleuze's three paradoxes of time are taken up and worked through, the antinomy we outlined is inscribed in all narrated fictions. The fiction-narratological necessity of this antinomy of tense is seen in all the combinations we discussed of the two poles *was* and *is*. All three literary forms more or less implicitly combine affirmative and negative elements. In (a) classical narrated fiction, presentification detemporalizes and negates the past tense's ostentatious claim to the past. In (b) modernity, the claim of narration relates to time as to a synthesis of all its dimensions. This is understood, for instance in Virginia Woolf's "Time Passes,"[69] as an absolute present tense or a passing, not simply of the present, but of time as a whole. What obtains in (c) altermodern asynchrony is: narration passes.

The asynchronous present tense points to the pre-existence paradox of the past, that it never is (never has been) present: the past is-past non-present. Nonetheless, we do not want to conclude with an apology of the contemporary novel, since the paradox of the present consists in calling for the very time it lets pass. Neither past nor narration return. Narration is—past.

Conclusion

The present tense in the twentieth-century novel constituted the starting point of our study because the methods of narratology and fiction theory make it possible to discuss the genre of the novel in all its aspects. The novel lies entirely within the field illuminated by both methods. This allowed us to take stock of a double shift of dominants.

In the history of the novel, there is a shift of dominants from the past tense to the present tense. This goes unnoticed at first, because the earliest present-tense texts present themselves as, for example, factographic anti-novels, and because the present-tense novels that follow present themselves as anti-fictional or anti-narrative. Given the way the problem is posed in the two methods applied here, narratology and fiction theory, the asynchrony we describe could not simply be found in the present-tense texts. Only after completing the second shift of dominants—from a predominance of the narrative pole to a predominance of the fictional pole—is (the present tense of) asynchrony openly visible.

Just as asynchrony can only be understood as a counter-model to the presentification operated by narrated fiction, a poetics of the present tense also cannot do without taking recourse to literature written primarily in the past tense. It does so not only to give a precise description of the renunciation of the past tense and the emergence of the present tense as narrative tense. Rather, the analyses of a poetics of time assume a fundamental bipolarity at all levels that "only" gives rise to different dominants. (At the phenomenal level of the novel, it is rare to find the past tense *or* the present tense exclusively, and asynchrony proves to be a figuration of time that complements presentification.) The primacy of the narrative or of the fictional aspect can then also be seen in the historical phenomenon, the present-tense novel. In parallel to the shift of dominants from past tense to present tense, then, we observed a historical shift from a dominance of narration in the novels of the nineteenth century to a dominance of fiction in the altermodern present-tense novels of the late twentieth century.

As long as the present tense is viewed only in the context of the present-tense novel, there seems to be merely a break with the nineteenth-century matrix of narrated fiction. Long before the clear present-tense forms of the (alter)modernist novel, however, our material indicates a present tense of unclear provenance that is mixed in syncretically with the epic past tense and is not used systematically until around 1900. We dedicated the third chapter to this *imaginary present tense* not simply because we wanted to get to the bottom of the prehistory of the fictional and narrative present tense or because we wanted to tell the passion story of the move away from the past tense, a move that comes at the price of various pathologies. Instead, this self-fictionalizing present tense made it clear how much fiction and narration depend on one another. An imagination that does not take the form of narrated fiction destroys itself. Narration and fiction prove to be complementary in the sense that in order to live up to their respective claims, they each have to rely on the other. The avowed claim of narration, retrospectivity, is not made good on simply by looking back and employing the past tense—only the present tense of the past of the present-tense novel is in a position to do so.

A poetics that understands its object to be temporal cannot conceive of it as atemporal. Time does not simply define things or set the expiration date for concepts. It raises the question of how objects are subsumed under concepts. Temporality relates to transformations and changes in conditions. Temporal correlations describe how, on the one hand, the unity of a substance is perceived under conditions subject to change, while on the other hand substantial transformation, that is, the present-ation of something *new*, is possible only within temporal correlations.

Temporal unity has the form *was/is* or *is/was*. Such a *temporal bipolarity* (Rödl) can be found not only in the figuration of time that is presentification, but also in the figuration of time that is asynchrony. Asynchrony has a *bitemporal* form of the same kind as presentification. This makes the differences between the approaches of literary history, historical (genre) poetics, and the poetics of time palpable once more.

(1) From the perspective of the history of literature, (present-tense) novels naturally emerge in their respective present, and

only from this perspective can claims about their chronological sequence be made.¹ And in a strict sense, it is possible to speak of a rejection of classical narrated fiction (in which fiction is created by means of the epic past tense) starting with the avant-gardes only from a literary *historical* perspective.² The avant-garde practically confirms the *systematic* boundary drawn by the classical matrix of narrated fiction between an artistic use of the past tense and an everyday use of the present tense (a boundary that at the same time represents a barrier to knowledge).

(2) (Genre) poetological discussions (for example, Georg Lukács's siding with narration against description) can also not simply be made congruent with the poetology of the works themselves (e.g., anti-narrativity), especially where establishing the present tense as the dominant narrative tense of the twentieth century is concerned. Already from the perspective of historical poetics, the novel that emerges or is "reinvented" after the "end of the novel" cannot unambiguously be located within a history of literary development.

(3) From the point of view of a poetics of time, we see that the altermodern novel's fictional narration is synchronous with classical narrated fiction and need not be understood either as a regression within the history of literature or as an avant-gardism in the poetics of genre. Calling contemporary present-tense novels *altermodern* novels, too, takes this asynchrony into account. In asynchrony, the methodological strands of system transformation and literary history coincide. The altermodern novel projects an asynchronous narrated fiction onto the basis of a present tense split in itself. In the literary agenda of altermodernism, there is a moment of anteriority, which does not, however, imply a conservative gesture: to say that time passes does not mean that we must hold on to it.

The altermodern novel produces asynchronicity not only in texts, but also in the way it positions itself in literary history—one might call this the existentialization of its method. In its asynchronous relation to events in literature, the agenda of altermodern narration can no more be understood to be *post*modern than it could be said to be *pre*modern. The insight into asynchrony—the insight that every present moment is synchronous with a moment that precedes it—leads the altermodern novel to locate writing prior to the present.

The asynchronous poetics of the present tense, which the altermodern novel differentiates in the strata of literary history, historical poetics, and time-poetics, has guided our investigation methodologically. Starting with this poetics, we have examined the capacity of the present tense to produce fiction and narration and shown how such a poietic present tense also opens up a new approach to language and to reading.

GLOSSARY

Altermodernism *Nonlinear continuation of modernism*: First used by Nicolas Bourriaud in an art-theoretical context, it initially named a re-translation of the cultural values of modernism to respond to the questions and problems of the twenty-first century. We use the term to designate a shift in the original intentions of the modern present-tense novel. The altermodern present tense critically engages with modernism and suggests an alternative to the obsession with the present in the modern present tense (asynchrony). In inventing a new understanding of the past (anteriority), the altermodern present-tense novel picks up—from the viewpoint of a poetics of time, not that of literary history—from classical narration.

Anteriority *Preceding*: By anteriority we understand the moment of a pure past (or pastness) that cannot be thought as a former present. Prior to any former present, there is always a preceding past. This anteriority gives rise to the image of a constant non-present preceding in which no direction of time has been fixed yet.

Anteriority is not a dimension that belongs to the past alone. According to the multidimensional models of time elaborated by Gustave Guillaume and Gilles Deleuze, present and future also exhibit anterior dimensions. This is the sense in which Reinhard Koselleck speaks of a "past future" and in which we discuss the figure of time of an asynchronous present.

Aporia of synchrony *Impossibility of synchronously experiencing and narrating*: In narratology, the impossibility of such a synchrony is traditionally seen to apply in the relationship between experience and narration. In our view, this methodologically conditioned restriction is the reason for the naturalization of retrospection as the only possible form of time of narration. The embedding of narration into medial conditions other than the conditions of orality, however, has increasingly revealed that retrospectivity is a medial consequence of orality and not a necessary form of narration.

As long as narratology maintains a formal demand for a retrospectivity of narration, the modern present tense, too, counts as anti-narrative. The altermodern present tense abandons the effort to synchronize experience and narration (which is quite possible in radio, television, or video) and at the same time recognizes the abstract nature of the narrative form of time. What previously counted as aporia of simultaneous narration is reinterpreted as asynchrony.

Asynchrony *Temporal difference within synchrony*: In an asynchronous, non-simultaneous present, there is a preceding moment synchronous to every present moment. The preceding moment (anteriority) differentiates any presence allegedly present to itself (any present present to itself). Since this moment always remains non-present, it is introduced into the present itself as a split.

Asynchrony is the figuration of time of the altermodern present-tense novel. It unites the contemporaneity of fiction with the retrospectivity of narration under the dominance of fiction. The asynchronous present tense brings to light an anterior moment in the present of fiction and a non-contemporaneous moment in narrative retrospection. Furthermore, the figuration of time that is asynchrony provides an answer to the question of the possibility of narrating the past: narration is—past.

Contemporaneity *Present*: Contemporaneity is the (hypothetically) pure form of time of fiction. Literary fiction only occurs in association with narration. The form of time that is contemporaneity is therefore encountered in our study only in synthesis with the form of time of narration, that is, with retrospectivity (which we isolate hypothetically as well). This synthesis we call figuration of time and have found it to occur in two variants: presentification (in narrated fiction) and asynchrony (in fictional narration).

The contemporaneity of fiction draws on mechanisms of linguistic deixis, which, starting from a speaker's *origo* (I–here–now), embeds statements in spatial and—even more importantly—temporal contexts. The form of time of fiction emerges from a strategic deployment of tense and deixis that results in a shift of the *origo* such that another *I*, another *here*, or another *now* can become contemporaneous.

Deictic shift *Shifting the field of indication*: Classical theories of deixis have drawn attention to a kind of linguistic indication that constitutes a system of reality from a *here–now origo*. In contrast, *deictic shift theories* analyze shifts of space, time, and person that can start with any one of the parameters. Concentrating on the shifting of individual parameters and the dynamic of their combination allows for a comprehensive description of the linguistic operations of fiction within narration.

Deixis *Linguistic indication*: Deixis is the practice of everyday linguistic indication, in which any reference depends on the coordinates of space, time, and person. In the classical theory of deixis, the three parameters form an *I–here–now origo* and thereby constitute a system of reality.

Reference generally can only be determined depending on the original coordinates of such a system of reality. Only by resorting to my *I–here–now origo* can I establish when "yesterday" is, where "there" is, and who "she" is. Fiction emerges when the spatial or temporal deictics are artistically forged in such a way that a deictic shift and a shift of references occur.

Dominant(s), shift of   The concept *dominant* originates in the poetics of Russian formalism. It designates axiomatic asymmetry in bipolar relations and is used to describe the dynamics of artworks. From the point of view of formalism, artworks are not static objects but events of contradiction. The literary text thus understood retains its aesthetic value so long as new dominants manage to emerge in the struggle of contradictions within the work and as long as new relations of contrast can be discerned thanks to which the relations within the work can be deformed.

We transfer the concept from the framework of analyses of individual works to questions of literary history and historical poetics. To understand literary artworks as products of language in which the poetic function is dominant also implies that the historical shift of dominants can entail entire genres falling out of or being newly included in the concept of literature.

In the twentieth century, we observe a shift of dominants from narrated fiction to fictional narration.

Fabula*, pl. *fabulas   Story, *histoire*, *Geschichte*: The terms *fabula* and *sujet* originate in Russian formalism and designate a fundamental relation that is created by all narrative texts. The dualism of two levels can be seen in the relation between fiction and narration, of (hi)story (*histoire*, *Geschichte*, plot) and its rhetorical shape, or of a text's reference and its literary materiality.

The *fabula* is determined by the dynamics of (hi)story, fiction, and reference. It is the object of narrative texts that is always ahead of the reader and that the reader is (always) trying to track down. The *fabula* of narrative texts is aimed at reference, at a dynamic space into which the action unfolds, and at persons whose subjectivity is formed in their story, as well as at a time that opens up to them.

Fiction   Fiction does not create a second world, but instead shifts our relation to this world. A shift of references is always tied to a medium (or a conglomerate of media) and its cognitive internalization.

This can be clarified by theories of deixis that conceptualize the dependence of the formation of meaning in language on the spatial and temporal position of the speaker, on an *I–here–now*. Fiction shifts these temporal horizons, spatial dimensions, and relations of the *I* to (the) other(s) on which the reference of linguistic expressions depends. In the deictic shifting of the *I origo* (in particular, the shift toward its alter ego), fiction achieves the medialization of an imaginary.

Fiction, counterfactual Concepts of fiction based on the idea that fiction is counterfactual are characterized by a particular ambiguity. To the extent that fiction is understood in opposition to actuality, it becomes unavoidable for fiction and actuality constantly to switch positions. With reference to Russian post-revolutionary utopian novels, Yuri Striedter was the first to remark that actuality appears to be more fictional than the double (utopian) fiction of the novel. Faced with the artificiality of modern actuality, Odo Marquardt sees the task of aesthetic thought precisely to be a kind of anti-fictionality. And Aleida Assmann thinks the collapse of the opposition of actuality and fiction, even to the point at which the question must arise whether the difference (between reality and fiction) is not itself fictive.

Fiction-narratology The methodological necessity of systematically combining the approaches of narratology and fiction theory in a fiction-narratology results from the material and formal syncretism of narration and fiction. Although narration and fiction can be heuristically separated and, in the history of literature, enter into different relations of dominance, examining literary prose exclusively from the perspective of fiction theory or exclusively from the perspective of narratology leads to blind spots. Such a blind spot, for instance, emerges in overlooking that the determination of the temporality of narration depends on defining, first, a form of time of fiction, and, second, its cooperation with narration. Only a bipolar, fiction-narratological approach can trace how the present tense restructures the temporal relations of narrated fiction into those of a fictional narration and thereby achieves a reinvention of the novel.

Fictional narration Narration and fiction always appear in combination, albeit in changing relations of dominance (shift of dominant). In nineteenth-century narrated fiction, narration (*sujet*) presentifies a fictive *fabula*. In the historical development that leads from the epic past tense to the present tense, the dominants of the relation between narration and fiction also shift. In altermodern fictional narration, an imaginary dynamics of writing feigns the invention of *fabulas* as well as processes of narration and employs the present tense for this purpose. Not least of all, this also involves a shift from the figuration of time that is presentification, characteristic of narrated fiction, to the altermodern figuration of time that is asynchrony.

Figuration of time We call figuration of time the composition of the two forms of time of narration (retrospection) and of fiction (contemporaneity), which may be linked in inverse relations of dominance: either (as in the classic novel) as presentification, in which a past event is made contemporaneous in narration with the aid of fiction; or (as in the altermodern present-tense novel) as asynchrony, in which a fictive narrative situation is created from out of contemporaneity, a situation that makes the constant emergence of pastness in the present legible.

Focalization *Orientation according to a point of view*: Focalization first originates as a narratological category in attempts to separate the question "Who is speaking?" (voice) from the question "Who is seeing?" (focalization). A delineation from older theories—in narrative theory (Stanzel) and the poetics of composition (Uspensky)—furthermore introduces a distinction between perspective and focalization that expresses a difference between seeing and knowing. Both sets of questions react to a two-in-one that is typical of the relation between narrator and character in classical narrated fiction. Moreover, the question of the point of view locates the narrator, who is necessarily located in his character, on different levels.

Focus Focus resembles a concentration in the character of the narrator's perspective. This also makes the character the starting point of the spatial and the temporal perspective. Focus extends the concept of focalization with spatio-temporal aspects. As a form of personal focalization, it refers to the deixis of space and time. The spatial focus thus approximates classical focalization. The temporal focus (aspect), which is more essential to the question of the narrative tense present tense, has not yet been examined in this context. We see in focus a trigger of deictic shifts and thus a trigger of fiction. We therefore extend the two-in-one of narrator and character, which is typical of focalization, by a third figure. By including the perspective of the reader, we view focus as the phenomenon of a third eye, which distinguishes it from the squinting that is characteristic of focalization.

Form(s) of time The opposition of the two forms of time, retrospection and contemporaneity, governs the novel. Narration, with its tendency toward retrospectivity, and fiction, with its manifestation in the contemporaneous, form mutually exclusive, integrating, and encompassing figurations of time.

(The) imaginary The imaginary is the substance of fiction, that which, as Wolfgang Iser writes, is most likely to come into a pure present in delusion. Under the dominance of narration in the nineteenth century, the imaginary does not attain to the stable form of a fiction and only appears in three precarious forms situated between delusion and fiction. It appears, first, when the difference between delusion and fiction (of the protagonist) remains undetected (by the protagonist); second, when the difference is undecidable (for the reader); and third, when delusion and fiction are indistinguishable (for the author as well). In the framework of the shift of dominants within the novel from narration to fiction, the development of a textual imaginary in the twentieth century is central.

Material The material is the first methodological level of analysis (prior to phenomenon and object). In Russian formalism, "material" designates, first, matter that lies before constructive or analytical treatment; second, the (material) level within a construction that to a certain degree resists analysis or treatment; and third and finally, a sensitivity that materializes by means of the construction. The material of this book is the present tense: as a linguistic tense it is located prior to poetic treatment. As a literary tense it resists the poetics of the novel for a long time. In the altermodern novel, the present tense makes the object of our investigation, the figuration of time that is asynchrony, accessible to perception in reading.

Metafiction *A reflection whose object is fiction*: To the extent that we no longer understand fiction as medial illusion, reflection on fiction can no longer be understood in exclusively negative terms as unmasking or a breaking with illusion (illusions of immediate reference or immediate experience). The metafiction of altermodernism instead reflects fiction in a way that allows it to break through to the imaginary as the substance of fiction. Seen in this way, Romantic parekbases or the self-reflexivity or self-indication of fiction typical of modernity are not metafiction. Moreover, they in no way revoke processes of fictionalization, since they only pertain to marginal conditions, not to the processes of fiction (deictic shift, medialization of an imaginary) themselves.

Narrated fiction Narration and fiction do not appear in isolation from one another but enter into changing relations of dominance. In classical narrated fiction, narration dominates over fiction; an (implicitly) factual *sujet* narrates the fictive *fabula* and to this end employs primarily the past tense. The switch of tense from past tense to present tense is the expression of a shift of dominants from narrated fiction to fictional narration that takes place over the course of the twentieth century.

Narration *Storytelling*: Instead of just the minimum requirements of narrativity, according to which it requires a sequential interlinking, we demand not just that narration provide a succession of events but that in narration, events supersede one another. In view of the form of time of narration, a "course of events" can be understood as a process of supersession, in which what is superseded in each case becomes an antecedent and anteriority continuously emerges. This is the foundation of retrospection as the temporal relation of narrative and narration.

Narration only appears in combination with fiction (hence the synthetic methodology of a fiction-narratology), even if the two are never in balance and one always dominates the other. Nineteenth-century narrated fiction stands over against twentieth-century fictional narration.

Non-contemporaneity   *Non-presentness*: Non-contemporaneity is the specific temporal mode of the imaginary. In the asynchronous present tense of altermodernism, in which both the contemporaneity of fiction and the retrospectivity of narration become manifest, fiction and narration are joined by means of a non-contemporaneous imaginary present tense. The non-contemporaneity of the imaginary can be seen as a motor of the reference to pastness assumed by the altermodern narrative tense (present tense). Non-contemporaneity performs a similarly foundational function in altermodern narration.

Object   The object is the third methodological level of analysis (alongside material and phenomena). The level of the object is a level of investigation determined completely by our method of a fiction-narratology. The concrete object of this book is asynchrony as the figuration of time of the altermodern present tense. It results from the forms of time of narration (retrospection) and of fiction (contemporaneity) and is produced by the present tense under the dominance of fiction. Presentification in nineteenth-century narrated fiction represents an equivalent figuration of time, into which the forms of time just named are conjoined by means of the epic past tense under the dominance of narration.

Phenomenon   The phenomenon is the second methodological level of analysis between the material, which is least predetermined by the method, and the object, which is completely determined by it.

The phenomenon examined in this volume is the present tense novel. It belongs to a historical poetics of the genre that is the novel. It does not emerge in the slow appropriation by the genre of a new tense. Instead, it emerges from the gradual overcoming of the contradictions between material (present tense) and the figuration of time of the classical novel (presentification) thanks to the inventions of form in twentieth-century experimental poetics. Our object, the figuration of time that is asynchrony, is constituted only in the course of this process.

Poetics of time   The poetics of time is a method in literary studies for reflecting on the character of literature as an art of time. We understand the introduction of a poetics of time to be not only a contrast to the questions that concern historical poetics on the one hand and to the goals of literary history on the other. We also see it as a reflection of the consequences that follow for both from literature's character as an art of time. While literary history merely locates works within a chronology, historical poetics anchors them in two ways—in a history of events and in a history of structure. Literary artworks are as much singular events as they are agents of a history of the genre that goes beyond individual works. In contradistinction, a poetics of time insists that literature cannot be fully accounted for by a chronological history of literature or by the history of a genre's development. It examines the potential of literary language to institute time. From the perspective of the poetics of time, for example, the altermodern novel of the past can pick up on traditional narration without falling back behind the achievements of the modern present tense.

Presentification Presentification is the figuration of time of the epic past tense in classical narrated fiction. According to Käte Hamburger, the combination of past tense verb and future adverb (in the famous example she uses, "tomorrow was Christmas") is an unmistakable indication of the fiction of personal narration. What is narrated in the past tense is fictionally present-ified by the reader. In presentification, what is past is present. It is not least because of this actualizing effect of the epic past tense that the past never appears as such, even though that is the implicit program of traditional narration.

As the novel's global figuration of time, presentification is also tied into a context of narrative functions, in which it takes the form of a loop: The narrating reconstruction runs ahead of the unpredictably future moments of a prospective course of events in order to then presentify them retroactively.

Furthermore, the figuration of time of narrated fiction has implications for the philosophy of time and tense. In the philosophy of time, presentification implies the synchrony of a past with the present it once was. For the bipolarity of tense in the philosophy of tense, this means that in presentification, the temporal pole of the past is absorbed into that of the present.

Retrospection *Looking back*: Retrospection is considered to be the prototypical relation of narration to what it narrates. No matter how the two levels of narration and narrative are labeled (we prefer *sujet* and *fabula*), the temporal relations between them are traditionally always determined as retrospection: the present *sujet* narrates the past *fabula*. The alleged reason is the impossibility of experiencing and narrating at the same time. In overcoming this aporia of synchrony, retrospection is recognized as an abstract form of time of narration that is not solely derived from the empirical conditions of oral narration but at the same time arises from a need for a connection with the past. The literary arts of time take account of this need. In elaborating anteriority as the form of time of altermodern narration, the asynchronous present tense succeeds in a refoundation of narrative retrospection.

Simultaneous narration *Synchronous narration*: The term designates a narration in the present tense in which the narration seems to be synchronous with the narrative (that which is narrated), that is, the *sujet* seems to be synchronous with the *fabula*. In altermodern present-tense narration, in contrast, the *sujet* detaches from the (implicitly factual) spatio-temporal conditions of narration and fictionalizes itself. As a result, the *fabula* comes into view again, and the figure of an asynchrony of *fabula* and *sujet* is created.

Sujet Narration, plot, discourse: The terms *fabula* and *sujet* are fundamental categories that name two levels that differentiate in all narrative texts, for instance as a dualism of the story and its rhetorical shape or as dualism of a text's reference and its linguistic materiality. The *sujet* is the constitutive act of the literary text (operated by either a producer or a recipient) and of all its games of hide-and-seek; it is the place of literary and rhetorical technique; it is the archive of the artistic canon of forms; it is the voice of narration, the scene of writing. While the *sujet* could also be replaced in all these aspects by the synonyms named above, we prefer the formalist term for three reasons. First, it contains a relation to time that is essential to our endeavor but disappears in later terminology. Second, the terms *fabula* and *sujet* do not specify any determinate relation between them (the *fabula* does not arise from the *sujet* the way that narrative arises from narration). Third, both these levels of the narrative text can equally be understood as objects of fiction (which is not the case, for instance, for the concept *discourse*).

Temporal mode By temporal mode we understand a layer of time that is not completely formed, a pre-form of temporality. Non-contemporaneity as the temporal mode of the imaginary is the basis both of the form of time of fiction (i.e., contemporaneity) and of the form of time of narration (i.e., retrospectivity).

Temporal poles Temporal statements join two poles of time (*was/is*) into a predicative unity that does not correspond to the form in which the objects fall under concepts. Rather, a statement in the form of S *was/is* A conceives of various states as the temporal unity of a substance for which the difference of these states is as characteristic as is this unity. *A fruit is/was a blossom* means: Fruit and blossom are not conceived of as different objects that fall under different concepts but are precisely to be thought as a unity of two poles of time.

The temporal knowledge of individual poetologies of the novel can be determined by the way in which they clothe the figuration of time of the novel in the form of temporal statements: the *was/is* of narrated fiction (in the figuration of time that is presentification) and the *is/was* of the asynchronous past novel.

Tense A poetics of the present tense examines the tense at the interface of a linguistic grammar and a philosophical grammar. Linguistic tenses do not depict time. In cooperation with aspect and mode, they form that linguistic image of time that we take on as our everyday, chronological understanding of time with the acquisition of language. Grammatical time has those three dimensions and must deploy all three to generate a linear course of time.

Tenses Tenses do not refer to points in time but belong to the deictic category of shifters. The deictic shifts they facilitate allow us to search for our present elsewhere than here and now. In terms of a philosophical grammar (Rödl), tense expresses a predicative unity of *was/is*. While a logical copula describes the way that objects fall under concepts, the temporal copula *was/is* marks the temporal unity of a substance in various states (poles of time).

Two-in-one Two-in-one is a figure Dorrit Cohn describes in psychonarrations of the late nineteenth century as the typical presence of the narrator in his protagonists. We follow this observation in order to outline a general principle of the constitution of fiction that links up with the procedures of deictic shifts. Fiction systematically transforms the parameters of deixis, condensed in an *I–here–now origo*, into two-in-one characters (doubling, a/syntopy, a/synchrony). The relation of the *I* to another, the creation of linguistic heterotopes, the interweaving of at least two times—all these are characteristic figures of a two-in-one.

NOTES

Introduction

1 Key terms are defined in the glossary pages 223–32.
2 On the topos of "liveliness" in aesthetics, cf. Armen Avanessian, Winfried Menninghaus, and Jan Völker, eds., *Vita aesthetica: Szenarien ästhetischer Lebendigkeit* (Zurich and Berlin: Diaphanes, 2009).
3 Walter Benjamin, "The Reading Box," *Berlin Childhood around 1900*, trans. Howard Eiland (Cambridge, MA: Harvard University Press, 2006), 141–2.
4 One recent example is Dieter Mersch's work on event and aura, according to which the artwork has its "own temporality of the moment, absolute present tense, like presence, which immediately overwhelm and accrue where language no longer speaks." Dieter Mersch, *Ereignis und Aura: Untersuchungen zu einer Ästhetik des Performativen* (Frankfurt am Main: Suhrkamp, 2002), 146.
5 Giorgio Agamben, *The Man without Content*, trans. Georgia Albert (Stanford, CA: Stanford University Press, 1999), 70.
6 Disengaging the (experience of) time produced in reading from an aesthetic experience of time not only explains why we prefer to speak of poetics rather than aesthetics or why we do not opt for an author-poetology. Systematizing the differences between the four types of novels we have isolated (classical narrated fiction, classical modernity, modern present tense, altermodern) is possible only once we understand the poietic capacities of literary language. Since what takes place in reading is not an experience of time but its production, and since the four types of novels each derive something different from the operative time of chronogenesis, none of them can claim to know more than the others. As we are primarily concerned with the know-how of the individual novel forms, an author-poetology would have limited value for

our inquiry. Individual (altermodern) present-tense authors might exhibit less naïveté in regard to the (fictional) perception of chronological time than their much-berated ancestors in narrated fiction. That does not, however, make the knowledge gained from the present-tense novel any more profound than the one we obtain from novels written in the past tense. Knowledge about the procedures of language is not the result of an individual or personal style.

7 For a categorization of the "subfield of aesthetics that is poetics" that is both historical and systematic, cf. Sandra Richter, *A History of Poetics: German Scholarly Aesthetics and Poetics in International Context, 1770–1960* (Berlin and New York: de Gruyter, 2010), 5.

8 This also has consequences for the history of theory, which can be read off contemporary semantics. "An English word that, considered etymologically, corresponds to πράξις, is *experience*, *ex-per-ientia*, which contains the same idea of a *going through* of action and in the action. The Greek word that corresponds to the word 'experience'—ἐμπειρία—contains the same root as πράξις, *namely* περ, πείρω, πέρας: etymologically speaking it is the same word." According to Agamben, "Aristotle hints at an affinity between experience and praxis when he says, 'with a view to action [το πράττειν], experience [ἐμπειρία] seems in no respect inferior to art [τέχνη] ... since experience is knowledge of individuals, while art is knowledge of universals, and action [πράξις] ... is concerned with the individual'" (Agamben, *Man without Content*, 74).

9 Thinking in terms of aesthetics, it would at most be plausible to pursue a poetic analysis of perceptible literary materiality, that is, a materiality accessible to *aisthesis*. But to grant that a *poiesis* of language has any knowledge other than the merely self-referential is to go beyond the (material aesthetic) framework that aesthetics applies to poetics. For aesthetics, creation would have to interrupt itself in its very practice—it would for a moment exempt itself from its own action—in order to be able to reflect on its practical-productive activity. This is what justifies the call for transgressing the immanence of poetics that is understood merely to circulate in the materials and forms of art. In the name of replacing this narrow production-*aesthetic* circle by the relation to experience, however, aesthetics invokes more than just reception, that is, reading. Aesthetic theory must remain unclear about what justifies our *poetics* of literary knowledge: the unavoidable

10 Dmitry Likhachev, "Poètika khudozhestvennogo vremeni," *Poètika drevnerusskoy poèzy* (Moscow, 1967), 212–352, here 213. The temporality of literature becomes the foundation of its aesthetic value. "What is most essential for the study of literature are the examinations of artistic time: of time reproduced itself in literary works, of time as the artistic factor of literature" (ibid., 213–14).

11 Cf. for instance Franz W. Seidler, "Das Praesens historicum im Englischen," *Die Neueren Sprachen* 17 (1968): 317–25. Another typical example of a literary history of the present tense is Udo Fries, "Zum historischen Präsens im modernen Roman," *Germanisch-Romanische Monatsschrift* 51 (1970): 321–38.

12 Peter Osborne, "The Fiction of the Contemporary: Speculative Collectivity and Transnationality in The Atlas Group," *Aesthetics and Contemporary Art*, ed. Armen Avanessian and Luke Skrebowski (Berlin: Sternberg, 2011), 101–23, here 118.

13 Ibid., 110.

14 Rüdiger Campe, "Form und Leben in der Theorie des Romans," in *Vita aesthetica*, 193–211, here 194.

The present-tense novel

1 Käte Hamburger, *The Logic of Literature*, 2nd rev. ed. (Bloomington, IN: Indiana University Press, 1993), 66.

2 On the history and significance of this example sentence within narratology, cf. Franz K. Stanzel, "'Morgen war Weihnachten': Erlebte Rede als Irritation von Grammatik und Erzähltheorie," *Unterwegs: Erzähltheorie für Leser*, ed. Dorrit Cohn (Göttingen: Vandenhoeck & Ruprecht, 2002), 62–7.

3 According to Hamburger, propositions in first-person narrations retain the status of statements (about reality). This is why, for her, only third-person narratives can be fictional. We develop a critique of this controversial assumption in Chapter 2. This conception, which understands narration as a speech act, must be revised when it comes to the deixis of tenses. In relation to personal and spatial deixis, it would be better to speak of a narrator's entry into the character and of the formation of a focus, that is, of a displacement (not disappearance) of the perspective to the interior.

4 Cf. Michael Scheffel, "Käte Hamburger," *Klassiker der modernen Literaturtheorie*, ed. Matias Martinez and Michael Scheffel (Munich: Beck, 2010), 156: "From her observation of a modification of the tense system of language, of the loss of the deictic function of time and space adverbs, and of the use of verbs of interior processes for third parties, Hamburger concludes that there is no real or fictive subject who expresses these propositions at a particular time and a particular place, and who, in this way, could articulate a 'field of experience or sensation' tied to a concrete person."

5 See John R. Searle, "The Logical Status of Fictional Discourse," *New Literary History* 6, no. 2 (1975): 319–32, here 326: "Now what makes fiction possible, I suggest, is a set of extralinguistic, nonsemantic conventions." Compare Ann Banfield, *Unspeakable Sentences: Narration and Representification in the Language of Fiction* (London: Routledge, 1982).

6 In her article, "Deictic Shift Theory and the Poetics of Involvement in Narrative," Mary Galbraith defends Ann Banfield against Genette's criticism: "When he argued that 'Narrative without a narrator, the utterance without an uttering, seem to me pure illusion and, as such, unfalsifiable,' he missed the key point of Banfield's argument: Fiction is just such an illusion" (*Deixis in Narrative: A Cognitive Science Perspective*, ed. Judith F. Duchan, Gail A. Bruder, and Lynne E. Hewitt [Hillsdale, NJ: Lawrence Erlbaum Associates, 1995], 19–59, here 44–5). This passage is all the more remarkable for highlighting the two positions from which we distance ourselves. We follow Galbraith in her objection to Genette, i.e., that he lacks a concept of fiction, but we do not go so far as to say that fiction can be seen as entirely divorced from narration, propositions, and their medial character. As we will show, fiction is not the illusion of a narrative without narration or a proposition without a propositional act. We do not understand the poetics of fiction as the creation of an object that would emancipate itself from its production in language.

7 Cf. Franz K. Stanzel, "Episches Praeteritum, erlebte Rede, historisches Praesens," *DVJS* 33 (1959): 1–12, here 2; Jürgen H. Petersen, "Erzählen im Prasens: Die Korrektur herrschender Tempus-Theorien durch die poetische Praxis," *Euphorion* 86 (1992): 65–89, here 70 and 79; and Dorrit Cohn, *The Distinction of Fiction* (Baltimore, MD: Johns Hopkins University Press, 1999), 79.

8 Cohn, *Distinction of Fiction*, 109–31.

9   Dorrit Cohn, *Transparent Minds: Narrative Modes for Presenting Consciousness in Fiction* (Princeton, NJ: Princeton University Press, 1978), 29.

10 Harald Weinrich, *Tempus: Besprochene und erzählte Welt* [1964], 6th ed. (Munich: Beck, 2001), 39.

11 Ibid., 14.

12 Within linguistics, too, the temporal interpretation of the tenses, and of the present tense in particular, is a point of contention. We will return to it in the context of the tenses' deictic meaning in Chapter 2.

13 The meaning of tense evolves from a phenomenon that can be empirically, i.e., linguistically, examined in literary texts to a criterion of global distinctions between narrating texts and other kinds of texts. Accordingly, the meaning of tense does not have to be defined in each individual case. Tense usage can be analyzed statistically and a clear distribution among two groups of tenses becomes apparent. In later interpretations of tense within textual linguistics, the separation into two text sorts (narration and description) hardly plays any role at all. Categories like deixis and aspect are given preference. Weinrich's distinctions become more significant for a different field of inquiry, namely narratology.

14 Weinrich, *Tempus*, 76. When, in what follows, we employ Weinrich's division into two groups of tenses, we too concentrate on the two "zero-tenses" present tense and past tense.

15 Ibid., 39–40.

16 Ibid., 65.

17 Ibid., 66.

18 Tzvetan Todorov, "The Grammar of Narrative," *The Poetics of Prose*, trans. Richard Howard (Ithaca, NY: Cornell University Press, 1977), 108–19.

19 In his study, *Zeit im Roman: Literarische Zeitreflexion und die Geschichte des Zeitromans im späten 18. und 19. Jahrhundert* (Munich: Beck, 2001), 25, Dirk Gottsche discusses Wilhelm Raabe as representative of a process of temporalization in bourgeois realism that he situates close to modernism. When it comes to the "discovery of time in the novel" in the late eighteenth and the nineteenth century, however, we are less interested here in the cultural context of a subjectivity and historicity (cf. ibid., 66) than we are in fundamental poetic changes on the narrative and fictional levels.

20 Wilhelm Raabe, *Die Chronik der Sperlingsgasse* [*The Chronicle of Sparrow Alley*] (Munich: Nymphenburger, 1980), 101ff. The extent to which Weinrich's distinction between narration and discussion marks the boundary between novel and chronicle can be seen in the chronicler's defiant reaction to the accusation that he lacks narrative coherence: "I do not write novels and can hardly be bothered with writerly counterpoint; what the past has brought me, what the present gives me, that is what I would like to tie together here, mounted in a pretty frame" (ibid., 12). The tense confusion evoked in the passage cited is the expression of the dissent between chronology and retrospection, which cannot be made to fit the clear narrative conditions of a chronologically progressing *fabula* and a retrospectively narrating *sujet*.

21 Nessa Wolfson, "A Feature of Performed Narrative: The Conversational Historical Present," *Language in Society* 7, no. 2 (1978): 215–37, here 219. In relation to spoken language, Wolfson continues: "It is simply one of the uses of the present tense, which, in English, is timeless and has no semantic value of its own. Rather, it is the switching between CHP [the *Conversational Historical Present*] and the past tense which I have labelled CHP alternation, which is the relevant feature, serving to mark off different events within the story." In her essay "Tense-Switching in Narrative," *Language and Style* 14, no. 3 (1981): 226–31, here 230, she takes into account the different (and literary) genres in which the CHP appears and argues against the *vividness* reading: "[W]e must point out that since the present tense has no time reference, and since it is not used to refer to present moment action, there is no basis for the explanation so often given that the present tense is used as CHP in order to make the audience feel they are reliving the event."

22 See below p. 225

23 Ivan A. Goncharov, *Oblomov: Roman v chetyrech chastyakh* (Leningrad: Nauka, 1987), 7; *Oblomov*, trans. David Magarshack (London: Penguin, 1954), 13.

24 William Thackeray, *Vanity Fair* (London: Penguin, 2001), 7.

25 Émile Zola, *Au Bonheur des Dames, Oeuvres Complètes*, vol. 4, ed. Henri Mitterand, 709–1043 (Paris: Cercle du Livre Précieux, 1967), 800; *The Ladies' Paradise*, trans. Brian Nelson (Oxford: Oxford University Press, 1995), 120–21.

26 Suzanne Fleischman, *Tense and Narrativity: From Medieval Performance to Modern Fiction* (Austin, TX: University of Texas Press, 1990), 24.

27 Walter Scott, *Ivanhoe* (London: Penguin, 2000), 15.
28 In her "brief analysis of the meaning of the concept 'presentification,'" Hamburger points out that "for the problematic of fictional narration, and also, most intimately connected with the phenomenology of the past tense," we should not lose sight of the double meaning of the term *presentification*. *Vergegenwärtigen* qua *repraesentatio* means both producing the present in the temporal sense as well as "imagining" and "representifying" it (Hamburger, *Logic of Literature*, 91–2).
29 We do not delimit Hamburger's and Weinrich's theses systematically, only historically. In so doing, we use them to explain a specific historical transformation. We are thereby following the formalist conception that assigns historicity of the concept of literature. One result of this approach is that all positivistic definitions of literature are reduced to synchronous cuts or periods in the evolution of the literary system. Cf. Yury Tynyanov, "The Literary Fact," *Modern Genre Theory*, ed. David Duff (Harlow: Pearson Education, 2000), 29–49; "On Literary Evolution" and "Problems in the Study of Language and Literature" (co-authored with Roman Jakobson), *Twentieth-Century Literary Theory: An Introductory Anthology*, ed. Vassilis Lambropoulos and David Neal Miller (Albany, NY: State University of New York Press, 1987), 152–62 and 32–4.
30 See below, p. 227.
31 As we will show later, the resumption of the *fabula* in narration in altermodernism is not a matter of regression (with which it did indeed return in Stalinism) but a new mode of criticism. This mode can be distinguished from the nihilistic reductionism of avant-garde modernism by its over-compliance with exactly those norms that drew their critical attention.
32 Sergey Tretyakov, "Zhivoe i bumazhnoe," *Literatura Fakta* (Moscow: Zakharov, 2000), 149.
33 Sergey Tretyakov, "Lyudi odnogo kostra," *Strana-perekrestok*, ed. T. S. Gomolitskaya-Tretyakova (Moscow: Sovetsky Pisatel, 1991), 309–440, here 318–19.
34 A first distinction between *fabula* and *sujet* (called "plot" and "storyline" in the English translation) is given by Viktor Shklovsky in a discussion of how to designate the descriptions of events in prose texts: "The concept of 'plot' is all too often confused with the concept that I arbitrarily propose to call the 'storyline,' which is just a description of events" ("The Parody Novel: Sterne's

Tristram Shandy," *Review of Contemporary Fiction* 1, no. 1 [1981]: 190–210, here 210). For an extensive discussion of the terms *fabula* and *sujet*, cf. Emil Volek, "Die Begriffe 'Fabel' und 'Sujet' in der modernen Literaturwissenschaft: Zur Struktur der Erzählstruktur," *Poetica* 9 (1977): 141–66.

35 Shklovsky examines the temporal dynamic that arises in the refiguring of the events of the *fabula* through the *sujet*. "Thus, from the very beginning, *Tristram Shandy* is characterized by the time shift ... Time shifts of this type occur quite frequently in the poetics of the novel" ("The Parody Novel," 191).

36 In its early formalistic understanding, the *sujet*, for example, is derived from the unfolding of tropes that are viewed as motifs of the text. The successive unfolding of the *sujet*—the allegoresis into characters and the unfolding of metaphoric comparisons to parables—meets the *fabula* at the moment in which it takes on a fully motivated form of person and action. To be interpreted as a story, it only needs to include a level of reference.

37 This dimension of Shklovsky's concept of *sujet* is treated by Russell West in his essay, "All *sujet* and no *fabula*? Tristram Shandy and Russian Formalism," *Erzählen und Erzähltheorie im 20. Jahrhundert*, ed. Jörg Helbig (Heidelberg: Winter, 2001), 283–302.

38 The development of the terms "fabula" and "sujet" primarily within narratology entailed a certain reduction of their scope. This is why it is no accident that contemporary deictic shift theory goes back to these formalist terms to work on the cognitive linguistics of narration under the dominance of the needs of fiction theory. Cf., for example, Judith F. Duchan, Gail A. Bruder, and Lynn E. Hewitt, eds, *Deixis in Narrative: A Cognitive Science Perspective* (Hillsdale, NJ: Lawrence Erlbaum Associates, 1995).

39 Theodor W. Adorno, *Aesthetic Theory*, trans. Robert Hullot-Kentor (Minneapolis, MN: University of Minnesota Press, 1998), 85. In relation to the historicity of art, Adorno speaks of an internal temporality of the artwork. "What appears in the artwork is its own inner time; the explosion of appearance blasts open the continuity of this inner temporality. The artwork is mediated to real history by its monadological nucleus. History is the content of artworks. To analyze artworks means no less than to become conscious of the history immanently sedimented in them" (ibid., 112).

40 On the formalist term "fabulalessness," cf. the explanation given in Boris V. Tomashevsky, *Theorie der Literatur, Poetik*, trans. Ulrich Werner (Wiesbaden: Harrassowitz, 1985), 215ff.

41 Tretyakov, *Lyudi odnogo kostra*, 328–9.
42 Vasily Rozanov, "Solitaria," *Izbrannoe* (Munich: Nejmanis, 1970), 1–80, here 34.
43 Particularly in the section "The A-Temporality of Fiction," Käte Hamburger defines the time-form of fiction as timeless without taking account of its narrative form of appearance (*Logic of Literature*, 89–98).
44 On this nineteenth-century development, cf. Gottsche, *Zeit im Roman*.
45 Ann Banfield ("Time Passes: Virginia Woolf, Post-Impressionism, and Cambridge Time," *Poetics Today* 24, no. 3 (2003): 471–516) explicitly accounts for the poetological moment of Woolf's compositional form. She shows that the mutual connection of parts can be traced to two short stories by Katherine Mansfield. Furthermore, at precisely the moment in which the parts are connected through the interval created by "Time Passes," a transition occurs from the short story to the composition of the novel.
46 See below p. 227.
47 In Russian formalism, the term "actualization" describes how literary artworks make structures of aesthetic objects perceptible or how they translate them into the semantics of the world of texts. There, they take the form of motifs, for example. There are well-known examples in Mayakovsky, for instance in his poem "Iz ulicy v ulicu" ["From Street to Street"], in which street and face are posited as homonyms and are successively actualized until the street makes faces:

> У-лица. Лица у догов годов рез-че. Че-рез ...

Vladimir Mayakovsky, "Iz ulizy v ulicu," *Polnoe sobranie sochineny* (Moscow: Gos. izd-vo Khudozhestvennaya literatura, 1955–1961), vol. 1, 38–9.

For an explanation of the process of "actualization," see Aage A. Hansen-Löve, "Zur Poetik der 'Realisierung' und 'Entfaltung' semantischer Figuren zu Texten," *Wiener Slawistischer Almanach* 10 (1982): 197–252.
48 Suzanne Fleischman notes in the context of a discussion of the terms *fabula* and *sujet*: "The implied priority of narrative structure over reality structure in the *fabula—sjuzhet* opposition relates presumably to the fact that this opposition was formulated with reference to fiction, the events of which obviously have no existence prior and independent of the text" (*Tense and Narrativity*, 95).

49 The fact that a few paragraphs later we read "(and the car went in at the gates and nobody looked at it)" does not contradict this observation, quite to the contrary. Virginia Woolf, *Mrs. Dalloway* (Oxford: Blackwell, 1996, 18).

50 Virginia Woolf, *The Waves* (Oxford: Blackwell, 1993), 74–6.

51 Cohn, *The Distinction of Fiction*, 96; Cohn makes this dogmatic point by citing Robert Scholes's text, "Language, Narrative and Antinarrative," *Critical Inquiry* 7 (1980): 204–12, here 209–10.

52 Virgian Woolf, *The Waves: The Two Holograph Drafts* (Toronto, ON and Buffalo, NY: University of Toronto Press, 1976), 215–21.

53 Cohn, *Distinction of Fiction*, 1999, 103.

54 Ibid., 104.

55 Woolf, *The Waves*, 74–7. While the second of Woolf's manuscripts uses double quotes to mark dialogue in this passage, there are passages in the first manuscript in double quotes directly next to others without quotation marks; *The Waves: Holograph Drafts*, 215–21, and 525–9. This editorial decision is based on the assumption that the use of the present tense is motivated by a proximity to dramatic form, in which the present tense is also the primary tense used. In her literary diaries, Woolf speaks of a "playpoem" (ibid., 21).

56 Interior monologue thus marks a historical threshold between classical narrated fiction and the altermondern present-tense forms insofar as its present tense is based on the non-contemporaneity of an imaginary. It thus avoids the narrative aporia of synchrony from the outset, even if it has not yet left behind narrated fiction's mimesis of a present-tense interior life.

57 John Updike, *Rabbit Angstrom: A Tetralogy* (New York: Knopf, 1995), viii.

58 Ibid., xii.

59 Ibid., 5.

60 John Updike, *The Poorhouse Fair, Rabbit, Run* (New York: Modern Library, 1965), n.p., quoted in Randall H. Waldron, "Rabbit Revised," *American Literature* 56, no. 1 (1984): 51–67, here 52.

61 Boris Uspensky, *Poetics of Composition*, trans. Valentina Zavarin and Susan Wittig (Berkeley/Los Angeles, CA: University of California Press, 1973), 71.

62 In *Rabbit Redux*, this involves a narrative style that, compared with the first volume, is at times very different. We find, for

example, passages spliced in from newspaper scenes or passages set in parentheses (for example, Updike, *Rabbit Angstrom*, 398). Such passages hastily refer to events or create contexts in the past tense: "She can be blithe. After he told her once … finding it there each morning" (ibid., 404). Usually, even at decisive points, the narrator (focusing/focused on by Rabbit) does not know more than Rabbit himself, for example when the question is whether Nelson and Jill are having sex or not (ibid., 475). At other points, however, the narrator shows himself to be authorial and removed from the succession of (present) events. This occurs not only for the sake of retrospective combinations and of making things understandable. It can also be completely proleptic: "Rabbit wipes her chin … and weeks afterward, when all is lost, will take out his handkerchief and bury his nose in it" (ibid., 526).

63 Cf. Bryant N. Wyatt, "John Updike: The Psychological Novel in Search of Structure," *Twentieth Century Literature* 13, no. 2 (1967): 89–96, here 92: "The work is narrated in the present tense, implying a further effort to convey a sense of immediacy and continuity over a much longer time span than that encompassed in his first novel. This technique is effective as long as the related action is continuous but it weakens when breaks occur (as they must in a story covering events over a period of many weeks) and has to strain to bridge the resultant voids, if the semblance of continuity is to be preserved."

64 In altermodernism, demonstrating the deceptions of "narrative reason" does not unilaterally lead to an "implosion of time" (Jochen Mecke, "Kritik narrativer Vernunft: Implosionen der Zeit im 'nouveau roman,'" *Zeit-Zeichen: Aufschübe und Interferenzen zwischen Endzeit und Echtzeit*, ed. Christoph G. Tholen and Michael Scholl [Weinheim: VCH, 1990], 157–76), but to an explosion of the generative possibilities for new narratives.

65 We develop the imaginary aspects of the modern present tense in Chapter 3, where we also describe the degree to which passages like the one from Rozanov participate in the internal focus of the interior monologue.

66 We could also speak of a sense-physiological overload threshold. This means that an "I" can only not narrate if it is involved in the events with its senses and intellectual abilities beyond a certain limit of capacity. This is not the case in watching a sports game, where a separation of the senses makes it possible simultaneously to watch and to speak into a microphone. Simultaneous processes of action and of narration are always possible up to the limit of

sense-physiological overload. It is possible to comment or describe synchronously as long as there is not too much to see or too much to hear and as long as none of the sense organs are overly strained (by lights that are too bright, by sounds that are too loud). Finally, there is a third conceivable variation, in which the connections between (optical, acoustic, etc.) sense data are so complicated that they overburden the cognitive capacities for processing them and rule out any narrative reproduction.

67 Or, as Weinrich (*Tempus*, 53) puts it: "Er [der Erzähler] erzählt also, *als ob* er bespräche"; Suzanne Fleischman (*Tense and Narrativity*, 115) translates this as: "a narrator narrates as if commenting."

68 Only in altermodernism does a third possibility appear. The present is furnished with an ontological difference, which constructs a fictional present.

69 Georg Witte, "'Einmal'—Aktualität als literarische Erfahrungsform: Am Beispiel von Lev Tolstojs 'Kreutzer-Sonate,'" *Jetzt und Dann: Zeiterfahrung in Film, Literatur und Philosophie*, ed. Anke Hennig, Gertrud Koch, Christiane Voss, and Georg Witte (Munich: Fink, 2010), 185–204.

70 Peter Weiss, *Der Schatten des Körpers des Kutschers* (Frankfurt am Main: Suhrkamp, 1978), 9; *Marat/Sade, The Investigation, The Shadow of the Body of the Coachman*, ed. Robert Cohen (New York: Continuum, 1998), 9.

71 Hubert Fichte, *Versuch über die Pubertät* (Frankfurt am Main: Fischer, 2005), 294.

72 From the viewpoints of poetics, aesthetics, and even hermeneutics, it is so unlikely that fiction would hide behind narration that justifying it by way of narrative practice itself is convincing. It needs to be explained by means of an epistemic regime. Cf. Aleida Assman, "Fiktion als Differenz," *Poetica* 21 (1989): 239–60.

73 Robert Walser, *Der Spaziergang* (Frankfurt am Main: Suhrkamp, 1978), 8f.; *Selected Stories* (New York: Farrar, Strauss and Giroux, 1982), 55–6.

74 The prospectivity of the *fabula* and the retrospectivity of the sujet have been further developed by Meir Sternberg (among others); see his "Telling in Time (I)," *Poetics Today* 11, no. 4 (1990): 901–48; "Telling in Time (II)," *Poetics Today* 13, no. 3 (1992): 463–540; "Telling in Time (III)," *Poetics Today* 27, no. 1 (2006): 125–235.

75 Cohn, *Distinction of Fiction*, 106.

76 From a narratological perspective, there is the secondary question whether the fictionalization of the present tense is not always achieved at the cost of the *fabula*, since both the fiction of narration and the narration of fiction work from out of the *sujet*.

77 The fact that fiction and narration emerge independently of one another thus has no effect on the question whether they can meet their own demands.

78 Wolfgang Hildesheimer, *Tynset* (Frankfurt am Main: Fischer, 1967), 5.

79 Ibid.

80 For the literary operation of cloaking the text's work of language in motifs, formalism uses the term "motivation."

81 Hildesheimer, *Tynset*, 7.

82 For Augustine, as is well known, there is only the present. Past and future are the "present of the past" and the "present of the future," and only present in the modes of memory and expectation. Cf. St. Augustine, *Confessions*, trans. Henry Chadwick (Oxford: Oxford University Press, 1992), 232.

83 In the third chapter we explain the three forms of problematic in/differences between non-reality and fiction: the imperceptibility, the indecideability, and the indistinguishability of imaginary products from fiction.

84 See below p. 66ff.

85 Johann Wolfgang Goethe, *Die Wahlverwandtschaften*, Werke, vol. 6, ed. Erich Trunz (Munich: Deutscher Taschenbuch Verlag 1977), 242–490, here 456–7; *Elective Affinities*, trans. R. J. Hollingdale, 1971 (London: Penguin, 2005), 261–2.

86 Cf. Hennig Brinkmann, "Zur Sprache der 'Wahlverwandtschaften,'" *Goethes Roman "Die Wahlverwandtschaften*," ed. Ewald Rösch (Darmstadt: Wissenschaftliche Buchgesellschaft, 1975), 236–62, here 253–4 and 246. His topic is short sentences that express unease, for instance, about the realization of love ("He [Eduard] sees Ottilie and she him; he flies towards her and throws himself at her feet."); about the death of a child ("The child lies motionless in her arms, the boat floats motionless on the water"); and about Ottilie's death ("'Promise me you will live!' she cries with gentle exertion, and at once sinks back. 'I promise!' he cried to her – yet he only cried it after her, for she had already departed." Goethe, *Elective Affinities*, 259 [mod.], 262, 293 respectively). Cf.

Hamburger's critique of this interpretation, which in her view is too committed to the content of the work (*Logic of Literature*, 118–19).

87   Hamburger, *Logic of Literature*, 117 [modified].

88   Otto Jespersen, *The Philosophy of Grammar* (London: G. Allen & Unwin, 1924), 258.

89   Franz W. Seidler ("Das Praesens historicum im Englischen," *Die Neueren Sprachen* 67 [1968]: 317–25, here 317) also writes about various other present-tense forms such as the *reflecting*, the *resultant*, the *registering*, or the *present tense of lingering*. For a first overview in the history of theory, see John R. Frey, "The Historical Present in Narrative Literature, Particularly in Modern German Fiction," *Journal of English and Germanic Philology* 45, no. 1 (1946): 43–67.

90   The expression is Fredericus Theodorus Visser's; on his work, cf. Udo Fries, "Zum historischen Präsens im modernen Roman," *Germanisch-Romanische Monatszeitschrift*, 20 (1970): 321–38, here 322.

91   Christian Paul Casparis, *Tense without Time: The Present Tense in Narration* (Bern: Francke, 1975).

92   Ibid., 33.

93   Ibid., 9–10.

94   Udo Fries argues against Hamburger and Weinrich but subscribes to Stanzel's thesis of an affinity of the "present tense as a narrative tense" to the "personal novel." He makes a narratological distinction between two functions of the historical present. In the "authorial novel," it is a stylistic means of representifying the event of the time of narration as a stylistic device "when, at the same time, the narrative situation is clarified over and again through the use of past tense forms." In the "personal novel," in turn, we may exclude "a particular presentifying meaning." All definitions of the historical present tense that operate with the term "presentification" must heed this distinction. The historical present can have a presentifying effect only in authorial narrative situations because readers' attention lies with the narrative act. "In novels with a personal narrative situation, that is, novels that seem to have no narrator, in which the reader's center of orientation lies in an acting person, the epic preterite can often have a presentifying function. In novels with a primarily authorial narrative situation, that is, novels where the narrating narrator is present, the past of the action is continually referenced through the narrative distance—the period of time between the narrator and

what is narrated, the past tense thus keeps its past function" (*Zum historischen Präsens*, 323).

95 Fries, *Zum historischen Präsens*, 336–7: "If we take the HP to be any present tense that—generally speaking—refers to the past—in the special case of the novel—to the time of action, then it is not sufficient to establish that the function of the HP is to vivify and presentify." It could also "have a different stylistic function … which has to be determined in every individual novel." On the term "narrative present," cf. Dorrit Cohn: "Kafka's Eternal Present: Narrative Tense in 'Ein Landarzt' and other First-Person Stories," *PMLA* 83, no. 1 (1968): 144–50, here 147.

96 Weinrich, *Tempus*, 2001, 56. Cf. also Elisabeth Leiss, *Die Verbalkategorien des Deutschen: Ein Beitrag zur Theorie der sprachlichen Kategorisierung* (Berlin and New York: de Gruyter, 1992), 245ff. Peter Hühn and Jörg Schänert have recently made the following claim: "Particularly since the seventeenth century, stories in poetry—and here they tend to differ from stories in novels—have primarily referred to inner phenomena such as perceptions, thoughts, ideas, sensations, memories, wishes, imaginations, or attitudes. The speaker or protagonist ascribes these phenomena to himself, in a monologic process of reflection or becoming-aware, as a story through which he defines his individual identity. Such processes can be conveyed in the present tense thanks to the gesture that they are only just now completed in 'pronouncing' them and communicating them—even before the introduction of actual actions or (very typical for poetry) as the decisive action itself. The time-form of the epic (presentifying) past tense, however, can also call up and/or remember already-completed processes of this kind to link them with actions that are (or should be) completed in the present of speaking" ("Einleitung: Theorie und Methodologie narratologischer Lyrik-Analyse," *Lyrik und Narratologie: Text-Analysen zu deutschsprachigen Gedichten vom 16. bis zum 20. Jahrhundert*, ed. Peter Hühn, Jörg Schönert, and Malte Stein [Berlin and New York: de Gruyter, 2007], 1–18, here 10–11).

97 Deborah Schiffrin, "Tense Variation in Narrative," *Language* 57, no. 1 (1981): 45–62, here 46.

98 Manfred Markus, *Tempus und Aspekt: Zur Funktion von Präsens, Präteritum und Perfekt im Englischen und Deutschen* (Munich: Fink, 1977), 26. Stanzel's "narrative situation," the manner of speaking, is also not suitable for a definition of the meaning of tense. Tense, instead, has contextual meaning (cf. ibid., 29–30).

99 Theo Vennemann, "Tempora und Zeitrelation im Standarddeutschen," *Sprachwissenschaft* 12 (1987): 234–49, here 239.
100 Leiss, *Verbalkategorien des Deutschen*, 250.
101 Hamburger, *Logic of Literature*, 102.
102 Leiss, *Verbalkategorien des Deutschen*, 250.
103 In this context, Deborah Schiffrin discusses a variety of linguistic approaches (for instance William Labov's): "Past events 'come alive' with the HP because it is formally equivalent to a tense which indicates events whose reference time is not the moment of experience, but the moment of speaking" (*Tense Variation in Narrative*, 46).
104 Martin Heidegger, *Being and Time*, trans. Joan Stambaugh (Albany, NY: State University of New York Press, 1996), 353.
105 We have already encountered a certain contemporaneous presentness of pasts in Zola's novel *Au Bonheur des Dames*. The contemporaneity of all pasts in narrated fiction does not change anything about its chronological order; the precedence of individual events is signaled by the past perfect. In contrast, the altermodern novel discovers an anti-chronological arrangement of time in anteriority.
106 The various poetics imply different understandings of history. (1) In classical narrated fiction, history is conceived of above all starting from diachrony. The asynchrony of two moments that overlap in fiction denotes a chronological order. The past is presentified, which makes it possible to place oneself in the past and to look back at a precedent journey in time. (2) Modernist novels are more driven by the idea of a synchrony, the idea of a contemporaneity that does not coincide with simultaneity. (3) In the altermodern notion of history, in turn, asynchrony seems neither to open up an alternative chronological arrangement nor the identity of a present. It designates an instant that deviates from itself.
107 In Vladimir Nabokov's *Speak Memory: An Autobiography Revisited*, this takes the form of a competition set up between literary language and photography with regard to the fictionality and factuality of memory. Nabokov sees himself provoked by the materiality of the past tense in photography. Counter to everything factual one might see in a photograph, presentification precisely means distancing oneself from it. Vladimir Nabokov, *Speak Memory: An Autobiography Revisited* (New York: Vintage, 1989).

108 Paul Ricœur, "Narrative Time," *Critical Inquiry* 7, no. 1 (1980): 169–90.
109 Cf. Heidegger, *Being and Time*, 242.
110 Reinhart Koselleck insists that the degree of fictionality of events (as the object of historiography) and structures (as the object of historical writing) is the same. This is why he argues for a temporalization of historical concepts: "[T]he facticity of events established *ex post* is never identical with a totality of past circumstances thought of as formerly real. Every event historically established and presented lives on the fiction of actuality; reality itself is past and gone ... The quality of reality in past, narrated, events is no greater epistemologically than the quality of reality contained in past structures, which perhaps reach far beyond the apprehended experience of past generations ... The fictional nature of narrated events corresponds at the level of structures to the hypothetical character of their 'reality'" (*Futures Past: On the Semantics of Historical Time*, trans. Keith Tribe [New York: Columbia University Press, 2004], 111–12).
111 Slavoj Žižek, *The Indivisible Remainder: An Essay on Schelling and Related Matters* (London: Verso, 1996), 33.
112 Cathy Caruth, *Unclaimed Experience: Trauma, Narrative, and History* (Baltimore, MD: Johns Hopkins University Press, 1996), 17.
113 Cf. Ansgar Nünning, *Von historischer Fiktion zu historiographischer Metafiktion* (Trier: WVT, 1995).
114 Quentin Meillassoux, "Time Without Becoming," lecture at Middlesex University, London, May 8, 2008. http://speculativeheresy.files.wordpress.com/2008/07/3729-time_without_becoming.pdf (last accessed October 31, 2014).
115 Claude Simon, *Les Géorgiques* (Paris: Minuit), 12–13; *The Georgics*, trans. Beryl and George Fletcher (New York: Riverrun Press, 1989), 8.
116 Thomas Klinkert has described this unfolding from documents in Simon; see his *Bewahren und Löschen: Zur Proust-Rezeption bei Samuel Beckett, Claude Simon und Thomas Bernhard* (Tübingen: Narr, 1996).
117 Simon, *Géorgiques*, 1981, 21; *Georgics*, 15.
118 Two cases of non-chronological *fabulas* would be interesting: on the one hand the attempt by an author to construct an achronological *fabula*, an approach whose limits Marie-Laure

Ryan has outlined ("Zeitparadoxien in Narrativen," *Jetzt und Dann*, 105–27); on the other hand, a non-chronological or not strictly chronological consciousness of time responsible for the achronological construction of the *fabula* by a reader/listener. According to Mikhail Bakhtin, we can assume a cyclical (seasons, planting cycles, calendars) and a dialectical (identity of beginning and end, death and birth) consciousness of time to be at work in most folklore and medieval novels. A chronological way of reading these texts is of course possible, but it produces hermeneutic difficulties: conceiving of the events depicted chronologically does not make sense of them ("Forms of Time and of the Chronotope in the Novel," trans. Caryl Emerson and Michael Holquist [Austin, TX: University of Texas Press, 1981]).

119 Gilles Deleuze, *Difference and Repetition*, trans. Paul Patton (London: Athlone Press, 1994), 82 [modified].

120 See below p. 224.

121 Foucault writes: "On each of the two levels, a different history is being written. *Recontemporaneous redistributions* reveal several pasts, several forms of connection, several hierarchies of importance, several networks of determination, several teleologies, for one and the same science, as its present undergoes change: thus historical descriptions are necessarily ordered by the present state of knowledge, they increase with every transformation and never cease, in turn, to break with themselves" (*The Archaeology of Knowledge*, trans. A. M. Sheridan Smith [London: Tavistock Publications, 1972], 5).

122 Anton Fuxjäger, "Der MacGuffin: Nichts oder doch nicht? Definition und dramaturgische Aspekte eines von Alfred Hitchcock angedeuteten Begriffs," *Maske und Kothurn* 52, no. 2 (2006): 123–54.

123 Peter Handke, *Der Hausierer* (Frankfurt am Main: Suhrkamp, 1967), 7–8.

124 See below p. 65.

125 The fact that it is not the motif of the V2 rocket itself that produces the asynchronous effect is obvious in a comparison with Christian Kracht's *Ich werde hier sein im Sonnenschein und im Schatten* [*I Will Be Here in the Sun and in the Shade*] (Munich: dtv, 2010). Kracht's novel does not develop the temporal implications of supersonic speed relevant for altermodern asynchrony. The author, known for present-tense novels such as *Faserland*, uses the past tense in this counterfactual novel that

does not take place in the present. A pop author, he trusts the present tense only to evoke the present. He does without it as soon as he wants to tell a past alternate history, one that was never present. This corresponds to his merely motivic use of the rocket: "Infinitely high up in the sky, the projectile of a German long-range cannon whizzed toward the east, coming from the north. Sometimes they fell down and hit the ground near us. It was pure coincidence, although of course we first perceived the impact and then the sound of the approaching projectile" (21). In Pynchon, in contrast, it is in the present tense that "A screaming *comes* across the sky" means "It *is* too late." The rocket's impact thus refers to an event that has always already taken place. It refers not only to the sensual difference between sense data but also to the temporal difference between sense data and sense dating. The translatability of time into space posited by the theory of relativity is mirrored by the differential spatiality opened up by the first sentence of Pynchon's novel: "A screaming comes across the sky" employs a bi-directional verb. Unlike Kracht's "to whiz," which exclusively refers to hearing, or other verbs like "to go," which only has one direction, away from the speaker, and thus has only one deictic person of reference, "to come" has a double direction. The first (present-tense) verb of Pynchon's novel has two deictic reference points, it is related to the speaker and the addressee, and it evokes a spatial image of corresponding complexity.

126 Thomas Pynchon, *Gravity's Rainbow* (New York: Penguin, 2000), 3.
127 Hans Joachim Schädlich, *Tallhover* (Reinbek bei Hamburg: Rowohlt, 1986), 267–8.
128 Ibid., 268.
129 Ibid., 18.
130 Ibid., 19.
131 Ibid., 39.
132 Ibid., 38.
133 Ibid., 43.
134 Ibid., 48.
135 Eva Horn, *The Secret War: Treason, Espionage, and Modern Fiction*, trans. Geoffrey Winthrop-Young (Evanston, IL: Northwestern University Press, 2013), 53.
136 Gavriel D. Rosenfeld has analyzed alternative histories of the Third Reich that appear in English, French, and German; see his *The*

World Hitler Never Made: Alternative History and the Memory of Nazism (Cambridge: Cambridge University Press, 2005).

137 Claude Bremond has proposed a logic of the *fabula* in his *Logique du récit* (Paris: Seuil, 1973).

138 Hillary P. Dannenberg, *Coincidence and Counterfactuality: Plotting Time and Space in Narrated Fiction* (Lincoln, NE, and London: University of Nebraska Press, 2008), 2.

139 *What-if-novels* combine the narrative *what happened* with the fictional *as if*. There are what-if-novels in classical narrated fiction, too. There, the dominance of narration over fiction suggests a *fabula* open to the future.

140 Andreas Martin Widmann has thematized a "binary typology" that distinguishes between "deviant historical narration" on the basis of the story/plot distinction. Against the established research tradition and a concentration on the events of the *fabula*, Widmann is interested not only in "story-counterfactuals," in which certain historical events are replaced by others. He also examines "plot-counterfactuals," in which "historical causes [are] swapped," and insists that they, too, be understood as *what-if* narratives (*Kontrafaktische Geschichtsdarstellung: Untersuchungen an Romanen von Günter Grass, Thomas Pynchon, Thomas Brussig, Michael Kleeberg, Philip Roth und Christoph Ransmayr* [Heidelberg: Winter, 2009], 348). Our interest in altermodern fictional narrations, however, requires more than an extension of narratology's rendering the story absolute. It also calls for the comprehensive integration of the parameters of fiction and narration into a fiction-narratology, which takes an understanding of time as its starting point. See below, Chapter 4.

141 In Chapter 4 we explain in more precise terms how the *what if* of this text, in which the narrative question of *what happened* is crossed with the fictional question of an "*as if*," combines the question of the directedness of *fabula* and *sujet* with the question of the directedness of time. We will also see to what degree it requires that the present be fictionalized as an asynchronous moment of decision.

142 See above p. 84.

143 The classical vocabulary has difficulty accounting for the use of the present tense in this chapter. It is obviously not a vivifying present tense. And the claim that there is no presentification of events here, but a placing oneself back among the events, is equally unsatisfactory.

144 Charles Dickens, *David Copperfield* (London: Penguin, 2004), 769.

145 "In the personal novel, where narrative distance is not named, it is generally easier to introduce the present tense as a narrative tense" (Franz K. Stanzel, *Die typischen Erzählsituationen im Roman: Dargestellt an Tom Jones, Moby-Dick, The Ambassadors, Ulysses u.a.* [Vienna and Stuttgart: Braumüller, 1955], 120). According to Stanzel, the present tense can only have a presentifying effect in novels narrated by the author, where the reader's center of orientation is the narrative act and the past tense does not already have a presentifying effect.

146 We are following the formalist intuition that the use of non- (or not-yet-) canonical forms in literature is motivated by pathologies.

147 In the third chapter we will look at a series of unstable precursors to such a pathologically motivated present tense in nineteenth-century narrated fiction.

148 So far, the questions of whether readers experience a fiction in an empirical sense or to what degree they must use their imagination for fiction to emerge at all, and whether fiction collapses at the point at which readers begin to imagine for themselves, have remained open. Karlheinz Stierle takes a purely hermeneutic approach; he asks how fictions are to be understood, not how readers receive or produce them ("Was heißt Rezeption bei fiktionalen Texten?" *Poetica* 7 [1975]: 345–87).

149 Dorrit Cohn, "Signposts of Fictionality: A Narratological Perspective," *Poetics Today* 11, no. 4 (1990): 775–804, here 791.

150 In the third chapter we will examine the interior monologue and trace the present tense in classical narrated fiction. This will allow us to describe the emergence of an imaginary present tense that can serve as the basis for fictionalizing the first-person narrative. We will also develop our thesis on the temporal character line that separates third-person from first-person narratives, a separation that asserts both a fictional and an imaginary temporality.

151 Erwin M. Segal thus also rejects both the concept of a fictional narrator—"There is no existing fictional narrator"—and the "perspective of a character in the fictional world." He reactivates the category of author because the narrator cannot invent himself. See "A Cognitive-Phenomenological Theory of Fictional Narrative," *Deixis in Narrative: A Cognitive Science Perspective*, ed. Judith F. Duchan, Gail A. Bruder, and Lynne E. Hewitt (Hillsdale, NJ: Erlbaum, 1995), 61–78, here 69.

152 Daniil Kharms ("On Phenomena and Existences, Nr. 2," *Incidences*, trans. Neil Cornwell [London: Serpent's Tail, 1993], 95–6) denounces his readers as alcoholics who cannot resist getting drunk on the meaning of a text over and over again, even when the author gives them complete emptiness.

153 Monika Schmitz-Emans, "De-zentrierte Perspektivik," *Perspektive in Literatur und Kunst*, ed. Kurt Röttgers and Monika Schmitz-Emans (Essen: Die Blaue Eule, 1999), 96–138, here 132–3. On the relation between the first and second persons in Calvino's novels, cf. also Anne Waldron Neumann, "Escaping the 'Time of History'? Present Tense and the Occasion of Narration in J. M. Coetzee's *Waiting for the Barbarians*," *Journal of Narrative Technique* 20, no. 1 (1990): 65–86, here 66.

154 Monika Schmitz-Emans, "De-zentrierte Perspektivik," 132f.

155 Cf. David Herman, *Story Logic: Problems and Possibilities of Narrative* (Lincoln, NE: University of Nebraska Press, 2002), 345.

156 Cf. Monika Fludernik, "Second Person Fiction: Narrative 'You' as Addressee and/or Protagonist," *Arbeiten aus Anglistik und Amerikanistik* 18, no. 2 (1993): 217–47.

157 Roman Kuhn, "Zweite Person Singular Präsens: Überlegungen zu *Ein Mann der schläft* von Georges Perec," *Der Präsensroman*, ed. Armen Avenessian and Anke Hennig (Berlin and New York: de Gruyter, 2013), 210–23.

158 The aporia of synchrony only exists in relation to the implicit present of the narrator, in which there is no place for a contemporaneous experience. It does not exist for the reader, who always constitutes the *sujet* and *fabula* contemporaneously anyway (see above, p. 84).

159 The classical position of this has been formulated by W. J. M. Bronzwaer: "The two I's are not identical: the second I is an object of the first I's writing just as the other characters in the book are. The narrator-I exists exclusively on the first level of time: that of the composition of the novel. The second I exists primarily on the second time-level: that of the time when the story unfolds. This is the time level of the narrative, and the tense-form used for this time-level is the past tense" (*Tense in the Novel: An Investigation of Some Potentialities of Linguistic Criticism* [Groningen: Wolters-Noordhoff, 1970], 51).

160 This can be expressed as follows: the event is (retrospectively) contemporaneous when viewed from the present of the narrator who looks back at the event, and (prospectively) contemporaneous

when viewed from the present of the character for whom it lies in the future. We will explain this in more detail in the following chapter.

161 Dickens, *David Copperfield*, 769.

162 See above p. 86.

163 In order to understand the simultaneity of *fabula* and *sujet*, more recent studies in deixis theory have been able to bring in cognitivist perspectives. Erwin M. Segal, for example, writes: "In summary, our model identifies two logically different structures, discourse and story, through which the reader simultaneously travels by the process of narration" (*Cognitive-Phenomenological Theory*, 67).

164 Käte Hamburger writes: "One may also say that the act of narration is a function, through which the narrated person, things, event, etc., are created: the narrative function, which the narrative poet manipulates as, for example, the painter wields his colors and brushes" (*Logic of Literature*, 136).

165 Here we can reconnect with Stanzel's (*Episches Praeteritum, erlebte Rede, historisches Präsens*) and especially Petersen's (*Erzählen im Präsens*, 70) arguments against Hamburger. In response to Hamburger's distinction between fictional third-person narrating and fictive first-person narrating, Petersen maintains that, for readers, this distinction does not exist. We believe, however, that this fiction theoretical position and narratology's criticism of it can be combined by distinguishing between fiction at the level of the *fabula* (third-person narration) and fiction at the level of the *sujet* (first-person narration and other types that arise in altermodernism).

166 Nonetheless, there are good reasons why in our genealogy of the present-tense novel we situate Updike before modernism and thus in proximity to narrated fiction. In Updike we also see a moment of regression in the narrative mode *He goes*. Like classical narrated fiction, Updike, too, allows narration to disappear.

167 This also results in an affinity between the present tense and the narrative second-person that has not yet been thematized in research on the present tense. It is possible, we believe, to demonstrate how the *you* of the reader becomes an *I* that obtains an *origo* position in the *fabula*. The slow translation of a reader-*origo* into the *fabula* is the result of a formal development in literary history from the establishment of focalization (the narrator-I in the character-s/he) in nineteenth-century narrated fiction via the interior monologue (the narrator-I in the character-I)

to the full synchronization of reader and character (for instance in the *narrative you*).

Readings in methodology

1. Matias Martinez and Michael Scheffel point to the empirical syncretism of both methods and propose a synthetic object, "fictional narratology" ("Narratology and Theory of Fiction: Remarks on a Complex Relationship," *What is Narratology? Questions and Answers Regarding the Status of a Theory*, ed. Tom Kindt and Hans-Harald Müller [Berlin and New York: de Gruyter, 2003], 221–37, here 221). Monika Fludernik even assumes that narrativity and fictionality mutually increase one another (*Towards a "Natural" Narratology* [London: Routledge, 1996], 38ff.).
2. Temporal relations vanish in particular when narratology considers fictionality only at the level of the *fabula*.
3. In Chapter 4, we will show why fiction and narration are to be regarded as forms of time that are necessarily related. This, in turn, explains why neither (aesthetic) narration nor fiction can come into its own when it is isolated from the other.
4. See below p. 37f.
5. The notable exception is Alexander Bareis, *Fiktionales Erzählen: Zur Theorie der literarischen Fiktion als Make-Believe* (Göteborg: Göteborgs Universitet, 2008).
6. Cf. Markus, *Tempus und Aspekt*, 33ff.
7. Galbraith, *Deictic Shift Theory*, 49.
8. Uri Margolin, "Of What Is Past, Is Passing, or to Come: Temporality, Aspectuality, Modality, and the Nature of Literary Narrative," *Narratologies: New Perspectives on Narrative Analysis*, ed. David Herman (Columbus, OH: Ohio State University Press, 1999), 144–66, here 150.
9. Pynchon, *Gravity's Rainbow*, 3.
10. What is designated as "future narration" frequently is not the relation between *fabula* and *sujet* but a certain chronologically prospective and open form of organizing the *fabula*. This, however, is a metaphorical use of "future" in the sense of potentiality. The form itself is similar to that of what-if-novels and the alternate histories.

11	Uri Margolin, "Shifted (Displaced) Temporal Perspective," *Narrative* 9, no. 2 (2001): 195–202, here 197.
12	Ibid., 195.
13	Fludernik, *Towards a "Natural" Narratology*, 256ff.
14	According to the historical development of relations between aspect/tense/mode as traced by Elisabeth Leiss (*Die Verbalkategorien des Deutschen*, 288), the future tense increasingly serves to analyze modes. As such, the importance of the future tense for fiction is likely to increase. An example of expressing a mode by means of the future tense is: "She will be in the bath." Theoretically, the organization of modal relations into fictional narration is to be expected; it may possibly already exist. There have been attempts at interpreting contingent narratives as future narratives (a kind of *what-if* structure) as well.
15	Beside the "belatedness of narration," we have also already encountered the inverse option, that of "anterior action," e.g., in Schädlich's *Tallhover*. Contemporaneous anteriority or past activity are typical pathologies in the narrative constellation of action and narration.
16	On the concept of "actualization" see above p. 241, Note 47.
17	It is primarily the dimension of fictionality that Margolin does not consider. This is evident when we consider that future narration structurally corresponds to prophecy; yet the properties of prophecy can be described, if at all, in a non-fictional context. In a fictional prophecy embedded in a fictional text, these properties would have to be referred to the time-relations existing between *sujet* and *fabula*, where what seems to be "futural" about the "prophesized event" would dissipate.
18	Marcel Beyer, *Kaltenburg* (Frankfurt am Main: Suhrkamp, 2009), 179; *Kaltenburg*, trans. Alan Bance (Boston, MA and New York: Houghton Mifflin Harcourt, 2012), 136.
19	Ibid., 305; 233–4.
20	References to the poetological tradition in this context generally reach back as far as the Aristotelian concept of *mythos*, a process with a beginning, middle, and end (Aristotle, *Poetics*, trans. Stephen Halliwell [Cambridge, MA: Harvard University Press, 1995], 27–142).
21	Simon, *Georgiques*, 31; *Georgics*, 21.
22	Gunther Müller, "Erzählzeit und erzählte Zeit," *Morphologische*

Poetik: Gesammelte Aufsätze, ed. Elena Müller and Helena Egner (Tübingen: Niemeyer, 1968), 269–86.

23   Interestingly, there is a priority of *fabula* over *sujet* in Seymour Chatman (*Story and Discourse: Narrative Structure in Fiction and Film* [Ithaca, NY: Cornell University Press, 1978], 62). This may be due to the fact that the starting point of his reflections is film, where the photographic apparatus requires a photographic referent that must already exist or be staged in order to be filmed.

24   There seems to be an interpretation of devices specific to film lurking in the background of Chatman's thesis. This is particularly evident in the connecting modalities of editing or montage, that is, in the creation of meaningful intervals, which suggest thinking (film) narration on the basis of just these zero forms.

25   According to a general characterization of focalization on an online portal of the basic terms of literary theory launched by Katrin Dennerlein (*Narratologie des Raumes* [Berlin and New York: de Gruyter, 2009]; cf. also the definition at *Literaturwissenschaftliche Grundbegriffe online*, http://www.li-go.de/definitionsansicht/prosa/fokalisierung.html, last accessed October 31, 2014).

26   Cf. Percy Lubbock, *The Craft of Fiction* (Minneapolis, MN: University of Minnesota Press, 2007), 55. This suggests both a misunderstanding of the linguistic nature of narration as well as an unresolved question concerning the question of media.

27   Gérard Genette, *Narrative Discourse: An Essay in Method*, 1972, trans. Jane E. Lewin (Ithaca, NY: Cornell University Press, 1980), 162.

28   Ibid., 163–4.

29   See Genette, *Narrative Discourse*, and *Fiction and Diction*, trans. Catherine Porter (Ithaca, NY: Cornell University Press, 1993), esp. 66–7 and 80.

30   In what follows, the French word *narration* is printed in italics to refer to this specific usage in Genette.

31   In contrast to this primary difference, however, one can imagine chains of media embedded both in the relationship between the oral and the written as well as in images. Images are media conglomerates that include at least four media: (1) picture/photograph, (2) film/cinematic image, (3) video image, (4) computer image—and it is too early to tell whether the development of visual culture is complete. While the number of media gradations has reached an apex in digital film (which goes

32 Since the introduction of sound to film, the differences between media in combinations of different primary media not only affect the act of medial actualization, but permeate all elements of narrative organization. They thus make new plot structures possible, for example.

   to show that not every medium creates a new narrative level), the contrast with literature shows that the specificity of media embedded in the media conglomerate of the image lies in the form of their embeddedness. Thus, for example, the relationship between seeing and speaking is not primarily, like that of image and video image, one of insertion.

32 Since the introduction of sound to film, the differences between media in combinations of different primary media not only affect the act of medial actualization, but permeate all elements of narrative organization. They thus make new plot structures possible, for example.

33 In a discussion of Virginia Woolf's essay on the cinema, Oleg Aronson speaks of a "totality of the cinematographic principle of impact" in classical literature even before filmic devices are used explicitly in the modernist novel ("Kino i kniga" ["Cinema and Book"], *Kommunikativny obraz: Kino, Literatura, Filosofiya* [Moscow: Novoe Literaturnoe Obozrenie, 2007], 351–2, here 351).

34 Genette, *Narrative Discourse*, 30.

35 Ibid.

36 Ibid.

37 Genette merely notes at one point that the so-called effect of homodiegetization "is never totally removed from a narrative in the present, whose tense always conveys more or less the presence of a narrator who—the reader unavoidably believes—cannot be very far from an action he himself present as so near" (*Narrative Discourse Revisited*, trans. Jane E. Lewin [Ithaca, NY: Cornell University Press, 1988], 83).

38 Ibid., 80–1.

39 Karl Bühler writes: "From the point of origin of the perceptual *here* all other positions are linguistically pointed out, from the origin now all other points in time" (*Theory of Language: The Representational Function of Language*, trans. Donald Fraser Goodwin [Amsterdam: Benjamins, 2011], 122–3).

40 Hamburger, *Logic of Literature*, 89.

41 Ibid., 66.

42 Gisa Rauh, "Über die deiktische Funktion des epischen Präteritum: Die Reintegration einer scheinbaren Sonderform in ihren theoretischen Kontext," *Indogermanische Forschungen* 87 (1982/83): 22–55. Manfred Markus (*Tempus und Aspekt*, 1977, 37), on the other hand, sees one of the two deictic positions, the

time of speaking or the time of acting, replaced in each case by an adeictic time of context.

43 Fludernik, *Towards a "Natural" Narratology*, 253.
44 Hamburger, *Logic of Literature*, 83.
45 Cf. Cohn, *Transparent Minds*, 188ff.
46 This widely discussed example derives from D. H. Lawrence's *England, My England*. It has been examined by Ann Banfield (*Unspeakable Sentences: Narration and Representation in the Language of Fiction* [London: Routledge, 1982], 94) and Brian McHale ("Unspeakable Sentences, Unnatural Acts: Linguistics and Poetics Revisited," *Poetics Today* 4, no. 1 [1983]: 17–45, here 35–6).
47 Daniil Kharms, *O yavleniyakh i sushchestvovaniyakh* (Saint Petersburg, 2003), 37–8; Kharms, *On Phenomena and Existences: No. 2*, 95.
48 Hamburger takes up Stifter's text at various points in her *Logic of Literature* (74–81, 123, 156) in order to explain the borderlines of fictionalization.
49 Marie-Laure Ryan, *Narrative as Virtual Reality: Immersion and Interactivity in Literature and Electronic Media* (Baltimore, MD: Johns Hopkins University Press, 2001), 135.
50 The extent to which permanent shifting of perspective on the part of a reader can be experienced as a dynamicization or, on the contrary, as excessively demanding, may be a matter of proficiency or, expressed from a critical perspective rather than an elitist one, of the degree of automatization in a reader's perception.
51 This links up with an observation that is of great significance for us, namely that space and time in fiction should be viewed as a "space-time-interval." We borrow the term from Yury Tynyanov, translating the Russian word *promezhutok* not as "interval," but as "space-time-interval." Cf. "The Interval," trans. John Glad and Sylvia Maizell, *Russian Literature Triquarterly* 5 (1973): 420–43.
52 Harald Weinrich, *Sprache, das heißt Sprachen* (Tübingen: Narr, 2006), 146.
53 Rauh, *Über die deiktische Funktion des epischen Prateritum*, 36.
54 We have altered it slightly for our purposes. In Wolfgang Klein the sentence reads "... Caesar came to Rome. A strong faction had formed around Pompey there" ('Wo ist hier? Präliminarien zu einer Untersuchung der lokalen Deixis,'" *Linguistische Berichte* 58

[1978]: 18–40, here 27). Gisa Rauh discusses it as well (see *Über die deiktische Funktion des epischen Prateritum*, 41).

55 The question of whether the event has "really" happened plays no role in recognizing the fact that it is a historical reference.

56 Émile Benveniste explains *anteriorité* as the second syntagmatic tense meaning (along with "perfection") of combinatorial time forms. He distinguishes between the temporal meanings of present, past, and future. "The proof that the form of anteriority does not carry any reference to time by itself is that it must depend syntactically on a free tense form whose formal structure it adopts in order to establish itself on the same temporal level and thus fulfill its proper function" (*Problems in General Linguistics*, trans. Mary Elizabeth Meek [Coral Gables, FL: University of Miami Press, 1971], 213). The missing reference to temporality is to be understood in terms of Jakobson's theory of linguistic shifters, which Benveniste discusses a few pages later. By shifter, he understands hollow linguistic forms that do not have a reference of their own. Their function consists in shifting meanings. This already implies that anteriority is deictic temporality (indeed, Jakobson's theory of the shifter provides the starting point for later deixis theory).

57 "до завтра еще далеко" Fyodor Dostoevsky, "Podrostok," *Polnoe sobranie sochineny*, vol. 13, 241. On this example, cf. also Wolf Schmid, *Elemente der Narratologie* (Berlin and New York: de Gruyter, 2005), 144.

58 Leiss, *Verbalkategorien des Deutschen*, 269.

59 Ibid.

60 Ernst Cassirer (*The Philosophy of Symbolic Forms, Volume 1: Language*, trans. Ralph Mannheim [New Haven, CT: Yale University Press, 1953], 219) emphasizes the connection between the spatial and temporal components of language, for "language designates time relations by the same means which it has developed for the designation of local relations."

61 Leiss, *Verbalkategorien des Deutschen*, 244.

62 Ibid., 270.

63 There are various justifications for theses about the atemporality of the present tense, for example in Manfred Markus, Harald Weinrich, or Theo Vennemann.

64 Leiss, *Verbalkategorien des Deutschen*, 246.

65 Ibid., 244.

66 Roland Barthes, *Camera lucida: Reflections on Photography*, trans. Richard Howard (New York: Hill & Wang, 1981), 86.

67 Leiss, *Verbalkategorien des Deutschen*, 245.

68 Kendall Walton, for example, maintains: "Fiction in this sense will be interchangeable with 'representation'" (*Mimesis as Make-Believe* [Cambridge, MA and London: Harvard University Press, 1990], S. 3); cf below p. 118.

69 "Пистолет, и кинжал, и армяк были готовы, Наполеон въезжал завтра." Lev Tolstoj, *Vojna i mir*, in *Polnoe sobranie sochineny* (Nendeln: Kraus, 1972), vol. 11, 369; *War and Peace*, trans. Richard Pevear and Larissa Volokhonsky (London: Vintage, 2007), 909 [modified]).

70 Cf. Hans Vaihinger, *The Philosophy of "As If": A System of the Theoretical, Practical and Religious Fictions of Mankind*, trans. C. K. Ogden, 1924 (London: Routledge, 2000).

71 If the reader believes that she or he can or must decide against the deictic-temporal structure of the text and opt for one of the two *origines*, the fiction effect dissolves. All that remains is a residue of agrammaticality.

72 Here we should recall the context we presented in the first chapter. We argue that, in order to form a story, a fiction can refer beyond its always contemporaneous presence if there is a third level of reference implied alongside the two narrative levels of *fabula* and *sujet*. Otherwise, *fabula* and *sujet* remain contemporaneous with each other, and the assumption that the *fabula* has to have happened before it could be narrated cannot obtain. The historical novel, according to Ricœur, negotiates the strict alternative between a fictional lack of reference and a narrative reference by implying reference.

73 Axel Bühler, "Karl Bühlers Theorie der Deixis," *Karl Bühler's Theory of Language*, ed. Achim Eschbach (Amsterdam: Benjamins, 1987), 287–99, here 298.

74 Ryan, *Narrative as Virtual Reality*, 95; she is referring to Richard Gerrig, *Experiencing Narrative Worlds: On the Psychological Activities of Reading* (New Haven, CT: Yale University Press, 1993), 5.

75 Ryan, *Narrative as Virtual Reality*, 95.

76 Roman Jakobson, "Shifters, Verbal Categories, and the Russian Verb," *Selected Writings, Volume 2: Word and Language* (The Hague: Mouton & Co., 1971), 130–47, here 131.

77 When Jakobson, in another text, compares a poetics of metaphor and a prose of metonomy, the status of prose, between prosaic and fictional language, is ambiguous. Jakobson had already discussed the double relation of metaphor and metonomy in 1935, and in 1960, the "poetic function" of language emerges from this double relation. Structuralist theories of prose then wondered whether it is possible to subsume narrative prose under the poetic function of language (cf. Stefan Speck, *Von Šklovskij zu de Man: Zur Aktualität formalistischer Literaturtheorie* [Munich: Fink, 1997]). From Jakobson's text it would seem to follow that in the special case of fictional narration prose exhibits the same double reference of code and message as the poetic function, but the direction from code to utterance is reversed. In Elisabeth Leiss's generalization, according to which "all morphologically recognizable grammatical categories are shifters" (*Die Verbalkategorien des Deutschen*, 5), we see a turning point: When they are instituted in grammar, the reference of shifters is reversed. They no longer refer from code to utterance, but at the same time also refer back to the code: they are *autonyms* as well. This does not result in a fictitious grammar, which would require an utterance, but in a poetics of grammar.

78 Aleksei Kruchenykh, "Sdvigologiya russkogo stikha," *Kukish proshlyakam* (Moscow and Tallinn: Gileya, 1992), 33–80, here 52.

79 On the "temporal perspective" expressed by verbal aspect, see below p. 135.

80 Kruchenykh, *Sdvigologiya*, 54.

81 Ibid., 68.

82 Robert Musil, *The Man without Qualities*, trans. Sophie Wilkins (New York: Alfred A. Knopf, 1995), 12. We are grateful to Simon Stuhler for pointing this passage out to us. He discusses similar questions in his *Phänomenologie des Lesens* (Leipzig and Berlin: Kirchhof & Franke, 2010).

83 Viktor Shklovsky explains that there is a differential quality, that is, a primary shift, appropriate to words that is lacking in the automatic nature of film recording ("Die grundlegenden Gesetze der Film-Einstellung," trans. Anke Hennig, *Poetika Kino: Theorie und Praxis des Films im russischen Formalismus*, ed. Wolfgang Beilenhoff [Frankfurt am Main: Suhrkamp, 2005], 208–20).

84 Cf. Bühler, *Theory of Language*, 118–19.

85 Walton, *Mimesis as Make-Believe*, 24.

86 Bühler, *Theory of Language*, 134–5.

87 Ibid.

88 Nelson Goodman conceives of "exemplification" as the specific mode of reference through which the *languages of art* are characterized ("Routes of Reference," *On Mind and Other Matters* [Cambridge, MA: Harvard University Press, 1984], 55–71, here 59). On exemplifying reference, cf. also Catherine Z. Elgin, *With Reference to Reference* (Indianapolis, IN: Hackett, 1983), 73ff. Elgin relates exemplification to metaphorical signification and thereby places it primarily on a semantic level.

89 In Gisa Rauh's terminology, one would speak of a dynamic between real deixis, imaginative deixis, and textual deixis. Rauh assumes that in imaginative deixis (which for her would count as fiction), deixis can be deployed at will by an author, who would be able to choose a type of deixis. This would create contradictions between individual centers of orientation and types of deixis. But authors of fictions do not remain within one type of deixis (namely, the imaginative), as Rauh—not unlike Hamburger—implies; "Über die deiktische Funktion des epischen Präteritum: Die Reintegration einer scheinbaren Sonderform in ihren theoretischen Kontext (Teil II)," *Indogermanische Forschungen* 88 (1983): 33–53, here 48.

90 Hamburger concludes that in literary fiction the past tense loses its deictic function. Rauh, in contrast, seeks to show that deixis is valid also and precisely in narrated fiction. For Rauh, fiction seems to be identical with imaginative deixis. Nonetheless, she neglects the moment (merely implicit in Hamburger's transposition of the *origo*) of a deictic shift achieved by the text itself. Rauh deemphasizes shift within modes of indication to such a degree that, for a reader, a difference between the experience of a fictional deixis and that of a real deixis is no longer plausible.

91 Lutz Rühling rejects Hamburger's theory by pointing out that her characterization of fiction is nothing more than a description of the qualities of "lived speech" ("Poetik und Fiktionalität," *Grundzüge der Literaturwissenschaft*, ed. Heinz Ludwig Arnold and Heinrich Detering [Munich: dtv, 1978], 25–51). While we acknowledge Rühling's objection on the level of empirical descriptions, we also understand that Banfield is in search of a *differentia specifica* and declares the epic past tense to be such a criterion of difference: "Banfield went on to show that the syntax of the literary style known variously as free indirect discourse, *erlebte Rede* (lived speech), or *represented speech and thought* (Banfield's term) is disallowed in nonnarrative contexts" (Mary Galbraith, "Deictic Shift Theory and the Poetics of Involvement in Narrative," 27).

92 Stephen C. Levinson provides an overview of the discussion concerning the priority given to spatial or temporal deixis (*Pragmatics* [Cambridge: Cambridge University Press, 1989], 85).

93 Segal, *Narrative Comprehension*, 17.

94 Segal, *Cognitive-Phenomenological Theory*, 69.

95 According to Gisa Rauh, tense does not lose its deixis, as Hamburger believed (*Über die deiktische Funktion des epischen Prateritum*, 37). Her objection is correct, but it lacks an understanding of the shift in the deictic shift. In Hamburger's misunderstanding of the shift as a loss of deictic quality, there is at least an acknowledgment of the shift's existence.

96 A genealogy of this and other exemplary sentences can be found in Franz K. Stanzel's "Morgen war Weihnachten."

97 Gisa Rauh combines perspective and spatial deixis: "Deixis is the linguistic expression of perspective, and a statement present the perspective of the one who counts as the encoder of this statement, and who thus forms the center of orientation" (*Über die deiktische Funktion des epischen Präteritum*, 52). Based on this definition, Rauh analyzes Stanzel's three narrative situations (first-person narration, personal narration, and authorial third-person narration). Rauh's deixis theory conceives of space entirely as perspective.

98 Ivan Turgenev, *Zapiski okhotnika* (Moscow: Nauka, 1991), 75.

99 Dorrit Cohn, "Kafka's Eternal Present: Narrative Tense in 'Ein Landarzt' and Other First-Person Stories," *PMLA* 83, no. 1 (1968): 144–50.

100 Franz Kafka, "Der Bau," *Beschreibung eines Kampfes: Novellen, Skizzen, Aphorismen aus dem Nachlaß, Gesammelte Werke in acht Bänden*, ed. Max Brod (Frankfurt am Main: Fischer, 1983), 132–65, here 134; "The Burrow," *The Complete Stories*, trans. Willa and Edwin Muir, ed. Nahum N. Glatzer (New York: Schocken, 1995), 325–59, here 327.

101 Osip Mandelstam, "The End of the Novel," *Critical Prose and Letters* (New York: Overlook Press, 1995), 198–201.

102 We also doubt that it is possible in purely narratological terms to integrate the focus novel and simultaneous narration (or by extension: the past tense and the present-tense novel) into a common paradigm, as Uri Margolin has tried to do. In his essay "Of What Is Past, Is Passing, or to Come: Temporality, Aspectuality, Modality, and the Nature of Literary Narrative," Margolin depicts the two paradigms of narration in the past tense

and ever-spreading narration in the present tense. He concludes that a paradigm shift has occurred where we detect a shift of dominants in the formalist sense (see above p. 147).
103 Stanzel, "Morgen war Weihnachten," 62.
104 In the first chapter we saw how the fictionality of novels was discussed in connection with the boundary between third-person and first-person narration. Hamburger delineates the two by claiming that first-person narratives are not fictional and that the epic past tense is not in effect in them. Much of narratology followed her in a stubborn reversal according to which the epic past tense cannot be considered to generate fiction at all because it has no presentifying effect in first-person narration.

The imaginary present tense

1 Cf. Felix Martinez-Bonati, "The Act of Writing Fiction," *New Literary History* 11, no. 3 (1980): 425–34, here 428.
2 Odo Marquardt, "Kunst als Antifiktion: Versuch über den Weg der Wirklichkeit ins Fiktive," *Funktionen des Fiktiven*, ed. Dieter Heinrich and Wolfgang Iser (Munich: Fink, 1983), 35–54, here 40.
3 Aleida Assmann, "Fiktion als Differenz," *Poetica* 21, no. 3/4 (1989): 239–60.
4 On this point, Kendall Walton's theory of an arbitrary fiction, based on agreement (*Mimesis as Make-Believe*, 1990), resembles Philippe Lejeune's assumption that reading autobiographies is based on an autobiographical pact between author and reader, an agreement on the status of what was read (*On Autobiography*, trans. Katherine Leary [Minneapolis, MN: University of Minnesota Press, 1989]). Admittedly, this is a matter of the belief in fictionality in one case and of belief in facticity in the other.
5 Cf. Manfred Spitzer, *Halluzinationen: Ein Beitrag zur allgemeinen und klinischen Psychopathologie* (Berlin and New York: Springer, 1988), 290–1.
6 "Now then to begin again with a few men and women and now to begin those of them as beginning. Now to begin again the history of Martha Hersland, to give a history of her as beginning. Then to go on with the history of Martha Hersland and of every one she ever came to know in her living. Now to begin with the beginning of the living of Martha Hersland. Now to begin the description of

the being in Martha Hersland in her beginning. Sometime there will be a complete telling of all young living, feeling, talking, thinking, being ... This is now some description of being ... Soon now there will be much description of the being ... This will soon be a description ... This is now a beginning of a description of Martha Hershland as beginning ... Sometime there will be a history" (Gertrude Stein, *The Making of Americans* [Champaign, IL: Dalkey Archive Press, 1995], 378).

7   Wolfgang Iser, *The Fictive and the Imaginary: Charting Literary Anthropology* (Baltimore, MD: Johns Hopkins University Press, 1993), 184.

8   On this motif, cf. Michel Foucault, "Fantasia of the Library," *Language, Counter-Memory, Practice: Selected Essays and Interviews*, trans. Donald F. Bouchard and Sherry Simon (Ithaca, NY: Cornell University Press, 1977), 87–109, especially 90ff.

9   Cohn, *The Distinction of Fiction*, 104.

10 Besides those already mentioned in the first chapter, they include Osip Mandelstam, Varlam Shalamov, and James Joyce.

11 Emmanuel Levinas insists "that time is not the achievement of an isolated and lone subject, but that it is the very relationship of the subject with the Other" (*Time and the Other*, trans. Richard A. Cohen [Pittsburgh, PA: Duquesne University Press, 1987], 39). Whether and to what degree there is also a spatial dynamic of shifting perspectives (of the gaze) at work here is a question we will discuss in relation to "Strindberg's" attempt to make a bill disappear right before the reader's eyes; see below, 156.

12 Alain Juranville, *Lacan und die Philosophie*, trans. Hans-Dieter Gondek (Munich: Boer, 1990), 88. This is not the context to discuss the various roles the imaginary played in the different phases of Lacan's theoretical development.

13 Ibid., 85. Juranville is playing here with *lettre en souffrance* (undeliverable letter).

14 Ibid., 86.

15 Ibid., 88.

16 Ibid.

17 Ibid., 387–8. Juranville is playing with the overlapping of the spatial and temporal aspects in terms like *avenir*, *devant*, etc.

18 The unfolding of the future is thus laid out in three different moments: "The moment that corresponds to a certain signifier is the moment in which it is established as one and in which it is

separated from it, and the moment of the placing of other signifiers in to its signifying. Its order is not pre-established—it is produced by the act of anticipation as its effect" (Juranville, *Lacan*, 386).

19 The formation of this loop can be described as the success of the work and—both on the side of production as well as reception—as a clue of aesthetic experience: "In a manner of speaking, aesthetic experience is effective both in utopian foreshadowing and in retrospective recognition. It perfects the imperfect world not merely by projecting future experience but also by preserving past experience ... On the receptive side, the aesthetic experience differs from other functions in the world of the everyday by a temporality peculiar to it: it permits us to 'see anew' and offers through this function of discovery the pleasure of a fulfilled present. It takes us into other worlds of the imagination and thereby abolishes the constraint of time in time. It anticipates future experience and thus discloses the scope of possible action. It allows recognition of what is past or suppressed" (Hans Robert Jauß, *Aesthetic Experience and Literary Hermeneutics*, trans. Michael Shaw [Minneapolis, MN: University of Minnesota Press, 2008], 10). This functionalization of the imaginary to create a teleology and to compensate for a lack could also be called the aesthetics of narrated fiction. The poetics of narrated fiction, which looks at its emergence, on the contrary reveals the risks involved in deploying the imaginary to transcend the world.

20 E. T. A. Hoffmann, *Der Goldene Topf, Sämtliche poetischen Werke*, vol. 1, ed. Hannsludwig Geiger (Wiesbaden: Vollmer, n.d.), 181–255, here 198–200; *The Golden Pot and Other Tales*, trans. Ritchie Robertson (Oxford: Oxford University Press, 1992), 20–1.

21 Ibid., 205–6: 27–8.

22 On the motif of discourse networks, cf. Friedrich A. Kittler, *Discourse Networks: 1800/1900*, trans. Michael Meteer (Stanford, CA: Stanford University Press, 1992); Uwe Wirth, "Der goldene Topf," *E. T. A. Hoffmann: Leben—Werk—Wirkung*, ed. Detlef Kremer (Berlin and New York: de Gruyter, 2009), 114–30.

23 Hoffmann, *Der goldene Topf*, 255; *The Golden Pot*, 83.

24 Nikolai Gogol, *The Diary of a Madman*, in *The Collected Tales of Nikolai Gogol*, trans. Richard Pevear and Larissa Volokhonsky (New York: Pantheon, 1999), 155–65, here 156; "Сегодня среда, и потому я был у нашего начальника в кабинете." Nikolay Gogol, *Zapiski sumasshedshego*, in *Sobranie sochineny*, vol. 3 (Moscow, 1994), 148–65, here 150.

25 Gogol, *Zapiski sumasshedshego*, 153.
26 Gogol, *Zapiski sumasshedshego*, 158–9.
27 "Англичанин большой политик. Он везде юлит": Gogol, *Zapiski sumasshedshego*, 164.
28 Gogol, *The Diary of a Madman*, 165 [modified].
29 Quoted in Iser, *The Fictive and the Imaginary*, 173.
30 The motif of the missing date turns up earlier in the diaries: "Тотчас же видно, что не человек писал. Начнет так, как следует, а кончит собачиною. Посмотрим-ка еще в одно письмецо. Что-то длинновато. Гм! и числа не выставлено." Gogol, *Zapiski sumasshedshego*, 156. "Let's have a look at another letter. A bit long. Hm! and no date. Shows at once that it wasn't written by a man. Begins properly, but ends with some dogginess" (Gogol, *Diary of a Madman*, 170).
31 Uspensky, *The Poetics of Composition*, 73.
32 Gogol, *Zapiski sumasshedshego*, 163; *The Diary of a Madman*, 164. Even if we do not adhere to a strict terminology here, we are nonetheless aware of the different orientations and shades of meaning of terms such as, for instance, delusion (phenomenal-hermeneutic), madness (social position), mental illness (noetic dysfunction), or psychopathology (depraved psyche). For a discussion of the relationships between unreasonableness, delusion, and joking (folly, lunacy), cf. Oliver Kohns, *Die Verrücktheit des Sinns: Wahnsinn und Zeichen bei Kant, E. T. A. Hoffmann und Thomas Carlyle* (Bielefeld: Transcript, 2007).
33 Gogol, *The Diary of a Madman*, 164.
34 Similarly loaded examples of resolute irresolvability can be found in Pynchon's *The Crying of Lot 49* and, more recently, in Martin Scorsese's *Shutter Island* (2010).
35 Gogol, *The Diary of a Madman*, 162.
36 Jakobson, "Shifters."
37 Gogol, *The Diary of a Madman*, 165. "Чи 34 сло Мц гдао. фсвбзпр 349." Gogol, *Zapiski sumasshedshego*, 165.
38 Jean-Paul Sartre, *The Imaginary: A Phenomenological Psychology of the Imagination* (London: Routledge, 2010), 185ff.
39 Fyodor Dostoevsky, *The Double: A Petersburg Poem*, trans. Constance Garnett (San Bernadino: Borgo Press, 2002), 3. "Было без малого восемь часов утра, когда титулярный советник Яков

	Петрович Голядкин очнулся после долгого сна" (*Dvojnik* [St. Petersburg: Azbuka klassika, 2007], 7).
40	A knowledge of intertextual relations is required to recognize in *The Double* the twin text of Gogol's *Diary of a Madman*, *The Coat*, or *The Nose*.
41	Dostoevsky, *The Double*, 8. "что не я, а что кто-то другой, разительно схожий со мною" (*Dvojnik*, 13).
42	For a narratological overview of focalization, cf. Matias Martinez and Michael Scheffel, *Einführung in die Erzähltheorie* (Munich: Beck, 2007), 64ff.
43	We will return to methodological reflections on a "transformative poetics of time" in the Conclusion, p. 235.
44	For an analogy with painting, cf. for instance Marie-Laure Ryan, *Narrative as Virtual Reality*, 3.
45	In analogy with late Gothic painting, it could be called Flemish perspective, for it is precisely not objectively/mathematically construed.
46	"Но обратите внимание на то, что за спиной Николая Ивановича нет ничего. Не то что-бы там не стоял шкап или комод, или вообще что-нибудь такое, а совсем ничего нет, даже воздуха нет. Хотите верьте, хотите не верьте, но за спиной Николая Ивановича нет даже безвоздушного пространства, или, как говорится, мирового эфира. Откровенно говоря, ничего нет. Этого, конечно, и вообразить себе невозможно. Но на это нам наплевать, нас интересует только спиртуоз и Николай Иванович Серпухов" (Kharms, *O yavleniyakh i sushchestvovaniyakh*, 37–8). "But take note of the fact that behind Nikolay Ivanovich's back there is nothing. It's not that there isn't a cupboard there, or a chest of drawers, or at any rate some such object: but there is absolutely nothing there, not even air. Believe it or not, as you please, but behind Nikolay Ivanovich's back there is not even an airless expanse or, as they say, universal ether. To put it bluntly, there's nothing. This is, of course, utterly inconceivable. But we don't give a damn about that, as we are only interested in the vodka and Nikolay Ivanovich Serpukhov" (Kharms, "On Phenomena and Existences: No. 2," 95).
47	The fact that focus turns up in both literary history and phenomenology at roughly the same time seems to support the thesis that focus and epic past tense are complementary.
48	She claims that "the present tense is increasingly advanced as a basic tense in contemporary narrative prose" (Fiona Björling, "As

Time Goes By... Tentative Notes on Present Tense Narration in Contemporary Fiction: A Comparison with Narration in Film," *Telling Forms: 30 Essays in Honour of Peter Alberg Jensen*, ed. Karin Grelz and Susanna Witt [Stockholm: Almqvist & Wiksell, 2004], 17–36, here 19).

49 The degree to which the past exceeds memory can be seen in the fact that even the remembered past dispossesses the I: "No one knows what an infinite host of images of the past slumbers in him; now and then they do indeed accidentally awake, but one cannot, as it is said, call them to mind. Thus the images are *ours* only in a *formal* manner" (Georg Wilhelm Friedrich Hegel, *Hegel's Philosophy of Mind, Being Part Three of the Encyclopedia of the Philosophical Sciences*, trans. William Wallace and A. V. Miller [Oxford: Clarendon Press, 1971], addendum to §433, 205).

50 Jacques Derrida, *Dissemination*, trans. Barbara Johnson (Chicago, IL: University of Chicago Press, 1981), esp. 95–133. The appropriation of focalization persons in narrated fiction is the literati's new talent and at the same time the intoxicating poison from which they perish.

51 Cf. Gogol, *The Diary of a Madman*, 161: "He's not going to have a third eye on his forehead because he's a kammerjunker."

52 "[L]ongtemps que je médite un roman sur la folie ou plutot sur *la maniere* dont on devient fou": Gustave Flaubert, *Œuvres complètes, vol. 14: Correspondance 1859–1871* (Paris: Club de l'Honnête Homme, 1975), 16.

53 Dostoevsky, *Dvojnik*, 94; *The Double*, 83–4.

54 Franz Kafka, "Die Wahrheit über Sancho Pansa," *Die Erzählungen und andere ausgewählte Prosa*, ed. Roger Hermes (Frankfurt am Main: Fischer, 1998), 350; "The Truth about Sancho Panza," *The Complete Stories*, ed. Nahum N. Glatzer (New York: Schocken, 1971), 430.

55 "The fantastic confronts us with a dilemma: to believe or not to believe?": Tzetan Todorov, *The Fantastic: A Structural Approach to a Literary Genre*, trans. Richard Howard (Ithaca, NY: Cornell University Press, 1975), 83.

56 Cf. Jorge Luis Borges, "Pierre Menard, Author of Don Quixote," *Ficciones*, trans. Anthony Bonner (New York: Grove Press, 1962), 45–55.

57 Dostoevsky, *Dvojnik*, 192; *The Double*, 183.

58 Aage A. Hansen-Love, "Nachwort," *Der Doppelgänger: Eine Petersburger Dichtung*, by Fyodor Dostoevsky, trans. E. K. Rahsin (Munich: Piper, 1986), 894–939, here 909.

59 Cohn, *Transparent Minds*, 180. "Fantastic stenography" does not denote a fantastic apparatus but Dostoevsky's technique of dictation.

60 Samuel Beckett, *Company*, in *Nohow On: Three Novels* (New York: Grove Press, 1996), 1–46, here 3–4.

61 Dostoevsky, *Dvojnik*, 50; *The Double*, 43. "Он сорвался с места, на котором доселе стоял, как прикованный, и стремглав бросился вон, куда-нибудь, на воздух, на волю, куда глаза глядят." "He started off and rushed away headlong, anywhere, into the air, into freedom, wherever chance might take him." In this reminiscence of the grotesque, with which the passage then coherently closes, delusion become intertextually identifiable again. [Translation altered to reflect tense usage in the original.]

62 This passage can also be interpreted as proto-cinematic. As earlier with Chatman, montage can be understood as a form of ellipsis that participates in the creation of film narration. We have discussed ellipsis as one of those systematically relevant cases in which a deception arises thanks to the status of the *fabula* in narrated fiction.

63 Peter Weiss' present-tense text *The Shadow of the Body of the Coachman* fails in figuring the spatial volume and holding capacity of a black carriage. It seems impossible to the protagonist that the carriage, which arrived undetected at the beginning of the narrative, could contain as much coal as can actually be found in the dark cellar. Weiss' story begins with factographic pathos and ends with mysterious darkness. It moves from the present tense back to a past tense, and if it did not begin again exactly where it ended, one could suspect a failure in Weiss' poetology.

64 August Strindberg, *Inferno*, trans. Claud Field (New York: Putnam, 1913), 96. The composition and publication history of the *Inferno* is a complicated one. Originally written in French, it was first published in a Swedish translation (not checked by Strindberg), followed by a heavily edited French version. The second, corrected Swedish version is generally used as the basis for the translation cited here, and conforms entirely in tense usage. We have therefore opted, in this case only, not to cite any "original."

65 Ibid., 20.

66 Ibid., 62.

67 Ibid., 105.
68 Ibid., 134.
69 Ibid., 130.
70 Ibid., 132.
71 This definition by Jaspers—the process of delusion is a successive unperceived course—is later strongly contested by Jacques Lacan. We would argue that such indistinguishability never exists in relation to a reality, but always only in relation to a literary fiction—the validity of which must first be contested in a discourse that reveals the nihilistic dynamic of delusional de-rangement; cf. Jacques Lacan, *The Psychoses*, trans. Jacques-Alain Miller and Russell Grigg (New York: Norton, 1997), 16–17; Karl Jaspers, *Strindberg and Van Gogh*, trans. Oskar Grunow and David Woloshin (Tuscon, AZ: University of Arizona Press, 1982).
72 Stuhler, *Phänomenologie des Lesens*, 35.
73 Strindberg is playing here with all the elements of *agon*/battle, *aleia*/chance, *mimicry*/deception and reversal, as well as *ilinx*/intoxication. Cf. Iser, *The Fictive and the Imaginary*.
74 Michel Foucault, *Madness and Civilization: A History of Insanity in the Age of Reason*, trans. Richard Howard (New York: Random House, 1965).
75 The "exposure of devices" is a major strategy of literary self-reflection in the poetics of Russian formalism.

Tense philosophy

1 On the unaesthetic radicalization of an absolute present tense into an eternal present tense, cf. Peter Hallward, *Badiou: A Subject to Truth* (Minneapolis, MN: University of Minnesota Press, 2003), 157: "the time of truth is the time of a properly eternal present, indifferent to both the inheritance of the past and the promise of the future."
2 Karl Heinz Bohrer, *Das absolute Präsens: Die Semantik ästhetischer Zeit* (Frankfurt am Main: Suhrkamp, 1994), 157.
3 Felix Philipp Ingold, *Der große Bruch: Russland im Epochenjahr 1913: Kultur – Gesellschaft – Politik* (Munich: Beck, 2003); Hans Ulrich Gumbrecht, *1926: Ein Jahr am Rand der Zeit* (Frankfurt am Main: Suhrkamp, 2003); Karl Schlögel, *Terror und Traum: Moskau 1937* (Munich: Hanser, 2008).

4   Jacques Rancière, *The Names of History: On the Poetics of Knowledge*, trans. Hassan Melehy (Minneapolis, MN: University of Minnesota Press, 1994), 49.

5   Fernand Braudel, *The Mediterranean and the Mediterranean World in the Age of Philip II*, trans. Sian Reynolds (Berkeley and Los Angeles, CA: University of California, 1995).

6   Jacques Rancière, "The Putting to Death of Emma Bovary: Literature, Democracy and Medicine," *The Politics of Literature* (Cambridge: Polity Press, 2011), 49–71.

7   Jacques Rancière, "On the Battlefield: Tolstoy, Literature, History," *The Politics of Literature* (Cambridge: Polity Press, 2011), 72–9.

8   Elisabeth Leiss, "Gustave Guillaumes Sprachtheorie: Am Beispiel der grammatischen Kategorien des Verbs," *Sprachwissenschaft* 9 (1984): 456–72, here 456.

9   On Deleuze's recourse to Guillaume's dynamic language theory against Saussure's oppositions, which he considered too static, cf. Daniel W. Smith, "Deleuze's Concept of the Virtual and the Critique of the Possible," *Journal of Philosophy: A Cross Disciplinary Inquiry* 4, no. 9 (Spring 2009): 29–42. In this same context, Henning Schmidgen, too, has commented on differential positionings and the critique of Lacan's phoneme opposition as early as *Difference and Repetition*; cf. Roland Braun, "Rezension von Henning Schmidgens 'Das Unbewuste der Maschinen,'" http://www.cultd.net/texte/antioedipus/schmid.htm (last accessed October 31, 2014).

10 John M. Ellis McTaggart, "The Unreality of Time," *The Human Experience of Time: The Development of Its Philosophical Meaning*, ed. Charles M. Sherover (Evanston, IL: Northwestern University Press, 1975), 278–96, here 279.

11 For a narratological study relevant in this context, cf. Mark Currie's *About Time*: "The A-theory is therefore a tensed theory of time, and goes by a variety of other names such as *presentism* and the *moving now* theory. B-theory, on the other hand, dispenses with the idea of the now, and therefore with the idea of events being past and future ... In terms of the debate between A-theory and B-theory, a similar claim can be made for fictional narrative: that fictional narrative is characterised by its special power to articulate a tensed theory of time to an untensed theory of time" (*About Time: Narrative, Fiction and the Philosophy of Time* [Edinburgh: Edinburgh University Press, 2007], 144 and 146).

12 Peter Bieri argues against the proofs of unreality in time from within an analytical tradition. These proofs, he writes, always take the detour of detecting an inconsistency in the experience of time. Starting from the validity of all experiences of time, Bieri replaces the distinction real-unreal with that of subjective-objective. Every experience of time thus relates to an objective time as subjective. The inaccessibility of a real time does not justify accusing the subjective experience of time of being unreal (*Zeit und Zeiterfahrung: Exposition eines Problembereichs* [Frankfurt am Main: Suhrkamp, 1972]).

13 McTaggart, "The Unreality of Time," 290.

14 Ibid., 284.

15 Bertrand Russell, *History of Western Philosophy and Its Connection with Political and Social Circumstances from the Earliest Times to the Present Day* (London: Allen & Unwin, 1946), 805.

16 Bertrand Russell, *Our Knowledge of the External World as a Field for Scientific Method in Philosophy* (London: Allen & Unwin, 1914), 136.

17 Prior to this time, the dominant, cultural-historical view of literature gave preference to the referentiality of the *fabula* and the factuality of its chronological course to the detriment of the mannerist artificiality of narration.

18 Examples include accumulations of weddings at the ends of folklore narratives, an excess of events in novels of adventure, and even possible solutions piling up at the end of detective stories.

19 Bertrand Russell, *Theory of Knowledge* (London: Routledge, 1992), 69.

20 In regard to the history of discourse, we should mention that the narratological distinction of simultaneity and synchrony appears around this time and prepares the gradual discovery of a differential quality of the present.

21 Russell, *Theory of Knowledge*, 74.

22 In the history of discourse, we now find ourselves at the point at which the perception of artworks can no longer be described solely as the perception of their material. Instead, temporality is integrated into the material, which takes the form of a transition from a concept of material to a concept of media, which necessarily has immaterial traits. This is particularly evident in synthetic media whose material movements take place

in time. Sound films, for example, make it possible to perceive the synchrony and asynchrony of visual and audial movements. Materials thus are to be not only synthesized but simultaneously synchronized.

23 The example of sports commentary on the radio often serves to illustrate a separation of the senses of speaking and seeing in which a contemporaneous experiencing and narrating is possible. If, however, the medium itself already synchronizes the senses, as television does, the aporia of an overemployment of the senses (*qua* sense overload) returns indirectly. When image transmission is interrupted, television commentators are, in principle, in the same situation as radio commentators, and could bring the event as close to their listeners (now deprived of the image) as their radio colleagues do. The image blackouts on German television during the 2008 European Football Cup matches, however, demonstrated that the synchronization of what is experienced and what is narrated—which radio commentators achieve effortlessly—overtaxed television commentators. Conveying what is not visible to the television viewer was too much for them because their synchronous medium always already relieves them of this burden.

24 Russell, *Theory of Knowledge*, 74.

25 Ibid., 69.

26 Simultaneity understood as juxtaposition encompasses syntopy and asyntopy as long as space is conceived as homogeneous and infinite. When time as its fourth dimension and the curving of time described by relativity theory are taken into account, the term "asyntopy" becomes ambiguous. Asyntopy can no longer only be taken to mean simultaneity. It must now contain a temporal coordinate and relate itself to either contemporaneity or non-contemporaneity.

27 Bertrand Russell, *ABC of Relativity* (London: Routledge, 1985), 36.

28 Ibid., 37–8.

29 Walter Benjamin, *The Arcades Project*, trans. Howard Eiland and Kevin McLaughlin (Cambridge, MA: Harvard University Press, 1999), 470.

30 Sebastian Rödl, *Categories of the Temporal: An Inquiry into the Forms of a Finite Intellect*, trans. Sibylle Salewski (Cambridge, MA: Harvard University Press, 2012), 128–9.

31 Ibid., 129.

32　Ibid., 130.
33　Ibid.
34　Ibid., 131.
35　See above p. 124ff.
36　On undetectability, undecideability, and indistinguishability in relation to the imaginary and narration/fiction, see above, p. 145, 156.
37　See above p. 65.
38　Rödl, *Categories of the Temporal*, 130.
39　This can be asserted against any linguistic theory that claims the present tense to be atemporal. We also see it as an objection to those who conceive of time deictically from a centered I-here-now *origo*.
40　Cf. Walter Hirtle, *Lessons on the English Verb: No Expression without Representation* (Montreal, ON: McGill-Queen's University Press, 2007); Leiss, *Die Verbalkategorien des Deutschen* (Berlin and New York: de Gruyter, 1992); Elizaveta Referovskaya, *Filosofiya lingvistiki Gyustava Giyoma: Kurs lekcy po zhazykoznaniyu* (St. Petersburg: Akademichesky proekt, 1997).
41　According to Jan Assmann, the relation of a "dual concept of time to the specific tense categories of Egyptian" is much more restrictive, since in Egyptian one "has the possibility of expressing oneself completely abstractly in relation to time. The form for this is the nominal sentence, which has no finite verb and no temporal reference. Temporal reference is found only in one form of Egyptian sentences, in sentences with finite verbs. There is an opposition here that arises from the original semito-hamitic aspect-opposition, which I understand as virtuality vs. resultivity. The verb forms of the virtual depict an operation as such, independent of the placement in time of its contemporaneous course; the forms of the resultative depict it, in the manner of a present perfect, as currently completed and enduring (insofar as its result is concerned)" (Jan Assmann, *Stein und Zeit: Mensch und Gesellschaft im Alten Ägypten* [Munich: Fink, 2003], 40–1).
42　In Russian, where the aspect system is much more developed than the tense system, aspects already give a direction to time, as Guillaume's contemporary, Erwin Koschmieder, pointed out in 1929: "Aspects are grammatical categories to express the relation to the direction of time: the perfective for the directional relation future → past and the imperfective for the directional relation past → future" (*Zeitbezug und Sprache: Ein Beitrag zur Aspekt- und Tempusfrage* [Darmstadt: Wissenschaftliche Buchgesellschaft, 1971], 35).

43 Giorgio Agamben, too, relates universal time and chronogenesis: "This capacity to refer to the pure presence of the enunciation goes hand in hand, according to Benveniste, with *chronothèse*, time-positing (literally, "chronothesis"), itself the origin of our representation of time. In this way, an axial point of reference is established with regard to our representation of time" (*The Time that Remains: A Commentary on the Letter to the Romans*, trans. Patricia Dailey [Stanford, CA: Stanford University Press, 2005], 66).

44 Only auxiliary constructions (*has* walked, *has* eaten) can motivate this irrevocable immobilization of the verb's activity in the participle to begin a new cycle (of action).

45 Cf. Gustave Guillaume, *Temps et verbe: Théorie des aspects des modes et des temps* (Paris: Champion, 1965), 60–1.

46 Cf. the motif of "futures past" developed by Reinhart Koselleck in his study of the same name, 40–1.

47 The analogous "defuturizing of the future" in the case of deploying relaxation or de-tension (1) in the future will not be discussed here.

48 "Par ailleurs, on notera l'emploi du present comme moyen de rendre plus vive, plus directe, l'impression de faits passes ... Dans le present *historique* il convient de voir surtout un moyen de dramatiser les evenements, les situations, en les mettant mieux en lumiere, sur un plan plus proche" (Guillaume, *Temps et Verbe*, 60).

49 Against the background of Soviet alphabetization campaigns under Stalin, the re-affirmation of the classical relation between *fabula* and *sujet* can be interpreted in the terms of an ontology of language, i.e., as the effect language had on an alphabetized generation without much experience of literary history.

50 It is unclear whether a pre-alphabetical knowledge of time has had a lasting effect in literature. Mikhail Bakhtin, for instance, criticizes the Greek novel's adventure time for its abstract contemporaneity and non-contemporaneity. According to his basic thesis and interpretation, "suddenly" and "just" are the central determinants of time in the adventure novel, which constantly attempts to synchronize two completely arbitrary series of time. The "reversibility of moments in a temporal sequence and their interchangeability in space" indicates connections that conform only to the pattern of contemporaneity/non-contemporaneity. They are, however, not yet intertwined in a reversal ("Forms of Time and of the Chronotope in the Novel," 100).

51 Benjamin, *Berlin Childhood*, 141–2.
52 Such a revolutionary language dispossesses its speakers, it allows them to take part in language, but denies them any possession of language.
53 Nonetheless, the manifestos (counter-languages) that follow one on the other, the "-isms" that replace one by the other can be analyzed as a literary epoch and its synchronous typology of binary grammatical actualizations of language.
54 J. M. Coetzee, "Time, Tense, and Aspect in Kafka's 'The Burrow,'" *Doubling the Point: Essays and Interviews* (Cambridge, MA: Harvard University Press, 1992), 210–32, here 231.
55 Edward Branigan, "Nearly True: Forking Plots, Forking Interpretations: A Response to David Bordwell's 'Film Futures,'" *SubStance* 97, no. 31 (2002): 105–14, here 110.
56 Gerald Prince, "The Disnarrated," *Style* 22 (1988): 1–8, here 6.
57 Gilles Deleuze, *Difference and Repetition*, 97.
58 The limits of the present can only be defined by and in language. The present especially is not restricted a priori to the present in consciousness (that is phenomenologically) restricted. Such a standpoint (marked by the metaphysics of presence) misrecognizes that it is language that constitutes temporality as such in the first place.
59 Deleuze, *Difference and Repetition*, 100.
60 Ibid., 102. Because it is inaccessible before the structuring of time by language, the difference between passive and active synthesis, or in Bergson's terms, between habitual matter and pure memory, is secondary for our approach here. Deleuze introduces yet a third synthesis, a synthesis of the future, which we will not discuss here because we think that there is no future narration (see above p. 98): "The present is the repeater, the past is repetition itself, but the future is that which is repeated ... A philosophy of repetition must pass through all these 'stages,' condemned to repeat repetition itself. However, by traversing these stages it ensures its programme of making repetition the category of the future" (ibid., 94).
61 Ibid., 82.
62 Ibid., 103.
63 Ibid., 104.
64 Ibid., 100: "This is the paradox of the present: to constitute time while passing in the time constituted." This tautology is exactly what readers and critics have been accusing the present-tense

novel of since its emergence. Cf. the recent polemic in an English newspaper: http://www.guardian.co.uk/global/2010/sep/18/philip-pullman-author-present-tense; last viewed on April 18, 2015.

65   In Kant, the antinomies of theoretical and practical reason, as well as that of judgment, force us "to look beyond the horizon of the sensible, and to seek in the supersensible the point of union of all our faculties a priori: for we are left with no other expedient to bring reason into harmony with itself" (Immanuel Kant, *The Critique of Judgment*, trans. James Creed Meredith [Oxford: Oxford University Press, 1952], B 240).

66   Immanuel Kant, *Critique of Pure Reason*, trans. F. Max Muller (New York: Anchor Books, 1966), B 97.

67   Immanuel Kant, *Lectures on Logic*, trans. J. Michael Young (Cambridge: Cambridge University Press, 1992), 600.

68   Oswald Egger, *Die ganze Zeit* (Berlin: Suhrkamp, 2010), 188.

69   Woolf, *To the Lighthouse*, 135–55.

Conclusion

1   A peculiar effect shows how problematic this claim is. In looking at the emergence of the asynchronous present-tense novel, it always seems that it has not yet been achieved, and even very recent novels still do not seem to fully live up to the concept. From the altermodern point of view, however, the present-tense novel seems to always already have been there, and the point of its emergence seems continually to shift back to earlier texts.

2   When it comes to the use of the present tense in the Russian avant-garde's factographies, we can speak, *in terms of literary history*, of a poetological rejection of classical literature. Yet it also involves the slogan *Down with the novel* and an advocacy of a documentary literature of the everyday.

INDEX

ABC of Relativity (Russell) 196, 276
About Time (Currie) 274
Act of Writing Fiction, The (Martinez-Bonati) 266
Adolescent, The (Dostoevsky) 118, 261
Adorno, Theodor W. 31, 240
Aesthetic Experience and Literary Hermeneutics (Jauß) 268
Aesthetic Theory (Adorno) 31, 240
Agamben, Giorgio 8, 13, 233, 234, 278
altermodern 8, 12, 16–17, 39, 43–4, 46, 48, 52–3, 57–61, 63–8, 70–1, 76-7, 79–81, 83, 83–92, 95, 100, 106, 133, 142, 144, 147, 148, 168, 184–7, 196, 199, 201, 208–12, 214, 216–18, 220–1, 223, 224, 226, 227, 228, 229, 230, 231, 233, 234, 239, 243, 244, 248, 250, 252, 255, 280
altermodernism 15, 20, 23, 52, 58–62, 65, 67–8, 75–6, 79–80, 83–4, 84, 96, 99, 113, 138, 144, 168, 184–6, 207, 209–10, 213–18, 221, 223, 228, 229, 239, 243, 244, 255

anteriority 53, 69, 92, 96, 117–18, 186, 191, 193–4, 197, 202, 206, 209, 221, 223, 224, 229, 231, 248, 257, 261
antifictional 8, 65, 142
aporia of synchrony 3, 40, 44, 77, 85, 87, 194, 195, 223, 230, 242, 254
Arcades Project, The (Benjamin) 276
Archaeology of Knowledge, The (Foucault) 250
Aristotle, 234, 257
Arnold, Heinz Ludwig 264
Aronson, Oleg 259
As Time Goes By (Björling) 168, 270
aspect 4, 8, 13, 59, 61, 66, 76, 80, 97, 125–6, 137–8, 147, 149, 177, 190, 202, 219, 227, 232, 237, 257, 263, 277, 279
aspect system 277
Assman, Aleida 142, 183, 226, 266, 277
Assmann, Jan 142, 183, 226, 266, 277
asynchrony 4, 6–8, 12, 53, 58–9, 65, 70, 75, 90–1, 95, 144, 168, 184, 186, 193–4, 196–7, 201, 213–15, 218, 219–21, 223, 224, 226, 227, 228, 229, 231, 248, 250, 276

Au Bonheur des Dames (Zola) 15, 25, 96, 213, 238, 248
Augustine, St. 52, 245
autodiegetic 63
Avanessian, Armen 233, 235

Bakhtin, Mikhail 250, 278
Banfield, Ann 18, 34, 236, 241, 260, 264
Bareis, Alexander 256
Barthes, Roland 30, 120, 262
Beckett, Samuel 1, 143, 176, 195, 249, 272
Being and Time (Heidegger) 9, 59–60, 190, 248, 249
Benjamin, Walter 3, 197, 207, 233, 259, 262, 276, 279
Benveniste, Émile 30, 117, 261, 278
Berlin Childhood around 1900 (Benjamin) 3, 207, 233, 279
Beyer, Marcel 96–7, 168, 257
Bieri, Peter 275
Björling, Fiona 168, 270
Bohrer, Karl Heinz 187, 205, 273
Borges, Jorge Luis 74, 80, 82, 173, 271
Branigan, Edward 30, 197, 209, 279
Braudel, Fernand 188, 274
Braun, Roland 274
breaking point, narratological 44–5
breaking point of fiction 15, 16, 40, 44, 45, 52, 65, 83, 199
Bremond, Claude 252
Brinkmann, Hennig 54, 245
Brod, Max 265
Bronzwaer, W. J. M. 254
Bruder, Gail A. 236, 240, 253
Bühler, Axel 122, 262, 263

Bühler, Karl 107–8, 114, 122–3, 125, 129–30, 132, 259, 262, 263
Burrow, The (Kafka) 137, 139, 208, 265, 279

Calvino, Italo 82, 254
Camera lucida: Reflections on Photography (Barthes) 120, 266
Campe, Rüdiger 14, 235
Caruth, Cathy 61, 249
Casparis, Christian Paul 55, 246
Cassirer, Ernst 261
Categories of the Temporal (Rödl) 7, 189, 191, 197–8, 200–1, 220, 232, 276, 277
Chatman, Seymour 30, 91, 99–101, 258, 272
chronotopos 24–5, 51, 79, 104, 108
co-presence 174
Coetzee, J. M. 4, 6, 185, 208, 254, 279
Cohen, Robert 244
Cohn, Dorrit 19, 36, 44, 48, 77, 81, 86, 109, 134, 137, 146–7, 166, 183, 208, 232, 235,
Company (Beckett) 176
composition 227, 241, 242, 254, 269, 272
Confessions (St. Augustine) 52
counterfactual 19, 36, 75–6, 81, 148, 226, 250, 252
course of events 16, 42–3, 74, 146, 149, 228, 230
Craft of Fiction, The (Lubbock) 101, 258
Critique of Judgment, The (Kant) 216–17, 280
Critique of Pure Reason (Kant) 216–17, 280

Currie, Mark 274

Dannenberg, Hilary P. 76, 252
David Copperfield (Dickens) 11, 70, 78, 86, 213, 253, 255
Deictic Shift Theory (Galbraith) 92, 236, 256, 264
Deixis in Narrative (Duchan, Bruder, Gail and Hewitt) 92, 133, 236 n.6, 240 n.38, 253 n.151, 255, 256
Deleuze, Gilles 7, 65, 190–1, 197, 210–12, 218, 223, 250, 274, 279
Dennerlein, Katrin 258
Der Hausierer (Handke) 67–8, 250
Der Präsensroman (Avenessian and Hennig) 244, 254, 263
Derrida, Jacques 168, 271
Detering, Heinrich 264
dialogue 4, 37, 127, 242
Diary of a Madman, The (Gogol) 6, 145, 150, 156, 159, 162–3, 169, 172–3, 180, 268, 269, 270, 271
Dickens, Charles 11, 70, 78, 86, 213, 253, 255
Die Chronik der Sperlingsgasse (Raabe) 21, 23, 213, 237, 238
Die ganze Zeit (Egger) 280
diegesis 101–2
Difference and Repetition (Deleuze) 65, 190–1, 210–12, 218, 223, 250, 274, 279
discours 30–1, 105
Discourse Networks: 1800/1900 (Kittler) 268
discussed world 20–1, 23, 29
Disnarrated, The (Prince) 279
Dissemination (Derrida) 178, 271
Distinction of Fiction, The (Cohn) 44, 48, 77, 183, 236, 242, 244, 267
documentarism 42
dominants, shift of 4, 12, 23, 56, 66, 76, 89–90, 141, 144, 219, 225, 226, 228, 226
Dostoevsky, Fyodor 6, 118, 145, 150, 163–4, 169–71, 174–8, 261, 269, 271, 272
Double, The (Dostoevsky) 6, 145, 150, 163–78, 269, 270, 271, 272
dream 3, 22, 169, 207
Duchan, Judith F. 236, 240, 253
Duff, David 239

Egger, Oswald 280
Egner, Helena 258
Elective Affinities (Goethe) 54, 245
Elgin, Catherine Z. 264
End of the Novel, The (Mandelshtam) 138, 265, 267
Eschbach, Achim 262
estrangement 23, 38, 89, 174, 183
event 3, 5, 7, 27, 33, 37, 51, 60–1, 70, 74, 87, 117, 119, 145, 149, 159, 161, 172, 174, 191–2, 206, 214, 227, 233, 238, 246, 249, 251, 254, 255, 257, 261, 276
Experiencing Narrative Worlds (Gerrig) 123, 262

fabula 4, 16–20, 27–8, 30–1, 33, 37–40, 42–8, 52–3, 58–60, 62, 64–71, 74–88, 95–7, 99–100, 103, 112–13, 132–3, 154, 156, 158, 177, 180, 185, 188–90, 193, 199, 200, 205–10, 213,

225, 226, 228, 230, 231, 238, 239, 240, 241, 244, 245, 249, 250, 252, 254, 255, 256, 257, 258, 262, 272, 275, 278
facticism 79, 100
factography/-ies 1, 15, 28, 30–1, 33–4, 39, 42, 45, 48, 59, 61, 61, 65, 121, 147, 182, 184–5
Fantastic, The (Todorov) 159, 172
Fichte, Hubert 46, 244
fiction, critique of 183–4
Fiction of the Contemporary, The (Osborne) 13, 235
Fiction and Diction (Genette) 100, 101, 103, 114, 120, 167
Fiction as difference (Assmann) 244, 266
fiction signal 81
fictionalizing 21, 52, 54, 61, 108, 121, 125, 137, 150, 200, 253
fictionalizing narration 212
Fictive and the Imaginary, The (Iser) 142, 144, 147, 160, 182–3, 227, 266, 267, 269, 273
film 29–30, 62, 92, 101, 103–4, 244, 258, 259, 263, 271, 272, 263, 279
Flaubert, Gustave 109, 138, 169, 188, 271
Fleischman, Suzanne 27, 168, 238, 241, 244
Fludernik, Monika 83, 108, 168, 254, 256, 257, 260
focalization 6, 34, 36, 100, 103, 107–9, 113–14, 131, 133–4, 137, 147, 163–5, 168, 170, 227, 255, 258, 270, 271

focalization person 170, 271
focus 6, 58, 66, 97, 106–7, 109, 134, 136–9, 147, 163, 164–70, 173, 175, 177–8, 185, 227, 235, 243, 265, 270
Forms of Time and of the Chronotope in the Novel (Bakhtin) 250, 278
Foucault, Michel 145, 184, 250, 267, 273
Frey, John R. 246
Fries, U. 55, 235, 246, 247
future 2, 13–14, 20, 27, 56, 60, 62, 69, 75, 93–6, 118–19, 133, 149–50, 152–4, 175–6, 179, 187–8, 190–4, 202–4, 210–11, 223, 230, 245, 252, 255, 256, 257, 261, 267, 268, 273, 274, 277, 278, 279
Futures Past (Koselleck) 223, 249, 278
Fuxjäger, Anton 250

Galbraith, Mary 92, 236, 256, 264
Geiger, Hannsludwig 268
Genette, Gérard 30, 91, 93, 99–106, 114, 120–1, 132, 167, 205, 236, 258, 259
Gerrig, Richard 123, 262
Glatzer, Nahum N. 265, 271
Goethe, Johann Wolfgang 54, 245
Gogol, Nikolai 6, 145, 150, 156, 159–60, 162–3, 169, 172–3, 180, 268, 269, 270, 271
Golden Pot, The (Hoffmann) 6, 150, 157, 172, 178–9, 182, 168, 269
Gomolitskaya-Tretyakova, T. S. 239

Goncharov, Ivan A. 24, 213, 238
Goodman, Nelson 264
Gottsche, Dirk 237, 241
grammar 21, 58, 93, 105–6, 119–20, 129, 131, 137–8, 162, 189, 201, 206, 232, 237, 246, 263
Gravity's Rainbow (Pynchon) 1, 4, 5, 15, 48, 69–70, 91–3, 95, 97, 100, 138, 212, 151, 256
Grelz, Karin 271
Guillaume, Gustave 7, 119, 189–91, 193, 202–6, 208–9, 211–12, 223, 274, 277, 278
Gumbrecht, Hans Ulrich 187, 273

Hallward, Peter 273
Hamburger, Käte 17–22, 24–5, 27–8, 33, 36–8, 44, 48, 51, 54–7, 81, 87–8, 91, 105–10, 112–17, 130–3, 136, 142, 148, 186, 198, 201, 210, 230, 235, 236, 239, 241, 246, 248, 255, 259, 260, 264, 265, 266
Handke, Peter 67–8, 250
Hansen-Loeve, Aage A. 175, 241, 272
Hegel, Georg Wilhelm Friedrich 271
Heidegger, Martin 9, 59–60, 190, 248, 249
Heinrich, Dieter 266
Helbig, Jörg 240
Hennig, Anke 244, 254, 263
Herman, David 254, 256
Hersland, Martha 266–7
heterodiegetic 48, 63, 87
Hewitt, Lynne E. 236, 240, 253
Hildesheimer, Wolfgang 15, 49, 52, 79, 108, 136, 195, 213, 245
Hirtle, Walter 277
histoire 31, 103, 188, 225
Hoffmann, E. T. A. 6, 150, 157, 172, 178–9, 182, 268, 269
homodiegetic 81–2, 259
Horn, Eva 74, 251
Hühn, Peter 247

Imaginary, The (Sartre) 162, 269
inactuality 51
Ingold, Felix Philipp 187, 273
interior monologue 16, 36, 136, 139, 141, 144–7, 169, 183–4, 242, 243, 253, 255
Interval, The (Tynyanov) 260
Iser, Wolfgang 142, 144, 147, 160, 182–3, 227, 266, 267, 269, 273
Ivanhoe (Scott) 27, 239
Iz ulizy v ulicu (Majakovskij) 241

Jakobson, Roman 5, 119, 122–5, 162, 239, 261, 262, 263, 269
Jaspers, Karl 181–2, 273
Jauß, Hans Robert 268
Jespersen, Otto 54, 246
Joyce, James 7, 34, 209, 213, 267
Juranville, Alain 148–9, 267–8

Kafka, Franz 63, 137, 139, 172, 208, 247, 265, 271, 279
Kaltenburg (Beyer) 96, 97, 257
Kant, Immanuel 216–17, 269, 280
Kharms, Daniil 63, 110, 112, 167, 254, 260, 270
Kindt, Tom 256
Kino i kniga (Aronson) 104, 259
Kittler, Friedrich A. 268
Klein, Wolfgang 260
Klinkert, Thomas 249

Koch, Gertrud 244
Kohns, Oliver 269
Koschmieder, Erwin 277
Koselleck, Reinhart 223, 249, 278
Kracht, Christian 250–1
Kremer, Detlef 268
Kruchenykh, Aleksei 125–6, 129, 263
Kuhn, Robert 254

Labov, William 248
Lacan (Juranville) 148–9, 267–8
Lacan, Jacques 148–9, 267, 268, 273, 274
Lambropoulos, Vassilis 239
Language, Counter-Memory, Practice (Foucault) 145, 267
Language, Narrative and Antinarrative (Scholes) 242
Lawrence, D. H. 260
Leary, Katherine 266
Lectures on Logic (Kant) 217, 280
Leiss, Elisabeth 57, 118–20, 247, 248, 257, 261, 262, 263, 274, 277
Lejeune, Philippe 266
Les Géorgiques (Simon) 1, 5, 15, 48, 62–4, 67, 80, 91–3, 98–100, 212–13, 249, 257, 263, 267
Lessons on the English Verb (Hirtle) 277
Levinas, Emmanuel 267
Levinson, Stephen C. 265
Likhachev, Dmitry 11, 235
Literary Fact, The (Tynyanov) 239
Logic of Literature, The (Hamburger) 17–22, 24–5, 27–6, 33, 36–8, 44, 48, 51, 54–7, 81, 87–8, 91, 105–10, 112–17, 130–3, 136, 142, 148, 186, 198, 201, 210, 230, 235, 236, 239, 241, 246, 248, 255, 259, 260, 264, 265, 266
Logical Status of Fictional Discourse, The (Searle) 18, 236
Logique du recit (Bremond) 252
Lubbock, Percy 101, 258
Lyudi odnogo kostra (Tretyakov) 15, 28–32, 42, 45, 239, 241

Madame Bovary (Flaubert) 169
Madness and Civilization (Foucault) 184, 273
Making of Americans, The (Stein) 143, 267
Man without Content (Agamben) 8, 10, 233, 234
Man without Qualities, The (Musil) 7, 126–7, 129–30, 195, 213, 263
Mandelstam, Osip 138, 265, 267
Mansfield, Katherine 241
Margolin, Uri 91, 93–5, 97, 100, 132, 256, 257, 265
Markus, Manfred 56, 247, 256, 259, 261
Marquardt, Odo 226, 266
Martinez, Matias 236, 256, 270
Martinez-Bonati, Felix 266
matrix of narration fiction, erosion of 37, 52
Mayakovsky, Vladimir 241
McHale, Brian 260
McTaggart, John M. Ellis 190–3, 274
Mecke, Jochen 243
media 13, 102–4, 114, 121, 195, 225, 258–9, 260, 275
Mediterranean and the Mediterranean World in

the Age of Philip II, The (Braudel) 188, 274
Meek, Mary Elizabeth 261
Meillassoux, Quentin 62, 249
Menard, Pierre, 173, 271
Menninghaus, Winfried 233
Mersch, Dieter 233
metafiction 62, 182, 185, 228
metafictional 28, 39, 61–2, 146, 152, 178, 180, 182, 184–5
metafictionality 62
metanarrative 95
Mimesis as Make-Believe (Walton) 128, 162, 263, 266
Mitterand, Henri 238
modernity 2, 7, 15, 28, 32, 34, 37, 45, 52, 59, 61, 66–7, 77, 195, 214–16, 218, 228, 233
moment 2, 4, 7, 11, 23, 32, 35, 43, 48, 53–4, 59–62, 67, 70, 74–6, 90, 92, 103, 109, 118, 120, 127, 130, 141, 152, 155, 158, 164, 170, 173, 177, 180, 183–4, 191, 196–7, 203–4, 206, 208–9, 221, 223, 224, 233, 234, 238, 240, 241, 248, 252, 255, 264, 267, 268
Müller, Elena 258
Müller, Gunther 99, 257
Müller, Hans–Harald 256
Musil, Robert 7, 126–7, 129–30, 195, 213, 263

Nabokov, Vladimir 248
Names of History, The (Ranciere) 188
narration, concurrent 93
Narrative as Virtual Reality (Ryan) 113, 123, 250, 260, 262, 270
Narrative Discourse (Genette) 30, 91, 93, 99–106, 120, 132, 205
Narrative Discourse Revisited (Genette) 105–6
Narrative Time (Ricoeur) 30, 60, 190, 149, 262
narrativity 2, 5, 33–4, 36, 39, 55, 60, 92, 94, 101, 127, 133, 142, 147, 193–4, 213, 221, 228, 238, 241, 244, 256
Narratology and Theory of Fiction (Martinez and Scheffel) 236, 256, 270
narrator 4, 18, 24, 27, 35–40, 42–3, 45–6, 48–50, 63, 70, 74, 77–9, 81–4, 86–7, 93–4, 96, 108–10, 113–14, 116–18, 127, 133–7, 139, 145, 149–50, 154, 156–8, 161, 163, 165–6, 169–71, 175, 177–8, 180, 182, 188, 195, 227, 232, 236, 243, 244, 246, 253, 254, 255, 259
Neal Miller, David 239
Nearly True (Branigan) 209, 279
non-contemporaneity 1, 7, 144–5, 147–8, 184–6, 213, 229, 231, 242, 276, 278
Nünning, Ansgar 249

Oblomov (Goncharov) 24, 213, 238
omniscient 165–6
On Autobiography (Lejeune) 266
On Literary Evolution (Tynyanov) 239
On Mind and Other Matters (Goodman) 264
On Phenomena and Existences (Kharms) 63, 110, 112, 167, 254, 260
origo 5, 88, 96, 107–8, 110,

113–17, 119, 121, 123, 131–3, 135, 146, 148–9, 177–8, 224–5, 226, 232, 255, 264, 277
Osborne, Peter 13, 235

Panza, Sancho 172, 271
Parody Novel, The (Shklovsky) 30, 64, 239, 240
perfect 20–1, 27, 46, 96, 117–18, 179, 248, 277
perspective of the character 118
Petersen, Jürgen H. 236, 255
Phänomenologie des Lesens (Stuhler) 263, 273
Philosophy of "As If", The (Vaihinger) 262
Philosophy of Grammar, The (Jespersen) 54, 236, 246 n.88
Philosophy of Mind (Hegel) 271
Philosophy of Symbolic Forms, The (Cassirer) 261
Pierre Menard, Author of Don Quixote (Borges) 173, 271
plot 19, 30–1, 60, 75, 77, 177, 180, 190, 209, 225, 231, 239, 252, 259
Plotting Time and Space (Dannenberg) 76, 252
Poetics (Aristotle) 257
Poetics of Composition (Uspensky) 42, 227, 242, 269
Poetics of Prose, The (Todorov) 21, 30, 237, 271
Poetika khudozhestvennogo vremeni (Likhachev) 11, 235
postmodern 61–2, 65, 82, 221
Pragmatics (Levinson) 265
presence 1–2, 8, 27, 56, 58, 88, 127, 144, 174, 188, 208, 224, 232, 233, 259, 262, 278, 279
presentification 2, 4–6, 12, 16, 27, 38, 43–4, 51, 54–5, 57–8, 62–3, 65, 75, 78, 90, 105, 114, 117, 120, 130–4, 133, 136, 149, 185–6, 198–9, 201, 204–5, 212–13, 215, 217–20, 224, 226, 227, 229, 230, 232, 239, 246, 248, 252
presentness 19, 27, 35, 37, 43, 55, 59, 77, 127, 149, 212, 214, 216, 229, 248
Prince, Gerald 279
Problems in General Linguistics (Benveniste) 30, 117, 261, 278
Problems in the Study of Language and Literature (Tynjanov and Jakobson) 239
prospection 79, 109, 198
Psychoses, The (Lacan) 273
Pynchon, Thomas 1, 4, 5, 15, 48, 69–70, 91–3, 95, 97, 100, 138, 212–13, 251, 252, 256, 269

Quixote, Don 171–3, 177, 271

Raabe, Wilhelm 21, 23, 213, 237, 238
Rabbit Angstrom (Updike) 40–3, 46, 85, 88, 213, 242, 243, 255
Rancière, Jacques 14, 188, 274
Rauh, Gisa 108–9, 114, 134, 259, 260–1, 264, 265
récit 30, 103, 105, 252
reference 2, 5–6, 10, 13, 15, 19, 30–1, 38, 48, 56, 59,

65, 69–70, 74, 86–7, 97,
  99, 107, 114, 118–25,
  127–30, 136, 152, 182,
  191, 199–201, 215, 224–6,
  228–9, 231, 238, 240–1,
  248, 251, 261, 262, 263,
  264, 277, 278
Referovskaya, Elizaveta 277
report 40, 46, 71, 107, 182
retro-referentiality 59
retrospection 4, 16–17, 19, 27,
  48, 53, 55, 60, 65, 79, 107,
  109, 142, 179–80, 186,
  198, 206, 223, 224, 227,
  229, 230–1, 238
retrospectivity 4–6, 16, 19, 30,
  52–3, 60, 105, 142, 184,
  206, 212, 214, 220, 223,
  224, 227, 229, 231, 244
Richter, Sandra 234
Ricœur, Paul 30, 60, 190, 249,
  262
Rödl, Sebastian 7, 189, 191,
  197–8, 200–1, 220, 232,
  276, 277
Rösch, Ewald 245
Rosenfeld, Gavriel D. 251
Röttgers, Kurt 254
Rozanov, Vasily 33, 37, 45, 241,
  243
Rühling, Lutz 264
Russell, Bertrand 7, 34, 124,
  190–7, 201–2, 205–6, 208,
  240, 273, 275, 276
Russian Formalism 30, 193, 225,
  228, 240, 241, 273
Ryan, Marie-Laure 113, 123,
  250, 260, 262, 270

Sartre, Jean-Paul 162, 269
Saussure, Ferdinand de 274
Schädlich, Hans Joachim 71, 251,
  257

Schänert, Jörg 247
Scheffel, Michael 236, 256, 270
Schiffrin, Deborah 247, 248
Schlögel, Karl 188, 273
Schmid, Wolf 261
Schmidgen, Henning 274
Schmitz-Emans, Monika 82, 254
Scholes, Robert 242
Scholl, Michael 243
Scorsese, Martin 269
Scott, Walter 27, 239
Sdvigologiya (Kruchenykh)
  125–6, 129, 263
Searle, John R. 18, 236
Secret War, The (Horn) 74, 251
Segal, Erwin M. 133, 253, 255,
  265
Seidler, Franz W. 235, 246
(self-)fictionalizing present tense
  220, 236, 237, 242, 244,
  247, 253, 260, 265, 267,
  272, 246, 247, 260, 261
self–reflexivity 31, 62, 68, 102,
  228
*Shadow of the Body of the
  Coachman, The* (Weiss) 1,
  45, 48, 52, 178, 195, 213,
  244, 272
Shalamov, Varlam 267
Sherover, Charles M. 274
Shifters (Jakobson) 5, 119–25,
  162, 261, 262, 269
Shklovsky, Viktor 28, 30, 33, 64,
  239, 240
Signposts of Fictionality (Cohn)
  19, 81, 86, 253
Simon, Claude 1, 5, 15, 48, 62–4,
  67, 80, 91–3, 98–100,
  212–13, 249, 257, 263, 267
simultaneity 57–8, 138, 185,
  191–2, 194, 196, 248, 255,
  275, 276
sketch 31–2, 51, 62

Skrebowski, Luke 235
Slow Man (Coetzee) 185
Smith, Daniel W. 274
Solitaria (Rozanov) 33, 37, 45, 241, 243
Speak Memory (Nabokov) 248
Speck, Stefan 263
Spitzer, Manfred 266
Stalin, Joseph 278
Stanzel, Franz K. 55, 78, 177, 227, 235, 236, 246, 247, 253, 255, 265, 266
Stein, Gertrude 143, 267
Stein, Malte 247
Sternberg, Meir 244
Stierle, Karlheinz 253
Story and Discourse (Chatman) 30, 91, 99, 100, 101, 258
Story Logic (Herman) 254, 256
Strindberg, August 6, 146, 163, 178–82, 267, 272, 273
Strindberg and Van Gogh (Jaspers) 181–2, 273
Stuhler, Simon 263, 273
superseding 197
synchrony 3, 19, 40, 42, 44, 52, 57–8, 70, 77, 79, 83, 85, 87, 113, 134, 138, 149, 185, 186, 191, 192, 194–6, 208, 223, 224, 230, 232, 242, 248, 254, 255, 275, 276

Tallhover (Schädlich) 71, 251, 257
Telling in Time (Sternberg) 244
Temps et verbe (Guillaume) 7, 119, 189–91, 193, 202–6, 207–8, 211–12, 223, 274, 277, 278
Tempus (Weinrich) 17, 20–3, 28–9, 36–7, 48, 55–6, 114, 147, 200, 237, 238, 239, 244, 246, 247, 260, 261
Tense and Narrativity (Fleischman) 27, 168, 238, 241, 244
Tense in the Novel (Bronzwaer) 254
Tense without Time (Casparis) 55, 246
Thackeray, William 15, 24–5, 238
Theory of Knowledge (Russell) 7, 34, 124, 190–7, 201–11, 205–6, 208, 240, 273, 275, 276
Theory of Language (Bühler) 107, 108, 114, 122, 123, 125, 129, 130, 132, 259, 262, 263,
Tholen, Christoph G. 243
Time and the Other (Levinas) 267
Time Passes (Banfield) 34
Time that Remains, The (Agamben) 278
Time Without Becoming (Meillassoux) 62, 249
Todorov, Tzvetan 21, 30, 159, 172, 237, 271
Tolstoy, Leo 244, 262
Tomashevsky, Boris V. 240
Towards a "Natural" Narratology (Fludernik) 83, 108, 168, 254, 256, 257, 260
Transparent Minds (Cohn) 36, 109, 134, 137, 146, 147, 166, 237, 260, 272
Tretyakov, Sergey 15, 28–32, 42, 45, 239, 241
Trunz, Erich 245
Truth about Sancho Panza, The (Kafka) 172, 271
Turgenev, Ivan 265
Tynset (Hildesheimer) 15, 49, 52, 79, 108, 136, 195, 213, 245
Tynyanov, Yuri 239, 260

Unclaimed Experience (Caruth) 61, 249
unreal 160, 183, 275
Unreality of Time, The (McTaggart) 190–3, 274
Unspeakable Sentences (Banfield) 18, 236, 260, 264,
Updike, John 40–3, 46, 85, 88, 213, 242, 243, 255
Uspensky, Boris 42, 227, 242, 269

Vaihinger, Hans 262
Vanity Fair (Thackeray) 15, 24–5, 238
Vennemann, Theo 213, 248, 261
Verbalkategorien des Deutschen (Leiss) 57, 118–20, 247, 248, 257, 261, 262, 263, 277
Visser, Fredericus Theodorus 246
Vita aesthetica (Avanessian and Völker) 2, 14, 233
vividness 55, 238
Volek, Emil 240
Völker, Jan 233
Voss, Christiane 244

Waldron, Randall H. 242, 254
Waldron Neumann, Anne 254
Walk, The (Walser) 3, 20–3, 28–9, 33–4, 48, 55–6, 114, 147, 200, 237, 238, 239, 244
Walser, Robert 3, 15, 46–7, 51–2, 68, 77, 79, 86, 96, 244

Walton, Kendall 128, 262, 263, 266
War and Peace (Tolstoy) 244, 262
Waves, The (Woolf) 2–3, 15, 34–7, 144, 195, 213, 218, 241, 241, 259, 280
Weinrich, Harald 17, 20–3, 28–9, 33–4, 36–7, 48, 55–6, 114, 147, 200, 237, 238, 239, 244,
Weiss, Peter 1, 45, 48, 52, 178, 195, 213, 244, 272
West, Russell 240
What is Narratology? (Kindt and Müller) 256
Widmann, Andreas Martin 252
Wirth, Uwe 268
Wish to become an Indian (Kafka) 63
With Reference to Reference (Elgin) 264
Witt, Susanna 271
Witte, Georg 244
Wolfson, Nessa 238
Woolf, Virginia 2–3, 15, 34–7, 144, 195, 213, 218, 241, 242, 259, 280
World Hitler Never Made, The (Rosenfeld) 251
Wyatt, Bryant N. 243

Žižek, Slavoj 249
Zola, Émile 15, 25, 96, 213, 238, 248

www.ingramcontent.com/pod-product-compliance
Lightning Source LLC
Chambersburg PA
CBHW052153300426
44115CB00011B/1650